INFORMATION SYSTEM MANAGEMENT

INFORMATION SYSTEM MANAGEMENT

Editor
Ankita Bansal

KALPAZ PUBLICATIONS
Delhi–110 052

INFORMATION SYSTEM MANAGEMENT
Information Science

Rs. 795

ISBN: 81-7835-087-4

Published in 2002 in India by
Kalpaz Publications
C–30, Satyawati Nagar
Ashok Vihar Phase-III
Delhi–110 052
E-mail: Kalpaz@hotmail.com

Lasertypesetting at: A.S. Printers
Printed at: Mehra Offset Printers, New Delhi

Preface

Today, 'Management Information System (MIS)' is a valid and meaningful term, placing emphasis on the elements that are the most significant. Information resource management, a subtle but important shift in the way MIS is viewed within a company. This change is characterized by the progression of titles under which the MIS function has operated. In the fifties the department head of MIS was called a computer manager or computer center manager. This implied that the central focus was the computer and that the manager was the custodian of this new electronic device.

In the sixties the term 'data processing' came into vogue, and the manager was called 'the manager of data processing' or 'manager of electronic data processing': now the department was called by the function it performed rather than the principal device that performed it. The late sixties brought increasing use of the word 'system'. A 'system' consisted of a computer, but also a host of input and output equipment, storage devices, software, applications, and the people that make the whole thing work. The emphasis shifted from the computer to the system. The seventies ushered in the term 'information' as apposed to 'data'. 'Data' is defined as raw numbers and files; thus, to be useful to management, data must be processed into meaningful information. The eighties brought a further shift to a new and imposing term—'information system management'. MIS, powered by sophisticated computer hardware and software with responsive communication to and form a variety of remote terminals to an integrated data base, has reached the stage where information has become a valuable resource in maintaining a competitive business.

Along with the evolutionary title change of MIS, the role of MIS within the organizational hierarchy has been elevated. Starting from a reporting position within the controller's function, the MIS operation now reports to the financial or administrative vice-president, or directly to the president. The title, too, has gradually evolved from manager to director to vice-president. The realization that information is a resource has brought the acknowledgment that its manager should be on the same level as managers of other equivalent resources.

The primary objective of this book is to provide a detailed practical guideline for managers and professionals in the area of information system management. It elaboratively discusses all essential aspects of information system management. It will prove highly informative to information system managers, decision-makers, administrators, network analysts and management students.

Editor

Contents

1

Introduction

Management can be defined as the process of achieving organizational objectives through the efforts of other people. Three important points of this definition may be emphasized. The first point is that management is a process—i.e., management consists of a number of interrelated steps or function which, when satisfactorily performed, lead to the achievement of goals. The second point is that without the establishment of specific impossible. The third point is that the successful practice of management involves people working together in harmony to achieve desired results.

The availability of quality information is, of course, a requirement for a smoothly functioning operation. The business manager is a practitioner of the art and science of management. It is his job to carry out the basic management functions necessary to attain company goals. Of course, the objectives pursued vary according to the manager's mission; however, the functions of planning, organizing, staffing, and controlling are performed by all managers.

Planning

To plan is to decide in advance a future course of action. Thus, planning involves making decisions with regard to (1) the selection of both short-run and long-run business strategies and goals; (2) the development of policies and procedure which will help accomplish objectives or counter threats; (3) the establishment of operating standards which serve as the basis for control; and (4) the revision of earlier plans in the light of changing conditions. The steps followed in planning and in arriving at rational decisions are:

1. *Identifying the problem or opportunity.* Meaningful planning may begin when a manager understands and has correctly defined the problem or opportunity which he faces. Information is needed to bring about awareness.

2. *Gathering and analyzing relevant facts.* To plan and made decisions, managers must have information.

3. *Determining suitable alternatives.* The manager must seek out the most attractive possible course of action. The appropriateness of the options selected is determined by the manager's skill by the quality of his information.

4. *Evaluating and selecting the most appropriate alternative.* The manager must weigh the options in light of established goals and then arrive at the plan or decision which best meets the company needs. Again, the correctness of this choice depends upon managerial skill and information quality.

5. *Following up on decision.* Broad plans may require supporting supplementary plans. For example, if the result of thee above steps is a

decision to acquire a computer, then additional plans must be made (a) to locate the new computer department in the organization, and (b) to staff it with operating personnel.

Organizing

The organizing function involves the grouping of work teams into logical and efficient units in order to carry out plans and achieve goals. In a manufacturing company, employees may be grouped formally into production, marketing, and finance divisions. In each of these divisions, workers may be further organized into smaller units.

The marketing division, for example, might consist of advertising, direct selling, and marketing research departments. Salesmen might be further organized by territory, by products sold, and by type of customer contacted. Managers at each organizational level receive formal authority to assign goal-directed tasks; they then must motivate and coordinate employee efforts if goals are to be achieved.

To sum up, organizing is the grouping of activities necessary to accomplish goals and plans, the assignment of these activities to appropriate departments, and the provision for authority delegation and coordination.

Staffing

Staffing consists of selecting people to fill the positions which exist in the organizational structure of the business. The staffing activity also includes (1) the training of employees to meet their job requirements, (2) the preparation of employees for promotion to positions of greater responsibility, and

(3) the reassignment or removal of employees when such action is required.

Controlling

The control function looks at the past and the present. It is a follow-up to planning; it is the check on past and current performance to see if planned goals are being achieved. The steps in the control function are:

1. *Setting standards.* Proper control requires that predetermined goals be established by planners. These standards may be expressed in physical terms or in monetary terms. The setting of a realistic standards requires quality information.
2. *Measuring actual performance.* Timely and accurate performance information is essential to control.
3. *Comparing actual performance with standards.* Comparison is action oriented. Computer can provide this information to managers on an exception basis only when performance variations are outside certain specified limits.
4. *Taking appropriate control action.* If actual performance is not up to the standard, it may be because the standard is unrealistic. Therefore, replanning may be necessary to revise the standard. Unfavourable performance may have to be corrected by reorganizing work groups or by adding more employees.

Management of new information systems

Plans beget subordinate plans, old plans require modifications, and new plans develop while old ones are in effect. Thus, it is impractical to insist on a special time sequence for the various functions. Quality information could support good decisions; good decisions should lead to effective performance of managerial functions; and effective functional performance should lead to the attainment of organizational goals. It is not surprising, therefore, that the acquisition and use of a computer may have important managerial implications.

With the emergence of business computing in the 1950s, many observes predicted that computers would be the managers of the future. This has not happened. Managers continue to be indispensable, particularly at higher managerial levels. What has engaged is the decision-making process because of the ability of computers to process and deliver information to managers on which decision making is based.

To illustrate, most managers today receive computerized reports on the status of work for which they are responsible: for example, reports on production quotas, orders, inventory levels, sales targets, accounts payable, and so on. The type of report, the amount of detail, the time horizon of the data, the degree of data aggregation and the source of data input are tailored to the manager's position in the organizational hierarch.

If the manager is at the operational level, the report will probably contain details of work in progress, such as sales per representative, quantity and cash value of each product sold, or cost figures for each unit in production in order to answer the question 'what is?'.

Middle managers responsible for control are more likely to receive summarized data, figures on branch or division performance. The reports may compare current data with historical data, or current data with planning projections in order to identify discrepancies that call for corrective action.

Computerized reports designed for top level managers concerned with strategic planning will contain operational figures for the organization as a whole and will try to answer 'what if?' questions. Without doubt, computers provide today's managers with more information, more timely information and better quality of information on which to base decision making than in the past.

Solutions to many managerial problems can now be programmed. Although the actual percentage of programmed versus non-programmed decision making varies from one industry to another, somewhere between 30 and 80 per cent of all decisions at operational and middle-management levels are programmable or semi-programmable given the current state of the art, especially in areas such as accounting, finance and manufacturing. For upper management fewer decisions are programmable, because many problems at this level are ill-structured (often called wicked problems), complex in nature, with variables that cannot easily be quantified. Personnel decisions fall into this category. So do decisions regarding goals and policies.

Top management's business acumen in promoting innovation, motivating the workforce and resolving disputes cannot be programmed. Indeed, there are many areas of business decision making that may never be automated. Nevertheless, many of the decisions of high-level managers are based on operational and control information generated by computer. In addition, the use of computerized planning and control models is becoming more common.

Computer decision support systems are of particular value in finding solutions to semi-structured problems-problems for which the solution requires managerial judgment and subjective analysis of information derived from a large number of, or complex, computations. For such problems, the manager plus the system can provide a more effective solution than either alone. Suppose a sales representative receives an order for a product to be delivered in four months' time. The order is passed to the production department where a computerized order processing systems conventional management information system-reports that the order cannot be filled in the time specified given the production schedule.

Instead of rejecting the order out-of-hand, the production manager uses a DSS to evaluate the consequences of refusing the order. A query language with a database management system is used to check the customer's record. Does the product that the customer wants to order have a generous mark-up? Is the customer a regular who places orders of high monetary value? The answers that the system supplies to these and similar questions will help the production manager to decide whether refusal of the order will represent considerable loss of profit to the firm and jeopardize future orders. If the customer is worth pursuing, the manager will consider options other than rejection.

For example, a scheduling model of the DSS might be employed to determine if the order of another, less important customer, could be delayed, thus opening a slot in the production schedule. A production spreadsheet program might be used to examine the price of overtime, subcontracting parts or substitute components to fill the order. A cost-benefit model might be used to determine the effect of a lower profit margin or loss of goodwill. Various combinations of options might be entered as parameters of a simulation model to determine possible strategies. The decision of whether to accept or reject the order will ultimately be the production manager's, but the information provided by the DSS will contribute to this decision.

On the market today are hundreds of business-oriented packages that may be incorporated in a DSS. These include packages for general ledger, billing, invoicing, cost-benefit analysis, investment analysis, insurance, manpower planning, mailing, order transaction, payroll, auditing, inventory management, shareholder accounting, cheque processing, tax calculation and so on.

Programs packaged exclusively for decision support are also available off-the-shelf. DSS executive software, designed to coordinate and monitor all software in a DSS system, is a sample DSS package. This software acts, in effect, like an operating system.

For example, when processing in a remote mode or when the DSS accesses remote databases, the DSS executive software will coordinate and control the teleprocessing software. Financial modelling language is another type of DSS package. FML consists of programs for financial forecasting, budgeting and management science computations.

Most FML include the following capabilities.

— Financial ratio analysis.

— Statistical analysis.

— Return on investment analysis.

— Forecasting and sensitivity analysis.

— What-if analysis.

— Graphics.

Sometimes, general purpose software, such as word processing, data management, communications, spreadsheets or graphics software can be integrated with DSS. Increasingly, products originally developed for functions outside the DSS spectrum have had features and interfaces added so that they can be sold as DSS software. For example, easy-to-use spreadsheet packages with self-documentation are available on the market for managerial use in decision making. Many of these packages include data manipulation, graphics and even word processing functions. While there are obvious advantages of combining functions in this way, rarely do such packages have the power of more specialized packages or custom developed DSS which are designed in-house to fit a particular managers's needs.

Expert systems can help managers to reach decisions. An expert system is a computer program that draws upon the knowledge of human experts captured in a knowledge base to solve problems that normally require human expertise.

Unlike conventional programming, an expert system does not follow an algorithm that details a precise series of stops to yield a precise result. Instead, processing is based on rules called heuristics, often called rules of thumb, that state relationships that are likely, but not guaranteed, to yield an outcome in an environment where information is uncertain or incomplete.

Consider the thought process of a banker in deciding whether a loan applicant is a good credit risk. After examining hard data, the banker will intuitively evaluate the likelihood of repayment. This is the type of problem that expert systems are designed to address-problems that cannot be reduced to mathematical formulas. Well-designed expert system imitate the reasoning process of human experts in solving specific problems within specific domains of knowledge.

At present, expert systems exist in only a few limited domains; however, their potential is vast. They may well change the way in which information is collected and evaluated in the future and may even replace some human managers on the job.

As a result of research in Artificial Intelligence (AI), progress is being made in areas such as voice recognition, natural language processing and computer vision that will also have an impact on the managerial role. For example, keyboards on terminals may be replaced with voice input, making it easier for managers to interact with computers. Natural language processing will help to eliminate the need for computers.

Natural language processing will help to eliminate the need for computer specialists to translate managerial requests for information into programming languages. This will increase the speed with which results are obtained and reduce the 'noise' of communication through an intermediary. Intelligent computer systems are projected for the future with the ability to query a manager to find out what type of information is needed and, based on this determination, self -program for the delivery of the required output.

The problems to be solved in artificial intelligence are formidable. As stated by Derek Partridge, a researcher in the field: 'Respect for the complexity and subtleties of human intelligence just keeps on growing'. People working on AI projects continually have to scale down their goals and objectives as they encounter unexpected hurdles. Furthermore, the lead time between AI prototypes and commercial products is proving to be quite lengthy. Some commentators, fear the increased reliance of managers on computers and processed information in decision making. The danger, they say, is that processed data filter out emotion, sentiment, mood and all of the irrational nuances of human situations. Yet effective management and decision making often depend on judgments based on the very elements which have been filtered out. It is argued that the manager who makes intuitive decisions that are just below the level of consciousness often has a clear vision of reality than managers who base decisions solely on data expressed in words or numbers.

In future, as more operations research models are put into use and progress is made in artificial intelligence, many functions not currently susceptible to computerization may become so and Kanter's percentage will have to be changed. But we are not yet close to Norbert Weiner's prediction that whatever man can do, computers will do.

Managers are still needed to recognize and infer patterns from non-quantifiable variables, interpret information, evaluate divergences between planned and actual performance, and determine corrective actions. Even programmed decision making requires managers initially to think through problems and establish decision rules for problem solutions. As Peter Drucker states:

> We are beginning to realize that the computer makes no decisions; it only carries out orders. It's a total moron , and herein lies its strength. If forces us to think, to set the criteria. The stupider the tool, the brighter the master has to be-and this is the dumbest tool we have. It shows us in fact, it compels us-to think through what we are doing.

Besides changing the decision-making process, computers have altered managerial span or control by changing the number and level of employees a manager supervises. They have also transformed the content of a manager's work.

Today, instrument tape may be fed into numerically controlled machines—machines that do the drilling without worker intervention. The semi-skilled or skilled workers who formerly operated drilling machines have been replaced by professional designers who prepare the instruction tape; the floor supervisor replaced by a worker who monitors production on a machine console. The emergence of the electronic office is another example of changes in job content and span of control for managers. Word processing has replaced conventional office procedures for the creation of correspondence, documents, reports and memos.

Electronic processing speeds computations and retrieval of data while electronic mail speeds inter-office communications. Teleconferencing reduces the need for business travel. These and other office activities listed have altered the duties of clerks, secretaries and administrative assistants and, as a consequence, the responsibilities of office managers. Productivity tools are not limited to the factory floor and clerical operations.

Furthermore, information systems to coordinate and control operations now make it possible to manage large enterprises with fewer personnel, particularly at middle management levels. There is evidence that computers are leading to a change in corporate structure, shrinking the traditional management hierarchy.

2

Management Information System (MIS)

The use of computer systems in all areas of business—accounting, production, marketing, sales—requires managers to manage computer resources within their departments. They must acquire hardware and software; oversee their installation and testing; control quality, privacy, security and systems maintenance; evaluate systems performance; direct employees who work at computer terminals; budget for systems acquisition and operations; design computer facilities; and participate in new systems development.

Although trained in business management, managers will undoubtedly have it personnel in their employ who require supervision. Managers are expected to know how information technology can improve their operations, how to generate the data they need, and how to evaluate the information that computer systems deliver. Most important of all, information technology presents managers with a challenge. They must learn to harness the speed and processing power of computers to achieve business goals and objectives.

System design and implementation

Information requirements determination may employ a variety of techniques, the appropriate technique being dependent on the situation. Development should encompass a process to accommodate requirements changes and provide assurance that the application as developed is an accurate and complete reflection of user requirements. A fundamental purpose for application development methods is therefore requirements development assurance. However, application development approaches or strategies differ in their power to achieve requirements assurance.

Once a strategy is selected, methods appropriate to it can be selected. Subsequent sections of this chapter describe the prototyping and life cycle development methods and relate them to the contingency approach to requirements development assurance. The underlying basis for the selection of a requirements determination strategy was uncertainty as to the ability of users and developers to know and elicit requirements. In the selection of an appropriate development strategy to assure correct and complete application development, there is uncertainty of requirements prior to and during development.

During application development, four contingencies affect the degree of uncertainty with respect to achievement of an application to deliver "real" information requirements. A common organizational response to requirements development uncertainty is to add control by adopting a single requirements development assurance method. Rather than forcing all projects to use a single requirements development assurance strategy, an alternative approach, which recognizes the differences in project-related factors, is as follows:

1. Measure contingencies and determine the level of development uncertainty.
2. Select a development assurance suitable for the observed level of uncertainty.

Four basic development assurance strategies, and the contingencies under which they are appropriate, are described below:

1. *Acceptance assurance strategy:* This strategy is to accept user statements of requirements as complete, correct, and firm and to develop as defined. There are no procedures to gain assurance that initial requirements are correct or complete or that requirements do not change during development. Examples of appropriate use of the "accept" strategy are file conversions, reports from existing files or databases, and some simple, single-user decision models. The contingencies these examples have in common are small size, high degree of structure, users who understand what the systems are to do, and developers who are experienced in this kind of task. When appropriate, the acceptance assurance strategy will lead to greater responsiveness to users who have well defined needs, elimination of frustrating assurance procedures for such users, and an increase in development efficiency.
2. *Linear assurance process*: If application requirements can be determined through a straightforward process with little or no subsequent modification, a suitable assurance strategy is to proceed from requirements specification to final development. As each step is completed, there are assurance procedures to verify conformance with requirements. There are "sign offs" to this effect. This is a linear

assurance process and is used in most formal life cycle methodologies. The linear assurance process is an effective strategy under a combination of contingencies that lead to a very low level of requirements changes after the initial sign-off on specifications. Application requirements for systems that are highly structured and for which user task comprehension and developer task proficiency are high may be effectively developed by this process. If the system is also small and involves only one or a few users, the linear assurance strategy may be effectively equivalent to an acceptance assurance strategy.

On the other hand, requirements achievement for even a relatively small system might not be assured by this process if the decisions to be supported are relatively unstructured, the user does not comprehend the task, or the developers have not previously produced such a system.

3 *Iterative assurance process*: Where requirements uncertainty during development is moderately high, the linear assurance strategy may not assure that application development meets real information requirements. For such applications, the linear assurance process of traditional life cycle methodologies can be modified to include iteration. Whenever requirements are found to be wrong or inadequate during development, the specifications are revised by a return to the requirements determination process with users. The sequence of activities in the life cycle can therefore be repeated as often as necessary in order to obtain the requirements and develop a system to achieve them. This approach

assumes that a correct and complete specification of requirements can be obtained if sufficient iterations are used. Examples where the iterative assurance process is applicable are large multiple-user systems and application areas that are new to the user or developer organization.

4 *Experimental assurance process*: A high level of requirements and achievement uncertainty during development may indicate the need for an experimental assurance process in which requirements development assurance is obtained through actual user experience with the system being developed. This experience is achieved by prototyping or simulation of the application. The prototype design method reduces uncertainty by producing successive approximations. Users and developers can readily identify the shortcomings of a prototype even when they were unable to specify application requirements in advance. Examples of applications with high uncertainty include decision support systems for upper management, interactive forecasting models, and unstructured systems to be implemented for multiple users.

Application of the contingency model require measurement of the level of each contingency, estimation of the overall level of uncertainty determined by the contingencies, and selection of an appropriate strategy. The strategy of experimental assurance in development of information system applications may be achieved by an evolutionary design method commonly called prototyping. Prototyping is used when requirements are difficult to specify in advance or when requirements may change significantly during development.

The prototyping methodology is based on the simple proposition that people can express what they like or do not like about an existing application system more easily than they can express what they think they would like in an imagined, future system. A prototyping methodology is initiated by a user who conceives of a problem or an opportunity to be solved by an information system.

Prototyping an application system is basically a four-step process, as described below and depicted in. There are two significant roles: the user and the system designer.

Identify the user's basic information requirements: In this stage, the user articulates his or her basic needs in terms of output from the system. The designer's responsibility is to establish realistic user expectations and to estimate the cost of developing an operational prototype. The data elements required are defined and their availability determined. The basic models to be computerized are kept as simple as possible.

Develop the initial prototype system: The objective of this step is to build a functional interactive application system that meets the user's basic stated information requirements. The system designer has the responsibility for building the system using very high level development languages or other application development tools. Emphasis is placed on speed of building rather than efficiency of operation. The initial prototype responds only to the user's basic requirements; it is understood to be incomplete. The early prototype is delivered to the user.

Use of the prototype systems to refine the user's requirements: This step allows the user to gain hands-on experience with the system in order to understand his or her information needs and what the system does and does not do to meet those needs. It is expected that the user will find problems with the first version. The user rather than the designer decides when changes are necessary and thus controls the overall development time.

Revise and enhance the prototype system: The designer makes requested changes using the same principles as stated in step 2. Only the changes the user requests are made. Speed in modifying the system and returning it to the user is emphasized. The number of iterations may vary considerably. There may be one of two reasons that iterative modification is ceased.

First, the user determines that the prototype is not useful and the working prototype is discarded. Second, the user is satisfied with the system and it becomes an "operational prototype." It may be modified at a later stage, but at this point it is considered usable any may be distributed to other users. Alternatively, it may "seed" the idea of a new major application and be used to provide initial specifications for the application development effort. The prototyping methodology, as outlined above, has several significant advantages in development of applications having high uncertainty as to requirements:

— Ability to "try out" ideas without incurring large costs

— Lower overall development costs when requirements change frequently

— The ability to get a functioning system into the hands of the user quickly

— Effective division of labor between the user professional and the MIS professional

— Reduced application development time to achieve a functioning system

— Effective utilization of scarce resources

A major difficulty with prototyping is management of the development process because of frequent changes. Also, there may be a tendency to accept a prototype as the final product when it should only be the basis for a fully-specified design. For example, a prototype may no handle all exceptions or be complete as to controls. It "works," but it is not complete. The model described above assumes only two participants: a user who is a functional expert and a system designer who is expert at the development of prototypes.

The prototyping methodology may be modified to accommodate a greater number of participants. Multiple users may be involved in prototype development when the application is useful across a broad area with many different user, or when it is so complex as to require input from several specialists.

Both situations require added time for communications and negotiation among users. They do not significantly affect the designer's time required to build the prototype. If an application requires complex technical or analytical skills, it may be necessary to have more than one designer, and this may add time to the prototype-building process. As users become more familiar with very high level development languages and gain experience with the use of prototypes, it will become more common for the user to also function as the system designer. In such cases, it is important that the user have access to computing resources. One approach is a service organization such as an information center.

Although there are a growing number of applications that should be developed using an experimental process strategy such as prototyping, a significant amount of new development work continues to involve major operational applications of broad scope. The application systems are large and highly structured. User task comprehension and developer task proficiency are usually high. These factors suggest a linear or iterative assurance strategy. The most common method for this large class of problems is a system development life cycle model in which each stage of development is well defined and has straightforward requirements for deliverables, feedback, and sign-off.

The system development life cycle is described in detail since it continues to be an appropriate methodology for a significant part of new development work. The basic idea of the system development life cycle is that there is a well-defined process by which an application is conceived, developed, and implemented. The life cycle gives structure to a creative process. In order to mange and control the development effort, it is necessary to know what should have been done, what has been done, and what has yet to be accomplished.

The phases in the system development life cycle provide a basis for management and control because they define segments of the flow of work which can be identified for managerial purposes and specify the documents or other deliverables to be produced in each phase. The phases in the life cycle for information system development are described differently by different writers, but the differences are primarily in amount of detail and manner of categorization.

There is general agreement on the flow of development steps and the necessity for control procedures at each stage. The information system development cycle for an application consists of three major stages: Definition, Development, Installation and operation. The first stage is the process which defines the information requirements for a feasible cost-effective system. The requirements are then translated into a physical system of forms, procedures, programs, etc., by system design, computer programming, and procedure development. The resulting system is tested and pout into operation. Not system is perfect, so there is always a need for maintenance changes. To complete the cycle, there should be a post audit of the system to evaluate how well it performs and how well it meets cost and performance specifications.

The three stages of definition, development. And installation and operation can therefore be divided into smaller steps or phases as follows:

Stages in life Cycle	*Phases in life cycle*	*Comments*
	Proposal definition	
Definition	Feasibility assessment	
	Information requirements analysis	
	Conceptual design	
	Physical system design	
Development		
	Physical database design	
	Program development	
	Procedure development	
	Conversion	
Installation and operation	Operation and maintenance	
	Post audit	

At completion of each phase, formal approval sign-offs are required from the users as well as from the manager of project development. Each phase also results in formal documentation. The information system development cycle can follow an iterative assurance strategy. For example, the review after the physical design phase may result in cancellation or continuation, but it may also result in going back to prepare a new conceptual design.

It is instructive to note that upon completion of coding of programs and beginning of program testing, the application is probably only about 60 percent complete. For example systems involving much testing, completion of coding may mark about the halfway point. Many errors in estimation of project completion dates can be attributed to failure to allocate adequate time to program testing and conversion. A major system development project is conceived as a component of the information systems planning process, but a proposal may come from other sources such as users and data processing personnel.

After a project is proposed, the next step in the definition stage is feasibility assessment, which is discussed briefly here. Once a proposed alternative is approved, the next phase is information requirements analysis. Following requirements analysis, a conceptual design phase produces a high-level design emphasizing the application as seen by its users. Upon completion of the definition stage most of the key decisions that affect the user have been made.

The definition stage is therefore critical in making sure the application will meet user needs. Although perhaps only 25 percent of total efforts has been expended, the important decisions that shape the remainder of the effort are in place. The definition stage must therefore not be neglected if applications are to satisfy the users. In a study by McKeen, it was found that projects which spend more time in the definition phase were more successful regardless of the outcome measure used. Both user satisfaction and ability to develop the application within budget were enhanced. The proposal definition phase is not necessary if the application was defined as part of information system planning. Otherwise, a simple procedure may be used for proposal of an application. Proposals may be for entirely new applications or for enhancements to existing applications. The proposal should not be complex but in a short one-or two-page document should provide sufficient justification to support a decision to proceed with a feasibility analysis.

User management approval, the proposal is reviewed by the management authority responsible for allocating information system development resources (user management, a steering committee, or the information systems executive).

When a new application is proposed, it normally goes through a feasibility study before it is approved for development. If the application is part of the predefined MIS master plan, it still should go through the feasibility assessment phase in order to evaluate alternative approaches to its development, even through the general idea has been approved with the rest of the plan. If a proposal is submitted outside of the plan, the feasibility study includes whether it is consistent with the existing plan and whether it should override the priorities of other applications already planned. Five types of feasibility are addressed in the study. They result in recognition of both the benefits and risks inherent in the development and implementation of the proposed application system:

1. *Technical feasibility*: Can the proposed application be implemented with existing technology? Analysis of project risk relative to technical feasibility includes not only whether the technology is available on the market but also its "state of the art" both in absolute terms and relative to the company's current technical sophistication.

2. *Economic feasibility*: Will the system provide benefits greater than the costs? The feasibility study presents intangible as well as tangible benefits in a formal way. A relatively detailed analysis of the costs of both development and operations of the various alternatives is also presented.

3. *Motivational feasibility: The* probability that the organization is sufficiently motivate to support the development and implementation of the application with necessary user participation, resources, training time, etc. This motivation is usually demonstrated by an owner or champion for the application who has sufficient organizational power to provide the resources and motivate others to assist and cooperate.

4. *Schedule feasibility*: The probability that the organization can complete the development process in the time allowed for development. Adding development resources does not always reduce the development time; in fact, adding staff who cannot be used effectively may impede development because of time spent in communication.

5. *Operational feasibility*: Will it work when installed? This analysis may involve a subjective assessment of the political and managerial environment in which the system will be

implemented. In general, the greater the requirements for change in the user environment in which the system will be installed, the greater the risk of implementation failure.

The feasibility study may be staffed in different ways. Some alternatives are:

1. Evaluation group with representatives from users, information systems, and other groups affected by the system. The head of the study group may be user or from information systems.
2. Evaluation person or group from information systems.
3. Evaluation person or group from users.

Each of the alternatives has advantages and disadvantages, and the selection of the staff for evaluation may depend on the type of the project and the organizational culture with respect to responsibility. For example, an evaluation group with many representatives has advantages when the application will have significant impact on several groups or on the fundamental operations of the organization.

The evaluation by information systems may be appropriate for highly centralized organizations in which the evaluation is primarily technical. The feasibility evaluation by users is consistent with user responsibility for information system resources. It establishes user commitment to the new system, and requires that user management be "sold" by the user evaluators. The feasibility report covers items such as the following:

— General description of the application

— Expected development schedule

— Schedule of resources and budget required for development

— Schedule of expected cost and benefits from operations

— Summary of evaluation with respect to technical, motivational, schedule, and operational feasibility

If the feasibility study includes several alternatives, the report should present the budget, expected benefits, schedule of resources required, etc., for each (including the alternative of "do nothing"). The choice of alternative is based on the relative feasibility of each of the alternatives. For instance, the following alternatives were considered for an accounts receivable system for one division of a large multidivisional company (after rejecting "do nothing"):

1. Dedicated minicomputer system with modification of a purchased software package
2. A minicomputer system for data entry with processing on the central computer using a generalized transaction processing package.
3. Online data entry to the central computer using an accounts receivable system developed by another division and modified as required.

The feasibility report is reviewed by the management of information systems and by the requesting department. If not part of the master plan, it may also be reviewed by the information systems steering committee. Once the feasibility study has been accepted and an alternative is approved, information requirements analysis can begin.

A contingency approach to selecting one or more methods for determining information requirements was outlined. In order to effectively obtain a complete and correct set of requirements, it is necessary to use a method or methods that take into account the extent to which requirements are already known versus their needing to be searched out or discovered. The result of the information requirements analysis or requirements determination phase of the application development life cycle is a report detailing the requirements for the application. The requirements consist of items such as the following:

— Reports (including the data items on the reports)

— Queries (both regular and ad hoc)

— Conceptual schema for database (From data modeling or other analysis)

— Functional requirements (including operational characteristics)

— User interface requirements

Conceptual design

In the proposal definition, some user needs were specified; in the feasibility assessment phase, additional requirements were identified and some fairly general design alternative were evaluated. The information requirements analysis phase elicited and documented a more detailed set of requirements. The conceptual design phase establishes a more complete user-oriented design for the application. It is useful to divide application design into a conceptual design phase and a physical design phase. These two phases can also be characterized as external design and internal design or general design and detailed design.

The conceptual design emphasizes the application as seen by those who will operate or use the outputs of the system; the physical design translates those requirements into specifications for implementing the system. The conceptual design establishes the inputs and outputs, functions to be performed by the application, and audits and controls. In general terms, conceptual design treats the actual processing functions as "black boxes" physical design specifies the actual processing given in conceptual design. Conceptual versus physical designs in application development are loosely analogous conceptual versus physical modeling in database development.

Typical contents of a conceptual design report are the following:

— User-oriented application description. Documents the flow of the application activities through the organizational units providing inputs and using outputs.

— Distinguishes manual operations from automated operations performed by the application system.

— Inputs for the application with general description of each (visual display screens, source documents, forms, queries, etc.)

— Outputs produced by the application with general description of each (visual display screens, query responses, printed outputs, reports, etc.)

— Functions to be performed by the application system.

— General flow of processing with relationships of major programs, files, inputs, and outputs.

— Outlines of operating manuals, user manuals, and training materials needed for the application.

— Audit and control processes and procedures for ensuring appropriate quality in the use and operation of the application.

The physical system design phase, also called internal or detailed design, consists of activities to prepare the detailed technical design of the application system. The physical system design is based on the information requirements and the conceptual design. In turn, it provides the basis for physical database design, program development, and procedure development. Testing is sometimes defined ad a separate phase, but testing is really part of each phase.

Some life cycles include physical database design in the physical system design phase; however, since the trend is toward more independence between programs and data and specialized skills are often required for physical database design, it is considered a separate design phase in this explanation. The results of the physical system design phase are specifications and designs for the following;

— System design showing flow of work, programs, and user functions

— Control design showing controls to be implemented at various points in the flow of processing

— Hardware specifications for the applications if new hardware is required

— Data communications requirements and specifications

— The overall structure of programs required by the application with procedural specifications on functions to be performed by each

— Security and backup provisions

— An application test quality assurance plan for the remainder of the development.

The physical system design work is performed by systems analysts and other technical personnel. Users may participate in this phase, but much of the work requires data processing expertise instead of user function expertise.

The work of the physical system design phase is to take the fairly high level, user-oriented requirements of the conceptual design phase and produce a specific technical design. This process is generally one of defining the "black boxes" that will produce the required outputs based on the inputs defined in conceptual design. There are a number of different methods an analyst may employ. By supporting the systematic process of expanding the level of detail and documenting the results, the methods aid in reducing the complexity and cost of developing application systems and in improving the reliability and modifiability of the designs.

Physical system design techniques achieve simplicity by subdividing the application system into small, relatively self-contained modules. System modules can be programs or procedures which are subsections of programs. System complexity is reduced because each module can be developed, coded, and tested relatively independently of the others. Reliability and modifiability are enhanced because a change can be made to a system module with minimal, well-understood effects on the rest of the system. The techniques are thus based on well-understood principles of systems theory.

The objectives of these examples of techniques for detailed design are similar, but each has unique features for defining and communicating system specifications. They can be used in communicating the design specifications to users, although they are not necessarily easy to understand for a person untrained in the technique. Another advantage of these physical design approaches is that they support the use of structured programming.

One problem with all of the techniques is that they require a large investment in training analysts and converting to the new procedures. Each requires a rather complete commitment and changeover; it is not easy to "borrow" elements from each and combine them. Since the early 1960s there has been ongoing experimental work in techniques for automating the system design process. The intent of these efforts has been to provide a means for specifying the information requirements of a system and automatically generating program code and database specifications. The problem is to develop a requirements language which is rich enough to provide the necessary information yet easy to understand. Another problem is developing adequate tools to generate code and organize data structures automatically.

The most comprehensive research project to date has been ISDOC at the University of Michigan. The ISDOS approach begins with a problem definer who defines the information needed, specifies timing and volume requirements, and provides algorithms and logic to produce output. The requirements are written in a Problem Statement Language.

The software system analyzes the problem statements and in a limited sense performs system design, complies programs, organizes files, and directs execution of the resulting application system. In other words, information requirements statements. The ISDOS system thus performs tasks associated with physical system design, physical database design, program development, some procedure development, conversion, and operation phases of the system development life cycle. The system is in limited experimental use.

The approach to physical database design for an application depends on the existing database and the approach followed for database requirements determination. There are three major approaches to meeting the data requirements for a an application.

1. *Create a new physical life or database:* This is appropriate if no database is used or a database is dedicated to the application; in either case the application "owns" the data and objectives of a database are violated. New data may be required and the files or database must be designed and created from data collected specifically for the application.

2. *Using and modifying an existing database*: This method is appropriate if an evolutionary strategy for database development is followed. It may require special functions to be evoked by the database administrator for restructuring the existing database as well as adding necessary data.

3. *Access an existing database by means of a user schema*: This approach is possible if a complete conceptual model of the enterprise, anticipating new application needs, was used as the basis for physical database design. New data may need to be added to the database, but the connection between the logical description of the data needed by the application and the physical database is easily made through the database management software.

The third alternative assumes that a complete data model of the enterprise will anticipate further application requirements. The second alternative is more likely even if a data modeling approach to database definition was followed. Fortunately, one of the advantages of database management systems is that the database can be restructured to accommodate evolutionary application requirements.

A primary output of the physical design process is a set of specifications that define programming tasks. The goal of the program development phase is to code and test programs required for the application. Testing of each module is performed on test data representing a fairly complete set of variations in input data in the user environment.

Problems encountered during the programming phase are typically a result of lack of complete specifications provided during conceptual or physical design. This often results in extensive reprogramming efforts when specifications are changed. The techniques for formalizing the conceptual and physical design process are aimed at alleviating this problem. Another problem in this phase is inadequate program testing prior to system test and conversion.

A number of program development techniques reduce program complexity and aid in achieving program correctness. Important examples are modularity, structured programming, application generators, and tailoring of application packages. The concept of modularity has already been discussed. The practice of subdividing a program into small, relatively well defined modules is generally accepted. Modularity aids in reducing program complexity and in enhancing reliability and modifiability. In most programming languages, modules can be programmed as subprograms with well-defined procedures for passing data values between them. Each module can be coded and tested by itself before begin integrated and tested with other modules.

In structured programming, a small set of basic coding structures is used for all program code, which generally results in programs that are straightforward in flow of logic. Structured programming is related to modularity in that use of the coding structures ensures well-defined modules. Structured programming is often termed "GOTO-less" programming because GOTO statements are discouraged or prohibited. The reason is that use of GOTOs can introduce unnecessary complexity. However, structures results in code which does not require GOTOs. The three primary coding structures in structured programming are illustrated.

Testing represents a critical factor in application development. It can take up from 15 to 50 percent of the total development effort depending on the size and complexity of the application. Formal approaches to system testing involve a discipline which begins early in the program development phase. There are three distinct phases of program testing:

1. *Module testing*: Each individual program module is tested using dummy routines for calls to other modules.
2. *Integration testing*: Group of program modules are tested together to determine if they interface properly. This may be done incrementally as they are developed until the entire program system is tested.
3. *System testing*: This involves testing of the complete set of application programs.

There is debate over what constitutes a correct or adequately tested program. Some errors will be revealed only after the system is in production; however, a system that is put into production with too many errors can be disastrous in terms of corrective activity required and organizational acceptance of the application. Criteria for program correctness vary widely and tend to be related to the method of generating test data.

It is useful to distinguish between reliability and correctness for programs. A correct program meets specification; a reliable program operates in an acceptable manner under both intended and unintended input data and operating conditions. In other words, a reliable program will perform satisfactorily under a wide range of correct and incorrect inputs; a correct program need only perform satisfactorily as long as the inputs are as specified.

An alternative approach to application development with high potential payoff in productivity is to purchase generalized software packages and modify them to meet the unique needs of the organization. Many applications, such as payroll, have similarities across organizations and across industries, suggesting the possibility of using generalized software instead of writing unique application software. There are tow alternative approaches to the use of generalized application software packages:

1. *Have organization adapt to the package*: The application software producers are fixed and the operating procedures of the organization are modified to conform to the software. This alternative may be desirable for an organization with applications where there are no significant unique organizational requirements or internal training is less expensive than modifying the software. Another situation is when cost limits or the urgency for the system to be implemented offsets the benefits of unique requirements that can be obtained only through delay and extra cost associated with unique application development. Small business, for example, can frequently afford the cost of conforming to a package but not the cost of unique development.

2. *Adapt package to organizational needs*: Recent trends, accepted by software vendors and purchasers, have been to provide general packages that can be easily modified because of modular design to fit unique organization requirements. The increasing cost of software development relative to packages makes it cost-justifiable to purchase a package and spend the same amount as the acquisition cost to modify it. Some vendors "tailor" packages themselves; others provide the source code for their clients to modify. The tailoring alternative is suited for situations in which the essential features are found in a package, but the purchasing organization desires unique features.

When the choice is made to purchase a software package rather than to develop in-house, it is still important to have complete, accurate system design specifications. The specifications provide the guidelines for evaluating different software packages and choosing the one that most closely meets the specifications. They also dictate how the chosen package should be modified, providing a basis for estimating the cost of modifications and assuring that it is done adequately.

Procedure development can take place concurrently with program development. Procedures should be written for all personnel who have contact with the system. This includes the following:

1. *Primary users*: This includes instructions for how to interpret a report, how to select different options for a report, etc. If the user can execute the system directly, as in online queries, it includes detailed instructions for accessing the system and formulating different types of queries.

2. *Secondary users*: This includes detailed instructions on how to enter each kind of input. It is more oriented to "how to" and less to "what" for different inputs.

3. *Computer operating personnel*: There are generally maintenance procedures to be performed by computer operators and/or control personnel. Procedures include instructions for quality assurance, backing up system files, maintaining program documentation, etc.

4. *Training procedures*: In some cases, a separate training manual or set of training screens is developed for the implementation stage and subsequent training.

One of two groups may be responsible for writing procedures: analysts or users.

The advantages of analyst-written procedures are technical accuracy, project control over completion, and conformance to the overall documentation; disadvantages are the tendency of analysts to write in technical jargon or technical abbreviations and to assume users have knowledge of the technical environment.

The advantages of user-written procedures are an appropriate level of technical description and instructions that are understandable; disadvantages are the difficulty of assuring clear, complete instruction.

A mixed strategy is one in which analysts and users work together to produce a technically correct, understandable manual. An effective procedures manual, one that communicates well and can be referenced easily, must be well designed. Several alternative layouts are shown.

Conditions under which are most appropriate are the following.

Format	*Conditions for use*
Conventional	Sequenced set of instructions for one job title or unit. Possible use for policy statements
Playscript	Sequenced set of instructions involving several job titles or units.
Caption	Unsequenced procedures or policies
Matrix	Two conditions determine a procedure or an action.
Decision	Several conditions and one or more procedures or actions.
Live specimen	Supplement for all of above.
Flowchart	Supplement to playscript, matrix, or decision table.

It is important that procedures be kept current to coincide with changes to the information system. A document numbering system that ties procedures to particular programs, modules, or data files is useful for this purpose.

The third stage of the information system development life cycle begins with conversion to the new application system. The rest of the system development life cycle refers to the life of the system in use. After the system is in production, changes and enhancements are made during the operation and maintenance phase of the system. Periodically, a post audit of the system is conducted; based on this activity, the system may be modified, enhanced, or replaced.

Conversion to the new application system begins after all programs and procedures have been prepared and individually tested. Three major activities prepare for actual conversion: acceptance testing, file building, and user training.

Acceptance testing is testing of the completed application and comparing it to specifications. It verifies to the user that the system meets performance criteria and operation requirements. The testing includes user inputs, operating and control procedures, and outputs. Differences between what users expected and what the system delivers are identified and resolved. The acceptance test was developed as part of the planning for the system.

File building refers to the collection and conversion to machine-readable form of all new data required by the application. File building can be a long and tedious process, and careful planning is important. *Ad hoc* file conversion programs may be employed if the required data is already in computer-readable form. If not, the data must be gathered, coded, and entered into the database. Sufficient time and human resources should be provided to "clean up" the data, that is, remove inaccuracies and inconsistencies and make the data complete.

User training may be relatively straightforward or a critical effort, depending on the degree to which the new application system affects existing jobs. If techniques such as job design are used, training will involve substantial reorientation of the users to their jobs. Proper user training is an important factor in overcoming user resistance to new systems. In a later section of this chapter, training as a subset of the implementation or change process will be discussed.

Conversion from the old system to the new takes place after acceptance testing, file building, and user training are complete. Conversion can be accomplished in several ways. The most careful method is to run the old and new systems in parallel; the new system is run under actual conditions and the results are compared with the old system for reliability and accuracy. After the new system has shown consistent results for a reasonable period of time it becomes operational and the old system is dropped. The drawback to this method is that it is expensive; both machines and employees work double time. Machine time can be costly if new hardware is replacing old and both must be maintained. More important, employees are required to perform essentially two full-time jobs, one of them being new and unfamiliar. Moreover, if the system has not been sufficiently tested and errors are detected during conversion, costly delays and employee frustration can cause serious problems. If parallel processing of the old and new systems is not feasible, the new system should be tested under simulated conditions of full volume before cutting over from the old.

Complete cutover is often referred to as "burning the bridges" because it is usually impossible to return operations to the old system once cutover takes place. Problems with the new system are corrected by "brute force" since no alternative is available. This is frequently a risky strategy, especially for systems such as payroll where very little delay can be tolerated. If possible, conversion should take place gradually, one portion of the system at a time.

A shoe manufacturer and importer, a division of a large company, waned a computer. The company hired a consultant to recommend computer hardware, prepare programs, and convert company records. The invoicing and inventory systems were to be the first applications, followed by accounts receivable and accounts payable. The first computerized invoices resulted in customer complaints. The inventory reports could not be compared with the parent company reports. The consultant was terminated, and he filed a lawsuit for fees due.

Some errors in development were highlighted in pretrial discovery:

1 The company had no experience with computers but still decided to implement all major applications at one time.

2 The manual system of inventory control had been developed by employees without formal training, resulting in somewhat unique features. The consultant never fully understood the existing system.

3 Live data items were used in the testing. This produced huge test outputs which could not be checked adequately.

4 The parent company system and the company's new system were not compatible, so the parent company inventory files were not copied. Instead, temporary input clerks were brought in to prepare data, but no programs were available to validate this input. The input data quality was poor.

5 No audit trails were included to identify corrections. No one knew what has changed or who made the changes.

6 No company personnel were assigned to the project. Lower-level employees were afraid to contradict the consultant; high-level employees refused to participate at all.

When the system appears to be operating without difficulty it is turned over to the information processing production function. This often requires not only approval by the user stating that they system meets predefined acceptance criteria, but also approval of the system operations and maintenance groups stating that it meets standards for documentation and maintainability. Any subsequent changes in the application are handled as maintenance.

Maintenance of an application can be classified as repairs or enhancements. Repairs are required when incomplete or incorrect coding renders the application defective. Enhancements are additions or improvements. Repairs dominate the maintenance activity for the first few months of operation. Later, most of the maintenance is enhancement. Sometimes maintenance is performed by the system developers, but often it is the responsibility of a separate maintenance group.

When an information system project is approved, its consequences are not certain; there are risks associated with it. The anticipated benefits may not be achieved, costs may be higher than planned, time for implementation may be greater than estimated, or performance of the hardware and software may be lower than anticipated. There are three factors, recognizable prior to implementation, that affect the inherent risk in a project: size, the degree of structure of tasks to be automated, and the level of technology of the project relative to the organization. Note that the first two are similar to the factors contributing to uncertainty of information requirements. The level of company-relatively technology introducers risk in system implementation but is relatively independent of requirements definition. Using combinations of high and low for these three factors, there are eight possible risk estimates for projects.

The contingency approach to project management is to organize and manage a project according to the level of risk in the project. Four types of tools and techniques are applied to obtain appropriate project management.

1. External integration tools and techniques to link the project with users. Examples are user project managers, users on project team, and user steering committee.
2. Internal integration tools and techniques to keep the project team working as a unit. Examples are project review meetings, minutes, and team participation in decisions.
3. Formal planning tools and techniques to structure and sequence tasks. Examples are critical path scheduling, milestones, and project approval processes.
4. Formal control tools and techniques to evaluate progress. An example is a series of formal status reports with variance analysis.

In general, the lower the structure of the tasks to be automated, the greater the need for high levels of external integration with user involvement. High level of technology relative to the organization generally is aided by high internal project integration and fairly low formal planning and control. High formal planning and control tend to be most useful for large projects with low technology.

Management may choose a portfolio of projects to balance the overall development risk. Typically, a high-risk project will also have the greatest expected benefits if implemented successfully. For instance, a balanced portfolio might include one or two high-risk, high-benefit applications as well as several low-risk applications with more modest expected benefits. A mixture of projects with different risks and different project organization and management will allow an organization to achieve acceptable results while taking some risks to implement large projects, unstructured projects, and using relatively high technology.

In one organization a well-designed system fails; a similar but poorly designed system in another organization succeeds. The reason can usually be traced to human rather than technical problems. Implementation of information systems is a process of organizational change; in this sense, implementation refers to the ongoing process of preparing the organization for the new system and introducing it in such a way as to assure its successful use. Recent research has focused on those human and organizational factors that affect the successful implementation of a new information system.

Theories of organizational change

Lewin's three-stage process of organization change was reviewed. This theory has formed the basis for most implementation research and is reviewed briefly below:

Stage	*Description*
Unfreezing	Increasing the receptivity of the organization to a possible change
Moving	Choosing a course of action and following it.
Refreezing	Reinforcing the "equilibrium" on the organization at a new level after the change has occurred.

Another model of organizational change that elaborates on the Lewin stages has been proposed by Kolb and Frohman. According to this model, an organizational "consultant" establishes a relationship with the "client" though a series of seven stages. The term "consultant" is used to refer to a person outside of the unit where the change is to occur. This key person is often termed a "change agent" and may be thought of as a catalyst for the change process. The success with which the consultant and client deal with important issues at each stage of the process determines the success of the overall change effort.

Models of organizational change are useful because they identify issues that must be faced in new information system design and implementation. Projects differ in their organizational impact. If a project is well defined at the outset and involves minimal organizational change, a purely technical solution may be adequate. However, most large application systems involve considerable organizational change and require many redefinitions and reformulations before they are complete. These conditions increase the likelihood that the system will not be implemented successfully without explicit change procedures. If the systems analyst is viewed as a "change agent" rather than a technician under organizational change conditions, the dangers of system failure can be reduced.

An active change agent can assure better communication with the user and minimize the possibility of misunderstandings. He or she stays involved through all stages of the process to assure that "refreezing" takes place, rather than leaving as soon as the technical system is installed correctly. Moreover, in the role of change agent, the analyst can recognize when his or her change skills and the project requirements do not match and take the necessary action to involve others with the required skills in the implementation effort.

Mechanisms

A recent study of implementation success and failure across multiple information system revealed that the probability of successful implementation of an MIS can probably be increased if special attention is paid to the following three key issues:

1. Gaining management and user commitment to the project
2. Gaining user commitment to any changes necessitated by the new system
3. Assuring that the project is well defined and plans are clearly specified.

Generally, user participation in the system design process is advocated in order both to increase commitment and to assure accuracy of requirements specifications. Involvement of primary users is usually advocated, particularly when system use is voluntary.

The more active the users in information requirements determination and in approval of user interface design, the more likely they are to accept the system and utilize it appropriately. Research has shown that user involvement in development can subsequently increase their satisfaction with the system, but a relationship between user involvement and propensity to use a system has not been clearly demonstrated. A significant problem with organizational change is resistance to the change by those affected. User resistance to new information systems can be as serious problem.

If use is voluntary, resistance will be manifested by avoidance of the system. If use is not voluntary, user resistance can cause significant problems in the way of disruptions, increased error rates, deliberate sabotage, or increased turnover. There are different approaches to overcoming user resistance, depending on the situation as well as the implicit theories of management and system designers. Three implicit theories to explain resistance are the following.

1. *People-oriented theory*: resistance occurs because of factors internal to the users as individuals or as a group.
2. *System-oriented theory*: resistance occurs because of factors inherent in the design of the system to be implemented.
3. *Interaction theory*: people or groups resist systems because of an interaction between characteristics related to both people and systems.

Strategies for implementation that are implied by different views of the problem of resistance are:

Theory	*Implementation strategy*
People-oriented	Educate users Coerce users Persuade users User participation
System-oriented	Educate users Improve human factors Modify packages to conform to organizational procedures. User participation
Interaction	For organizational problem before introducing system Restructure incentives for users Restructure relationships between users and designers User participation

The significant point of the interaction theory is that for a system with a large number of users who are impacted differently by the system, the first two approaches are too simplistic to overcome all resistance. Although user participation is often advocated for either obtaining greater commitment or improving system quality or both, there are situations where it is not appropriate. For insane, if a new design is mandated even though it is unpopular, and appearance of user involvement without substantive user influence in the design can increase user resentment and resistance.

System design

The specificity of information systems, namely their handling information affects necessarily the design and management procedures which have to comply with the basic characteristics and the variety of information. Many handbooks, textbooks and articles on information systems provide definitions of informations attempting to unveil the basic characteristics of the concept. According to Webster's International Dictionary, information is something received or obtained through informing, such as

> knowledge communicated by others sour obtained from investigation study, or instruction,
>
> knowledge of a particular event or situation: intelligence, news,
>
> facts or figures ready for communication or use as distinguished from those incorporated in a formally organised branch of knowledge data.

Other definitions attempt to make a distinction between concepts lie knowledge, facts, data, and information. Knowledge may be defined by one's understanding of reality, which may be obtained through the learning process and realized "by our senses and our mind's ability to form abstractions". Similarly, "knowledge is the clear perception or learning guided through experience or ruminative cognition", "It is the longest-lived, most persistent sort of information".

Data are "symbolic surrogates which are generally agreed upon to represent people, objects, events, and concepts", whereas other stress upon their being isolated facts or raw facts of observation. "Quantified data intellectually processed become information and produce knowledge". Similarly," Data processing is a set of activities which transform data into information". Information is produced from data and is, consequently, considered "the result of modeling, formatting, organising or converting data in a way that increases knowledge for its recipient". According to information "is an aggregate of facts so organised, or a datum so utilized as to be knowledge or intelligence", information is, on the other hand, "meaningful data, whereas data, as such, have no intrinsic meaning or significance".

And further "Information is the concept relating to data, which are otherwise meaningless to some specified human purpose or objective". The definition in is more flexible as it considers information to be "knowledge, intelligence, facts or data, which can be used, transferred, or communicated". A similar view is expressed in according to which "information is data that have been organised and communicated." Information has qualities such as availability, language or recognizable representation, but, first of all, meaning.

"Information is that which adds to, changes, or repeats a representation of what is known or believe to be known". These and other definitions of information and data may be of theoretical interest. For practical application in information system design there is no need to exclude data from information because information systems have, usually, to handle data as well and provide their users with information which may well include, or solely consist of data.

The latter type of information, if to be distinguished or emphasized, is usually called data information. The concept of information and data is very clearly presented in, where the term data refers to "pieces of non-discursive information", as opposed to discursive information. Information, in its turn, is defined in broader terms in as "the message conveyed or intended to be conveyed by a systematized body of ideas, or its accepted or acceptable substitutes". These definitions of information and data and the explanations given on and are working definitions and explanation accepted for the present text as well.

In human society information is being continuously generated, communicated and used. The flow of information is shown in the following figure, which depicts a most simplified model of the information chain. Generators of information are scientists, technologists, economists, statisticians, journalists, etc., who communicate the information generated by various communication channels at their disposal.

Communication of information, the art of the transfer of information, may be classified according to the channels of communication:

Documentary channels

— Personal correspondence, etc.

— Published, usually printed

— Unpublished or semi-published, usually duplicated

Audio-visual channels

— Exhibitions
— Demonstration
— Personal observations
— Films
— Television
— Visual aids to written and oral communication
— Person to person, face to face
— Person to group or audience
— Several persons to several persons.

The users of information are situated at the receiving end of the information chain and create a demand of information which is, or hopefully might be, communicated to them as the generators may supply it. As the emergence of the demand and the supply of the same item of information does not necessarily coincide, a time-lag between the generation and the use of information may appear. This time-lag has to be bridged by the storage of information which must be built into the communication phase.

Users need information for various purpose, such as policy making, decision-making, learning, general orientation, etc. Users may need information for absorbing it in order to generate new information. In other words, users may also be, but not necessarily, generators of information. On the other hand, specific groups of users absorb information in order to be able to communicate it to other users, the so-called and users. Thus the community of users may be subdivided into end users and intermediate users who role and place in the information chain has to be distinguished.

Lastly, there is an adverse flow of information, directed from the users to the communicators and generators of information, representing the *feedback* of the users, their reaction to and appreciation of the information supplied in meeting their demand. Apart from the qualitative assessment involved in some very rough quantitative statements can be made concerning the various communities shown in the graph.

End users represent by far the biggest group. End users who also generate information is a much smaller sub-group which might to set equal to the group of information generators the population of which is, therefore, vastly inferior to that of the end users. By far the largest group is that which is not shown in the graph, namely the mass of those persons who need information but do not actually use information channels and sources available to them.

The largest group of communicators, such a librarians, information specialists, editors, etc., certainly outnumber the originators of information but form a smaller group than the vast mass of actual and potential end users. Intermediate users form a small subgroup within the communicators. This subgroup contains, for example, the personnel of extension services, advisory and consultancy services, etc.

Before turning our attention to the information systems demarcated above, and their design and management, it seems appropriate to mention those rather well known barriers to communication which affect the information transfer process, and the consequences of which have to be duly considered when designing and managing efficient information systems. Barriers of communication are imposed mainly by distance, time, content and form, language and costs.

The physical (geographical) distance between the originator, the communicator and the user may limit seriously the communication of information. Such limitations may be overcome by technical means facilitating the transfer information from one place to another and by the storage of information at the centres of communication and information.

In many cases information is needed rather quickly, without delay. Other barriers (place, contents and form, language) may affect the timely presentation of the information required. It should be noted, nevertheless, that the time barrier is, to some extent, generally overrated in the practice of information services, but such experience must not deter information services to provide information requested as quickly as possible and to deploy all means of shortening the response time. Information storage is another most important means which may help to remove tome barriers.

Content and form may limit very severely the acceptance, understanding and absorption of information. The way and the level of the presentation, the terminology, the signs and abbreviations used, the form and outlay of the information may facilitate or complicate its use. Impressive style and editing, eventually the processing and repacking of information may help to remove such barriers.

The lack of knowledge of the language of the information source limits its use and decreases the reservoir of information which may be used and applied. This barrier can be removed either by broadening the language knowledge of the users (which is a very slow process, if undertaken at all) or by translation services which will result in quicker transfer of information but will, nevertheless, be rather consuming time and efforts, and, thus, increasing the time and cost barriers to communication.

Information is costly, information services are expensive services. Information, if considered as a commodity, is expensive to purchase. Economic considerations, lack of sufficient financial means are barriers which are difficulty to remove. Information systems must be, therefore, designed very carefully as regards both availability of services and economic feasibility.

The first industrial revolution in the 17th and 18th century in Europe, the rapid development of science and technology in those and the following centuries generated a tremendous increase of scientific, technical and other professional literature and a similar increase of the number of scientists, research workers, technologies etc. Both growth phenomena were closely interlinked as a result of which the overall demand and supply of information increased in an exponential manner.

The appearance of the scientific and professional journals in the 17th century and the increase of their number to approximately 100 thousand at present, the emergence of the abstracting and indexing journals in the 19th century and the increase of their number to several thousands, the appearance of research and technical reports, patent specifications and standards and the annual increase of the publication of such information sources by more than 1million items show clearly some main elements of the phenomena called document explosion, literature explosion or information explosion. These apparent consequences of the underlying knowledge explosion called for methods of document and information handling different from the traditional methods applied by libraries.

The notion of documentation emerged thus at the end of the 19th century when the International Institute of Bibliography (IIB), the predecessor of the International Federation for Documentation (FID), was founded in 1894. Several methods of what now is generally called information processing were introduced during the last decades of the 19th century and the first part of the 20th century. The application of modern technologies: reprographic technology (the first description of a plan of a microfilming system was published in 1907 by the IIB), communication technology and computer technology to both document processing and services, and information processing and services provided more effective technical means to cope with the flood of information characteristics for present times.

The rapidly growing flow of information and documentation resulted in the higher level of division of labour among libraries and information centres. Systematic co-operation of libraries and information centres has led to the emergence of local, sectorial, regional, national and international information systems and networks, not necessarily using highly sophisticated communication tools and channels. Information systems and networks help to overcome the difficulties caused by the information explosion,

- to integrate individual efforts of libraries and information centres,
- to organize resource sharing and effective co-operation,
- to improve services by raising the quality and efficiency of library and information work.

System theory and the system approach study the library as a sophisticated, complex information system consisting of interrelated subsystems. Every library is an *open system* which is closely interrelated with its social environment and is continuously communicating with the environment through various interfaces. As the result of a similar argumentation every information centre or any specific type of an information centre (information analysis centre, data centre, etc.,) can also be considered an open system the basic structure of which is analogous to that of the system mentioned above in respect to libraries. A common attribute of the open system is its exchange of matter, energy and information with its environment. In case of open information systems the following four main interfaces serve to establish contacts with the environment:

the input interface for the input of acquisitions and the inflow of other type of information from the environment, affecting the behaviour of the system,

the user interface for the output of information, that is the information services, The interface is permeable for the counterflow of information from the user to the system in the form of feedback as well,

the interface for the input of material and financial resources necessary for the functioning of the system,

the interface for the inflow (and outflow) of human resources (manpower).

The basic model of the information system does not depend upon the specific characteristic of the institution which collects, stores, processes and disseminates information. The structural isomorphism of such models allows to apply the same model to any type of library and information centre.

What is the significance of the system approach in its application to libraries and information centres?

The structural isomorphism of the systems which may model both libraries and information centres, the logical homology of these systems provide not only the practical basis, but also the philosophical background for the analogous handling of libraries and information centres.

Information systems in the information chain

These lectures will concentrate on those information systems which collect and process mainly documentary information stored chiefly, but not exclusively, as written (printed, near-printed) information and on various communication media. Some of these media physically transform the written text in an encoded form which can be retransformed by technical operations.

These information systems include institutions such as libraries, information centres, information analysis centres, data banks and similar institutions which may employ intermediate users as communicators or which may co-operate with extension services, advisory and consultancy services, etc., which employ intermediate users.

Libraries and information centres will be considered as the basic type of information systems with the understanding that the term information centre will be used as a generic term for libraries, information centres, information analysis centres, data banks, clearing houses, etc. This terminology does not imply any value judgement on the role and importance of libraries, on the one hand, and information centres, on the other. Both are the results of historical development and had, and still have, their specific role to play in the process of communicating information. It is the firm belief of the author that, in order to be effective, information centres have to be built upon libraries, or, more specifically, have usually, to include a library component which has to serve the users both directly and through the information centre. The systems which these institutions may represent, are information systems for science, technology, agriculture, medicine, social sciences, business and commerce etc., in short all activities engaged in social and economic, scientific and technical, and cultural development.

3

Organisation

The management control systems support the management control levels in the organization by providing "management" information. They rarely captured and process raw data. They mainly aggregate and manipulate data already captured and stored in files in order to trace trends, provide forecasts, deal with exceptions, and respond to ad hoc inquiries. These systems include structured decision systems, which make structured decisions, thus replacing the human decision maker, and decision support systems, which provide information for unstructured and semistructured decisions. The next section describes computerized transaction processing systems. Note that a TPS processes transactions but does not make any decision.

Since a computerized SDS does make automatic decisions, it is logically a different entity. However, we can incorporate such automatic decisions into the computerized processing of transactions and thus combine the two logical systems into the physical TPS. We then outline the structure of the typical decision support system. A DSS is not only logically different from a TPS and an SDS, but it also implies human-machine interaction and specific software and hardware elements that are not necessarily part of the conventional TPS. The distinction between the three types of systems—TPS, SDS, and DSS- is illustrated in the following examples of a partial inventory management system. The lower part of represents the physical system of supplies entering the warehouse. This system fulfills customers' orders.

The upper part of the figure illustrate how a customer's order is processed. In this process the computer does not make a decision. After an ordered item is issued from the warehouse, the relevant files are updated and, if necessary, a stock status report can be generated. In processing such transactions the computer performs only clerical operations. Continuing with the same example, we now let the computer make a programmed decision on whether to issue the ordered items.

The process includes both the processing of the transaction, and the making of an automatic decision by the computer. The automatic decision can be more complex and use models that access information from various files. For example, a decision to purchase stock additions can be made. The decision-making process in this case may be complex; it uses a programmed model and accesses two files. Yet, the process can be completely structured, and thus produce an automatic decision.

Again, the SDS involved can be incorporated into the routine processing of the purchasing transaction, or it can be a distinct independent processing step to be followed later by a transaction processing step. Depicts a DSS providing information to a human decision marker who is considering the same purchasing problem. This time the manager is making the decision; the system supports him or her by providing data and by quickly calculating the results of various alternatives considered by the manger. The purchasing decisions supported by the DSS may have to do with inventory items that are extremely expensive.

Each day hundreds or thousands of activities occur within an organization. Each activity triggers one or more transactions. For instance, a customer's order may initiate an order entry transaction, a billing transaction, and an accounts receivable transaction. A record is made of each transaction describing some important facts-what happened, when it happened, who was involved, how much money was involved, how many items were involved, etc. The transaction may be recorded manually, mechanically, magnetically, or electronically.

The recorded transactions are called *data*. This raw data can be analyzed in various ways to meet the unique information needs of the organization. Virtually any type of information can be produced from the data. The data, however, represents thousands of facts, which, presented separately, would only confuse. The data must be processed to convert it into information. This is the task of a transaction processing system. The TPS handles the major part of the work load of an information system. It records and stores most data needed by the information system, and it also generates most reports and documents needed by operational users.

Every organization, small or large, simply cannot survive without a TPS. The TPS can be manual and process a small volume of transactions; or it can be computerized and process very large volumes of transactions. As example of the latter, consider the TPS that processes the annual income tax returns in the United States. The Internal Revenue Service maintains its National Computer Center in Martinsburg, West Virginia. The centre processes the data individuals and organizations report to the regional IRS service centers around the country.

The TPS processes thousands of magnetic tapes per week in a batch-processing mode, updating master files that in 1980 contained records on 110 million individuals and 22 million businesses and organizations. The transactions-including tax returns, tax return amendments, and changes-are processed weekly. Describes the transaction processing cycle of the IRS. The source documents are recorded on magnetic tape at the regional centers through hundreds of direct data entry devices at each center. The tapes are shipped by air and automobile to the national center, which every Saturday begins processing the tapes it receives over a week's time. First they are sorted by Social Security number onto tapes. Then they are run against the master file containing the current records of the U.S. tax payers.

The records against which there are transactions are separated into a "transaction register", which is then updated by the weekly transactions. The updated file is then put through an analysis run, which produces notices and reports for the regional centers and the IRS national office in Washington. The updated records are then merged into the master file, and the processing cycle begins again.

There are four interconnected computerized processing cycles of a wholesale operation. Each cycle consists of several computer applications. For a description of most common computerized business applications. The first cycle, customer order processing, beings with the receipt of a customer order. The order is processed, leading to a request to draw from stock the quantity ordered; a packing slip together with the merchandise is prepared and sent to shipping; a bill of lading is prepared and sent to the customer with the merchandise.

The second cycle, accounts receivable processing, beings with the receipt of a document recording the shipment. The document is processed, leading to invoice copies being sent to the customer and to accounts receivable. The customer processes the involve and mails cash. The accounts receivable application processes the invoice. The cash receipt is processed by the cash receipts application then updated by the accounts receivable application. The third cycle, inventory processing, begins with the preparation of a purchase requisition as stock reaches a reorder level. The requisition is processed, leading to a purchase order being sent to a vendor. The vendor process the order and ships it, together with a packing slip and a bill of lading. These documents are processed by the receiving application and the stock is added to inventory. Note that the vendor's order processing is external to the wholesale business.

The fourth cycle, accounts payable processing, beings with the receipt of the vendor's invoice. The invoice is processed and a check is printed. The vendor cashes the check; the cancelled check is processed by the reconciliation application, and then recorded by the accounts playable application. Note, again, that the vendor's receivables application is external to the wholesale business.

The four cycles are integrated both by output of one serving as input to another and by some shared master files. A customer master file integrates customer order processing with accounts receivable processing; a product master file integrates customer order processing with inventory processing; a vendor master file integrates inventory processing with accounts payable processing.

Many organizational activities occur periodically rather than continually. Employees are paid weekly, or monthly; students' grades are turned in at the end of each term. The source documents recording these activities are gathered into a batch; this group of documents is then processed in a batch, and files are updated in one large batch on a scheduled date. Batch is usually the most economical way to provide periodic processing, when it is not necessary for files to reflect all transactions up to the latest minute. The transaction processing cycle consist of five stages: recording and data collection. Conversion and verification, data validation, file updating and processing and reporting.

An organization's performance of a transaction is generally recorded on a document or a form. The form may direct a transaction to take place, or record its performance, or confirm its performance. The capture of data is a necessary first step in processing a transaction. The initial recording of the transaction is critical.

The design of the recording procedure has a substantial impact on speed and accuracy of recording and on subsequent efforts to detect and correct errors. Accuracy, completeness, and authenticity of the input transaction data affect all subsequent processing and therefore warrant particular consideration. Furthermore, the volume of data collected can reach staggering proportions. The cost of data collection is often one of the largest single components of operating an information system. It follows, then, that the choice of data collection device is one of the most important design characteristics of an information system. There is a large variety of data collection devices. These differ in means of recording and sensing information, degree of automation, speed, portability, cost, accuracy, and the like. The form on which each transaction is recorded can be filled in manually, electronically, typewritten, or be partially preprinted. Some coding may take place, such as assigning a standard and compressed representation of data recorded in the source document; for example, sex may be signed a one-letter code. Preprinted forms and coding reduce the probability of erroneous recording.

Data conversion is the process of transforming data from a human-readable medium to a computer-readable medium. Recorded transactions go through a data entry process that converts the data into a computer input medium, such as a diskette, or magnetic disk. The converted records then become the transaction file. A typical system may use different types of devices to meet a variety of requirements and data sources. These include key transcription devices, optical font typewriters, bar-code readers, and online terminals.

The converted computer-readable result of these devices comprises magnetic disk documents that can be read by optical readers, and the lime. If the fields in a transaction record are known in advance, there is greater incentive to covert by a medium that reads prepared documents rather than by a medium that requires initial recording on a form. Remote terminals are now extensively used for direct entry of transaction data into the computer system. In such cases actual source documents are not prepared, and the stages of recording and data conversion are thus integrated: the original recording is computer-readable. Examples are automatic tellers in banks and point-of-sale terminals in retail businesses. You have to watch, though, that controls are properly devised in such systems, for the absence of a source document may cause control problems.

The data conversion activities may introduce errors. It is therefore necessary to check the conversion into computer-readable form. The process of insuring that the data recorded on a source document has been accurately transcribed to a computer-readable form is called verification. Verification can be performed by either rekeying the source document or sight proofreading.

Data validation

Verification refers to the accuracy, completeness, and authenticity of converted source documents. It can be handled manually or by a computer program, and does not require a comparison against master file records. Validation, on the other hand is always a computerized process involving a transaction file having records already verified and a check of relations between transaction records and master file records. Data validation is thus the process of screening transaction records against a set of validation criteria designed to detect certain types of inaccuracy, unreasonableness, or incompleteness. Validation checks are usually applied to individual characters and fields and/or to combinations of several fields from the transaction record, either alone or in conjunction with the content of one or more master files. Data validation tests should normally be made at the earliest possible point in the transaction processing cycle in order to reject, suspend, and correct invalid records.

A computer program, usually labeled *edit program*, reads in the transaction records and tests for all detectable errors. The edit program may, for instance, determine that each customer number in the transaction record matches a currently active customer. The edit program produces a new transaction file containing only valid records. It also produces a list of records rejected for errors. The rejected records are then corrected and reentered through the edit program. This process is continued until the input transactions are free of error. The rejected records represent potentially valid transactions. It is essential to ensure that they are either correctly reentered into the system or discarded as erroneously prepared transactions.

A sound control technique is to write the rejected transactions onto a separate "suspense file" together with a code of the edit criteria that led to the rejection. By holding rejected records in suspense, the edit program ensures that they will be correct and not lost or unduly delayed. To recapitulate, the stages of data verification and validation are intended to correct erroneous transactions before they reach the processing stage of the transaction processing cycle. At this stage computer programs perform file update, computation, and retrieval. Errors can result from an erroneous recording of a transaction or from a faulty conversion of the data to a computer-readable form. In most batch information systems, the verification and validity checks take place prior to the processing stage for the following two reasons:

1. The update and retrieval programs are usually too complex to contain the extra validity checks.

2. The processing programs are normally executed in fixed time intervals in one or several computer sites. Input preparation, on the other hand, is a continuous process throughout a certain time period and is distributed in many locations. Error corrections will be more efficient if done close in time and distance to the transaction occurrence.

Modern technology makes it possible for the recording, data verification, and data validation stages to be integrated by direct recording of data into a microcomputer or an intelligent data entry device. The separation between the stages is determined by the technological and economic alternatives available to a specific organization.

When the input transaction file has been edited, corrected, and cleared for use, file processing occurs. Processing the transaction file may take various forms and involve this file alone or this file in conjunction with one or more master files. Sorting is a common example of processing the transaction file alone. Sorting is the arrangement of records into some predetermined order, using a field in the record as a sorting key. There are many ways to sort records, depending upon the file media and equipment used.

Sorting is an important data processing activity, requiring a significant part of the information processing effort. If it is performed prior to input editing, the purpose is to detect duplicate transaction file in the same order as the master file to which it applies. Sorting may also be performed prior to printing output in order to have the data in a form that is convenient for distribution-for example, arranging a customer bills output file by zip codes before printing it. Processing the transaction file may involve other master files, from which data is retrieved only. One example is the processing of sale transactions for billing. Such transactions may contain a customer's number only; the customer's name and address are then obtained from the customer name-and-address file. Another example is the processing of a batch of inquiry transactions, such as requests to print various student records. For each transaction of this type, the student master file is accessed and a record retrieved for painting.

Updating is an example of processing the transaction file in conjunction with one or more master files. The master files are the permanent files of the organization and are maintained on a regular basis. Examples are the personnel file, the accounts payable file, and the general ledger file. The format of fields in master file records usually remain constant even though the field contents my change frequently.

Master files must be kept accurate by updating fields in the records, by adding new records, and by deleting old ones. For example, student are deleted from a student file once they graduate, and incoming students are added to the file periodically. The procedure for updating the master file depends on the type of file organization, and the processing methods.

Tthe record in the master file to be updated is read, updated, and then written onto an update file. In a sequential processing system, we usually assume that processed sequentially. Updating a file essentially involves reading of each master file record. If their is no transaction that applies to the record, the record is rewritten without change. If there is a transaction that applies to the record, the record is updated with changes; transactions reflecting new entities are used to add records to the file.

The relevant record should be deleted, then the record is simply not rewritten onto the updated file. In essence, the current master file is rewritten to produce a new, updated file. This approach of sequential batch processing of a salesperson master file. Inputs to the monthly salespeople update and analysis computer application consist of keyed receipts of gasoline and room and board expenditures incurred by the salespeople, as well as adjustments. The keyed receipts represent transaction records that update or add to variable fields in salespeople's records. They do not alter fundamental information stored in master files. For instance, they alter they year-to-date expenditure field in the salespeople's record, but not the address field. The keyed adjustments represent change or addition records, which are used to alter data fields considered constant in the master file, such as salespeople's names and addresses, or to add a new salesperson. This type of record adds to file contents, alters contents, and/or adjusts for errors. After keyed data is edited, the transactions are sorted by salespeople's numbers and processed by the analysis and update program. This processing entails totaling and posting expenditures to master file records, adding and deleting salespeople records, and printing a report.

The previous salespeople master file was produced as output from the last monthly process. The salespeople master file output from this month's process will, in turn, become the input to next month's process. Batch processes normally produce other output files, which can be used in other applications. For instance, the salespeople update program can produce a check file that will be used by a check program to print checks for reimbursing the salespeople.

The sequential process may seem cumbersome and somewhat archaic. You are right; however, in many organizational applications that do not require online update and retrieval of data, this process is still the backbone of data processing. Batch processing is also applicable when direct access storage devices are in use. In such cases some sorting and rewriting operations can be skipped, provided that the master files are not sequentially organized. However, the basic principle of operating in batches is not changed so long as the orientation of the TPS as a whole is not online.

The reporting stage provides the interface between the TPS and the users of its output. Effective reporting that aids the user in his or her perception of relevant information can substantially contribute to the usefulness of the system. Not all outputs from the system are reported. A large proportion of outputs may be stored in the data base without being reported in detailed form. Other outputs are stored for future processing. A payroll TPS, for example, can produce several outputs, including files, printed reports, documents and microfilmed reports. The TPS produce three major types of output: preplanned reports, preplanned responses to inquires, and transaction documents. Preplanned reports are preplanned as to content and format. They cover a predetermined time period and report either a status at a point in time or a flow during the period. Preplanned responses to inquiries are generally associated with limited output, usually with respect to part of the records in a master file.

A transaction document is an item such as an invoice, pay-check, bill or purchase order. Transaction documents can initiate some action, such as a purchase order, and they an be used to report a confirmation of a completed action. A documented designed for return and use in processing the completion of a transaction is known as a turnaround document. Examples are optically readable forms sent with customer billings with the request that they be returned with the payment. Transaction documents can also provide background information to the recipient and be used for reference purposes. The various reporting techniques and reporting media are each associated with costs and benefits. Some of these are

1. Preprinted paper forms
2. Computer generated paper forms
3. Optically readable forms
4. Computer output microfilm (COM)
5. Hard-copy terminal output
6. Soft-copy (Visual display) terminal output

The form of displayed output can vary. An alphanumeric display uses only a limited number of characters (the alphabet, numerals, special characters). Alphanumeric output is almost always a tabular display; only rarely in narrative from. Graphic display present information by means of graphs and patterns. Compared to tabular reports, graphic reports are not used very widely by transaction processing systems.

The various stages of the transaction processing cycle can take place in physically adjacent locations or in locations far apart. Also, the transactions and the computer can by physically separate. Similarly, there are various means of moving the transaction inputs to be processed and moving the output back to the users. Local processing is the term used when the transactions and the processing are physically adjacent; remote processing is the term when they are physically separate.

Remote processing may rely on mail, couriers, and transportation facilities to move inputs and outputs. In most cases, however, it relies on data communication facilities and on remote data entry devices to send transaction records in batches and to receive reports and documents. So long as processing and updating of files (including validation of transactions against master file) are not involved, this remote job processing should be classified as part of a batch transaction processing system. It does not merit any special discussion, since conceptually it was covered in the preceding sections.

Facilitics that are dependent on a distant data processing system linked by communication lines are thus equipped to perform part of the transaction processing cycle. Typically, they have data entry equipment that enables them to convert source documents into computer-readable input transactions, and they may also have printing equipment that can produce reports and documents. In other cases, such equipment may include a microcomputer. This approach allows the remote facility to handle data verification also. Transaction inputs is then verified and corrected at the point of entry, before it is communicated to the data processing center for processing. When data collection has an immediate effect on existing master files, the discussion applies to online transaction processing systems, to which we now turn.

In contrast to the delay inherent in periodic batch processing, online transaction processing can provide immediate data validation, or immediate updating and processing, or immediate reporting, or all these stages combined. In an online environment, the user is actually provided with direct access to files and computer programs via remote terminals and communication lines. The user can enjoy an immediate, real-time response. One of the main characteristics of an online processing system is that the sequence in which transactions are received is random, and each terminal may be treated as a separate transaction input source.

Transactions are processed continuously rather than periodically. Files are online and available to the system at all times for data validation and file updating. Errors in transactions my be detected immediately and corrected by the person making the data entry, rather than left for periodic processing, where erroneous transactions are returned to the source individual. The master files are continuously up to date and, thus, almost immediately reflect the occurrence of all events (provided that the transactions are immediately entered).

These advantages of online transaction processing are not gained without substantial costs. Extra computer time is required for processing and use of terminals; the application software and the system software are more complex than for batch processing; and a relatively heavy investment in acquisition and operation of terminals, communication lines and devices, direct access storage devices, mainframe computers, and additional control features is necessary.

Often online processing entails only part of the transaction processing cycle. This has to do mainly with the stages of data collection and data conversion and verification: transactions may be entered directly through terminals, immediately verified for correctness, then batched and processed at a subsequent time, as with batch processing. The advantages of this mode of delayed batch processing over conventional batch processing are the immediate capture of transactions in a computer-readable form and the immediate feedback for error correction.

Imagine a central warehouse connected online to a computer. The warehouse receives stocks from suppliers and issues stock items to manufacturing units. These transactions have to be entered and the inventory master file has to be updated immediately to constantly reflect quantities on hand.

A warehouse clerk, equipped with a computer terminal, enters each transaction into the system as it occurs. At the end of the data transmission, the system sends and acknowledgment to the terminal. This technique assures the clerk that the computer correctly received the transaction.

As soon as the transaction is received at the computer, the following tasks are performed:

1. The transaction (including date and time) is recorded onto a file called the transaction log. The transaction log is used for recovery from an error or a malfunction.

2. The transaction is verified and validated (including comparison against a master file

record) to make certain it is acceptable. This task is under the control of an edit program that can directly access the master inventory file.

3. If the transaction is erroneous, the system rejects, it, displaying the reason for rejection on the screen with an error message. The erroneous transaction is entered as an error record into a suspense file stored on a direct access device. The error record includes a code that indicates the error type, date and time, transaction type, and the content of the transaction. The error record is maintained until the corrected transaction is entered from the terminal.

4. An update program makes the master file record current. There are four types of transactions in our warehouse example, each requiring its own unique handling. Each type is identified by a transaction code:

   ADD- Add a new master record for a new stock item

   DEL- Delete an existing master record for an item that will not be stocked any more

   ISS- Quantity of an item issued

   REC- Quantity of an item received

Sometimes a failure destroys the current inventory and suspense files or makes them inaccessible to the system. When this occurs, it is impossible to proceed until the master files have been restored to their prefailure status. Therefore, the warehouse clerk is not allowed to access the system until it is operating with correct information. The restoration of service is accomplished by executing a computer program that recovers all the necessary information. The copies of the master files and the transaction log as of the beginning of the day are inputs to the recovery program. This recovery program repeats all the transaction processing up to the point of failure. The output of the recovery program is the reconstructed master files, which allow the system to be restarted at the point of failure. Once again, the warehouse clerk can access the system.

Structured decision systems

The files maintained by the various transaction processing systems serve both the operations and management modules of the information system. The difference between the modules is revealed in the various computer programs, not in the data files. We therefore distinguish between the data base and the model base of an information system.

The *model base* is the collection of application programs using the *data base*. The term *structured decision system* refers to information systems that make structured decision. While the TPS supports the activities of the operations level, the SDS makes decisions that are within the realm of operational and management control levels. The various SDSs cannot develop before the applicable TPSs are developed, since the automatic decisions made by an SDS are the result of processing data maintained by a TPS.

Any SDS incorporates programs that instruct the computer to process some relevant data by employing one or more decision models. A decision model represents a human decision-making process that is completely structured, and hence, programmable. The SDSs can be developed by one of two complementary approaches. First, as more and more transactions are collected and can use this data. Second, the organization can adopt known models or develop custom-made models, then use them to process either currently stored data or new data that was not collected before due to the lack of models.

A simple batch-mode SDS that determines reorder quantities based on this model. This SDS is activated at predetermined time intervals. Its input is a customer orders file that is one of the outputs of the customer orders TPS. This file is first sorted by stock item number of facilities more efficient processing. The records in this file contain the quantities of each item to be sold.

The reorder program accesses the updated inventory master file. Each item record in this file contains the safety stock, customers' back orders for the item, balance on hand, and quantity on order. For each item that has customer orders, the reorder program uses the relevant fields in both files and computes the new quantity to order. It then updates the inventory item master record with the new quantity on order and prints a line for each item that needs reordering.

What does this contrived SDS do? It makes reorder decisions that were once made by the firm's buyer, and it makes them in a faster and more accurate way. It uses data that was captured and processed by the customer orders TPS and by the inventory TPS.

Decision support system

This safety stock model accepts an inputs the data about demand for inventory items, the vendor lead times, and the order frequencies. It processes this data and produces an automatic decision. The demand forecasting then becomes an unstructured decision that cannot be converted to a computer program. It requires assumptions review the resulting forecast, change some more, and so on. He or she will finally select one of the forecasts and establish it as the figure used by the safety stock model. There are several implications in this short example, including the following:

1. Many decisions at the senior management level are unstructured or semi-structured.
2. The decision makers at this level must resort to assumptions, intuition, and experience when making such decisions.
3. The decision-making process is an interactive human-machine process. The machine supports the decision maker by evaluating various alternative solutions, and the decision maker selects one alternative and, thus, culminates the decision-making process.
4. The computer system provides supporting information to the decision maker by accessing the data base and using one or more models from the model base.
5. The interactive process takes place in a relatively short time. The senior manager cannot wait hours for the results of his or her processed assumptions. The process, therefore, normally requires an online mode of system operation.
6. The internal data base may have to be augmented by external data, such as those relating to business cycles. This data is not routinely captured by the TPS.
7. A prerequisite for the success of the interactive decision-making process is a convenient interface between the decision maker and the model base and between the decision maker and the data base.

These implications indicate, in effect, the necessary components and tools of a decision support system. Unlike TPSs and SDSs, DSSs are used to help solve the semistructured problems typical of the senior manager's world. They rely on the decision maker's insights and judgment at all stages of problems solving- from problem formulation, to choosing relevant data, to selecting the alternative solutions, and on to evaluating the solutions.

The term decision support system (also referred to as "management decision system," "management support system," or "strategic planning system") has been subject to a wide range of definitions. At one end is the narrow, specific definition of the DSS as "an interactive, computer-based system which supports managers in making unstructured decisions". At the other end is the more global assessment that a DSS is an aid in decision making and implementation; succinctly put, the DSS serves as an "executive mind-support system". It is one of the many tools a manager can choose to aid in daily decision-making activities.

The decision support system is not an "automated manager," but rather a "right-hand person," standing ready to support, not replace the manager. The hallmark of a good decision support system is not its sophistication or efficiency, but its ability to increase the effectiveness of the manager who employs it. Another definition, which clearly distinguishes a DSS from an SDS, asserts that "a DSS is a computer-based information system used to support decision-making activities in situation where it is not possible or not desirable to have an automated system perform the entire decision process".

Regardless of how a decision support system is defined, conceptually it must possess four essential components: data, decision models, a user-system interface, and decision makers. A DSS supports a semistructured decision; it is designed to support a decision maker in any stage of the decision-making process. The decision maker can choose those functions of the DSS that support some stage while not using other functions. For instance, a decision maker may require the use of data but not models.

The key to successful human-machine cooperation is this principle of specified DSS support. Early DSS literature defined DSS-appropriate problems as those that are semistructured. The degree of problem structure is, indeed, central to DSS. At one extreme, if a decision problem can be completely structured then an SDS can replace the human decision maker. At the other extreme, if no structure can be imposed on the problem, decision support is impossible. It is only between these extremes that DSS is relevant.

A problem is semistructured when it is possible to impose some structure on the problem, such as when a decision maker is willing to accept a certain data set or certain models as relevant to the problem situation. Thus, DSS can be defined as systems applicable to problems that can be at least partially, but not completely, structured. It does not matter to which stage of the decision-making process the structure is applied. Indeed, DSS literature has examples of support for all phases-intelligence, design of alternative solutions, evaluation of and choice among alternatives, as well as monitoring the implementation of the chosen solution. Of course, they type of support will vary from stage to stage since the nature of the activities varies. For instance, relatively few DSSs support the design stage, which typically requires the system to have more problem domain knowledge than is the case for other stages.

Before delineating the typical components of a DSS, we wish to remind you of the fundamental premise of the systems approach. Systems, regardless of their specific contexts, share a common set of elements. A DSS, being system, has a specific environment, mainly the users and their decision situation; the system impacts the user by providing some outputs; the system consumes some resources; and, the system has some internal structure, comprising components and their interrelationship.

The purpose of a DSS is to support a decision-making process. DSS can support decision makers in many ways, including the following:

1. Retrieving single items of information
2. Providing a mechanism, for ad hoc data analysis
3. Providing prespecified aggregations of data
4. Estimating the consequences of proposed decisions
5. Proposing solutions

Providing each of these types of support is likely to require different DSS capabilities. This, in turn, will lead to different components and arrangements. DSS literature seems to agree about three generic components of a DSS. These hardware/software components correspond to the conceptual components specified.

The dialog management subsystem provides and manages the framework in which outputs are presented to the user and in which inputs are specified by the user. The dialog between the user and the system is two way: output representations define the context for and prompt subsequent user inputs. An ideal dialog management subsystem has three elements.

1. *User interface*: Concerned with the syntactic aspects of the interaction, the interfacing with specific input and output devices and issues relating to the style of interaction. The specific design of the user interface element depends on the proficiency of users and the frequency of use.

2. *Request constructor*: Provides the two-way transformations between users' requests and the specific modeling and data access repertory. In one direction, it translates users' requests for data to valid database queries, and users' model references to corresponding model-invoking commands. In the opposite direction, it translates requests issued by the model base subsystem for the incorporation of user-supplied parameters in a specific mode. The specific design of this element reflects the vocabulary of the element, and the constraints imposed by the data base and model base subsystems of the DSS.

3. *Control element*: Guarantees the smooth operation of the dialog management subsystem; determines the mode of system's use, which can vary between "system-prompted" mode and completely "user-driven" mode. This reflects the structure level of the supported decision situation (system-prompted mode for highly structured situation; suer-driven mode where no predefined sequence of activities can be provided by the system).

The intelligence phase of the decision-making process involves scanning the environment in search of problems or opportunities. These problems or opportunities are recognized by accessing relevant data. In the case of a marketing decision, for instance, data must be accessed on each of the company's products as a first step in determining which products are to be phased out. This data might include such items as dollar sales, physical volume, total unit cost, and price per unit. Data such as this will normally be systematically collected from the internal environment as part of a routine TPS.

However, a DSS, as distinguished from a TPS, will often require collection of data concerning other environments. This may include data concerning competitors' actions, general societal trends, customer demand, or legal and/or governmental constraints. This type of data may be collected routinely or on an ad hoc basis. The relevant data is collected and stored in a data base to await the scanning stage.

A manger armed with the objectives of the firm begins the ongoing search for problems or opportunities. This search can take one of three forms, depending upon the type decision to be made and the level of the decision maker. A structured continuous search is usually performed in order to make decisions that are well defined and regular. The user may extract isolated data in order to perform such functions as monitoring the work flow and scheduling operations of a production department, or he or she may receive prespecified standard reports that act as input to the design stage of the decision-making process. Data may also be retrieved by a structured, but ad hoc, search in order to make infrequent decisions. Plant location is such a decision since it will normally occur infrequently.

The necessary intelligence gathering activities can be clearly structured. The output from such a search usually suggests the process to be used to analyze the situation, but it can also indicate the need for human intervention before the process can begin. Finally, there are problems and opportunities for which the search must be done heuristically through examination of data by the manager. This type of decision is usually made by senior management. The intelligence phase primarily provides the managers with easy access to the data base. The data retrieval capabilities of the DSS must therefore be rapid. This, of course, has many implications for the design of a DSS. The output from such a search generally identifies the situation but leaves the rest of the decision process to the manager. Sometimes the manager employs some programmed models to manipulate the relevant data and come up with alternative solutions.

The management of data—the ability to store, retrieve, and manipulate—is thus fundamental to a DSS. These activities are performed by the data management subsystem, which contains four generic elements. These four elements are

1. *The database management system*—provides an access mechanism, to data in the data base. The DBMS provides such services as data sharing and integration, data definitions, data manipulation, and data integrity. The DBMS also shields the other subsystems of the DSS from physical aspects of access to the data base.

2. *The query facility*—Serves as the front-end element of the data management subsystem and as the subsystem's interface to the model management and dialog management subsystems. It accepts requests for data from these subsystems, determines how these requests an be filed, translates the requests to DBMS-specific commands, and finally returns the requested data to the issuing subsystem.

3. *The data directory*—Provides the basis for answering preliminary questions submitted by the query facility concerning availability and source of data, or their exact meaning. This element contain meta-data . It is much needed in ad hoc DSSs, the directory's function is internal to the DBMS element and might then disappear as an independent element.

4. *The staging element*—Provides access to sources of data that are external to the DSS. It is an interface between the DBMS element and its DSS-specific data base and other organizational data bases or remote data bases. It structure reflects the nature of external data sources from which data is extracted. For instance, if remote data bases are to be accessed, some data communications facility is included in the staging element.

The model management subsystem

The model base will usually consist of a wide range of models, depending upon the type of decision to be made and the organizational level at which it is applied. The model building blocks and subroutines may include such standard applications as linear programming, capital budgeting, time series analysis, analysis of variance, and multiple regression.

A series of operational, tactical, or strategic models can be constructed functions in the decision-making process. It can make the decision, propose the decision, or estimate the consequences of proposed decisions. There is an equally wide range of modeling techniques to support decisions. The decision model assumes the role of decision maker when the decision is programmed and the process is routine. Conventional transaction processing deals primarily with this type of decision, but many decisions are based on data that enters the system through transaction processing.

The models used to make decisions usually involve relatively simple computational or statistical techniques such as simple and multiple correlation, sample selection, factor analysis, or other standard calculations. An example of the decision-making capabilities of a decision model is an insurance renewal rate and actuarial assumptions. The method differs from that of an SDS only in that the judgment of the underwriters is used to decide whether the standard calculations apply to a particular policy. The underwriter works with the DSS to arrive at the appropriate decision.

Another important type of model used for this type of decision making is the analytical decision model. It arrives at the optimum decision by representing the real world situation in mathematical form. Probably the most widely used of these optimizing techniques is linear programming. This technique can be employed at both the operational and the tactical levels. It is useful at the operational level when specific values for the parameters are known. At the tactical level these values may not be known and probabilistic estimates may have to be substituted. Probability distributions often serve this function.

The DSS is usually used at the tactical level for decisions that are only partially programmed. Such models are normally employed in the allocation and control of a firm's resources. They would typically be used to perform such management control activities as financial planning, personnel requirement planning, and routine capital budgeting-applications that require much subjective data because of the element of uncertainty involved. Because of this uncertainty and the interaction of several variables, the output from this type of decision model can only propose decisions.

The decision models used for strategic level decision making are normally broad in scope and employed to estimate long-term consequences of the decisions proposed by senior management. They function as a sort of "crystal ball" to enable managers to see the future scenarios that would result from their present decisions. The types of decisions made at this management level involve an even large amount of uncertainty and therefore, are nonprogrammable. Often the only way to approach such a decision is to employ a heuristic procedure. This will not lead to an optimal solution but will provide a decision that is generally superior to many alternative approaches.

The best use of models in this situation is an interactive human-machine process. The manger proposes the alternatives and the model supplies the predicted consequences. The simulation model is most commonly used for prediction purposes. It attempts to duplicate the real world under varying states of nature for a given set of parameters. Since a state of nature represents a random event, it is often necessary to generate a random variable for use in the simulation model. The random variable may represent, for example, varying levels of demand relevant to a marketing decision.

Simulation models are well suited to the complexity of strategic level decision making. They are able to deal with problems that cannot be handled by other methods. They are also very versatile, enabling the manager to perform sensitivity analysis on various parameters. This sensitivity analysis capability aids the manager in interpreting the results of the model. From these results the manager can gauge the risk inherent in his or her decisions and modify them accordingly. Any support beyond direct access to raw data invokes the application of a model. In fact, the management of models and modeling activities is what distinguishes DSS from TPS and SDS. The ability to invoke, run, change, combine, and inspect models is a core service of a DSS. The model management subsystem has the following generic elements.

1. *The model base management system*—Resembles, conceptually, the service of the DBMS with regard to data. It provides storage and retrieval facilities for programmed models. It supports the generation of models, perusal of models, updating of model parameters, and restructuring of models. An integral part of the MBMS is a model directory, which provides information about models in response to users' inquiries, or in support of the model executor's efforts to integrate several models into a super model. Another part of the MBMS can be staging element that extracts models from remote, online computerized model bases.

2. *The modeling command processor*—The interface between the model and dialog management subsystems. It accepts and interprets modeling instructions from the query facility element of the dialog subsystem. Interpreted instructions are then routed to the corresponding elements: inquiries about models are forwarded to the MBMS; model-building instructions to the model executor.

3. *The model executor*—The heart of the modeling subsystem. It controls the actual running of models by linking together attachable models retrieved from the model base. It also interacts with the request constructor element of the

dialog subsystem to obtain from the user the parameters and data that are needed by the models being run.

4. *The data base interface*—Connects the model and data management subsystems. It allows running models to retrieve data from the data base and to store outputs on the data base. It translate model requests for data into valid query formats, and query outputs to the internal data structure of the model.

The preceding description of the three subsystems of a DSS represents a full-blow generic schema. Its full implementation depends on the type of architecture that links the subsystems. The architecture, in turn, depends on the type of decision situations that are supported, on the users, and on the resources of the DSS. In practice, DSSs may not exhibit all the elements of the three subsystems as distinct entities.

The most important conceptual component of a DSS is the user. A decision support system cannot be considered advantageous unless the user employs it to increase his or her effectiveness. The DSS and the user work in tandem to arrive at the best solution.

Once the intelligence and design phases have been completed, a choice must be information to support a choice, but it cannot make the final decision. This requires the intervention of the human decision maker. The decision maker may employ many different methods to arrive at a decision. He or she may prefer a very structured approach in which the output from decision models can be employed to directly determine the decision. More often than, not, the decision-making process of the user will be very unstructured and informal, involving a great deal of intuition and business common sense.

As observed by the developers of one DSS, "Mangers don't really know how they make decisions, and, on top to that, they don't want to reveal the details of decision making of which they are aware, as these tend to be important specifics". This is particularly true in the case of ill-structured problems. Whatever the method employed by the decision maker, it is important for the technical specialist to be aware of individual orientations when designing a specific decision support system.

The DSS should take into account the user's tasks, abilities, cognitive preferences, and ways of arriving at decisions. Because the decision maker makes the policy decisions and, in effect, becomes the model formulator, he or she works with an analysts in translating informal decision models into formal, computerized models. This enables the decision maker to take an active, creative part in the development of the decision support system. This DSS user-orientation has several implications. The traditional orientation toward technical characteristics, with applications developed from the perspective of operations researchers and management scientists, was myopic. If failed to anticipate how useful such systems could be to all levels of management. The user-orientation allows the full potential of such systems and of the decision maker to be realized. A decision support system can extend the decision maker's capabilities in several ways. It can improve interpersonal communication by providing the user with tools for persuasion.

By establishing a common conceptual basis for decision making, it can provide the decision maker with a vocabulary and discipline that facilitate negotiations and increase organizational control. A DSS also helps the decision maker expand his or her experience by providing a means to explore alternatives. When we refer to the "user" of a DSS, we actually refer to a range that varies from one person to many. Individual users may be the ultimate decision maker; and interested party; a "chauffeur" who supports the ultimate decision maker; or a "feeder". This range implies a great variety of DSS configurations.

The labels of "institutional" and "*Ad hoc*," which are applied to the DSS, can also relate to the number and type of users. Institutional Dss is utilized for repetitive decision-making tasks. An important example of this is the portfolio management system developed by Gerrity. The PMS system involves a computer-based information system used by several portfolio managers within a bank, each addressing the portfolio management problem in a different manner. In contrast, an ad hoc DSS is developed and utilized for problems that are nonrepetitive. It is used for support of decision making in infrequent situations, particularly those with a one-shot, high-payoff nature. An example of this is a corporate merger decision.

Much of the DSS literature implies that DSS must be used by mangers, or perhaps even upper-level managers. However, while many DSSs are used by managers, many others are used by nonmanagers. In fact, many students have developed microcomputer-based DSSs using software resources such as Lotus 1-2-3 for support in solving problems in marketing or finance courses. The principal users of PMS are not mangers in the traditional sense, but rather investment decision makers. GADS, a DSS that has been used in a number of decision situations involving geographic boundaries has had users who were not managers.

DSSs are used in organizational settings and do not only support lone decision makers. DSSs are often used to coordinate decision-making activities among the multiple, interdependent participates in a decision. Two types of decision support, personal support and organizational support, are distinct and so warrant discussion. Personal support involves a DSS designed for direct and individual use by a decision maker. For example, personal support of departmental budgeting should provide the departmental mangers with easy ways to enter, manipulate, and display forecasted values.

Decisions requiring organizational support involve large, interdependent organizations and coordination as for calculations. For example, organizational support for budgeting should provide storage facilities for disaggregated, detailed budgets at the departmental level, and the integration of these by division and for the company as a whole. As these examples illustrate, the same task may require both personal support and organizational support. This distinction between personal and organizational support has implications for the DSS hardware and software resources. DSS can be implemented on a mainframe, on a microcomputer, or on both. While most of the early DSSs were mainframe based and used mainframe software packages, there can be a three-tiered structure: an organization can use a DSS with a spreadsheet package at the microcomputer level for local personal modeling; a micro-mainframe link can be used to handle medium-sized application; and decision situations that require more intensive DSS resources can be run on the mainframe, using a large software package.

There is some discussion akin to the old chicken-egg controversy over which came first: the capability or the need the software and hardware innovations from which new managerial uses of computers were developed, or the growing need for decision support systems from which stemmed the needed software and hardware. Regardless of the sequence of events, it is evident that the unique characteristics of a decision support system dictate specific hardware and software resources.

A DSS must have certain general capabilities in order to be beneficial to a user. Since the DSS will support users at several different levels of the organization, for both structured and nonstructured decisions, its primary strengths should be flexibility, ease of use, and adaptability. Flexibility implies that it can reflect the decision processes of different users and can adapt to their changing needs. These capabilities generate specific design criteria for both hardware and software.

The software used for system development should allow for rapid creation and modification. The system design should allow for quick and easy extensions. The human interface between user and computer should occur through a dialog, with a vocabulary readily comprehensible to the user.

The hardware employed should provide display devices that can be used to communicate with the user. Thus, the resources available for DSS fall into five major categories: people, hardware, software, data, and design methodologies. Design methodologies, used to construct a DSS, are diverse.

People are the resources for DSS design and operation skills. Many roles are involved in developing and operating a DSS. These roles can be played by humans, or, alternatively, by other resources, dependent on the availability and cost of human and nonhuman resources.

For example, the staging element can be a hardware-software mechanism, or a human; data extraction from external data bases will then, respectively, be either computerized or manual.

DSS data can be internal, operational, and maintained by the TPS, or it can be external, in a manual or a computerized form. Again, these resources can be substituted: an organization can elect to subscribe to an information utility in lieu of collecting the relevant data itself.

The greatest number of advance directly related to decision support systems have occurred in the area of software. The myriad user needs have dictated the creation of broad range of software tailored to individual user needs. Software for decision support systems can be provided by a vendor, developed by an in-house staff of specialists, or formulated by the users themselves. Software developed in -house can use either a high-level, general-purpose language such as FORTRAN or APL, or a special-purpose language.

Software is needed to manage the data base and the model base. The large amount and varied composition of the data collected for decision support systems necessitate a sophisticated data management system. This is provided by a well-organized data base manipulated through a data base management system. The software that probably best addresses the complexity of the data base, as well as the differing needs of the users, is that of a relation DBMS.

The relational DBMS assumed the onerous task of structuring the data so it can be easily manipulated by the computer. All the manger has to do is tell the system, in a non-technical language, what information is wanted and in what format. This type of DBMS is particularly well suited to top management level decision makers because it is easy to use, provides for quick and easy inclusion of new data, and allows incorporation of data from the external environment.

The complete orientation toward the user makes this type of DBMS of particular value to the decision maker. However, the cost implications of increased overhead time, greater storage, and redundancy of data may offset these relational DBMS advantages. The model base represents the core of the decision-making process. It supports a wide variety of managerial decisions by reflecting the way the manger thinks and by assisting the manger in reviewing alternative solutions. Its basic purpose can be simply stated ad aiding in the planning process.

The complex manipulation of large amounts of data through several iterations necessitates a development language that is flexible and user-oriented. As in the case of the DBMS, software for model base development and management can either be purchased ready-made from software vendors, computer manufacturers or time-sharing services, or it can be developed from scratch using a nontechnical programming language. Packaged models give the user great flexibility. They can be used separately or as building blocks to construct more complex models. The user can define subroutines in a language such as BASIC and incorporate them into the packaged model. Once the model is constructed, it can just as easily be modified.

Sensitivity analysis can be performed through the use of a "what if" command, which allows changes in certain parameters to be quickly assessed. There may also be a "goal seeking" or "reverse what if" command to determine what change is required in one variable to produce specific changes in another variable. A number of functions beyond the standard algebraic and trigonometric functions are also provided by modeling software. Software for curve-fitting and extrapolation of data, as well as standard business routines such as computing net present value and depreciation, can be specially useful to managers at all levels. Many packages allow for probabilistic specification of variables. The model base in most effective when the various models used are integrated. This requires the use of a model base management system very similar in concept to the data base management system. Arrays of data in the form of output of the various models are normally stored separately. The MBMS allows, by means of simple commands, for the consolidation of the content of the arrays, as in the case of financial analyses of several companies in a certain industry. These commands also enable the user to specify the exact format of the output report. The formats can be either prespecified or create as needed.

The MBMS can perform the following tasks: periodic run of well-established models; of a model or set of models; sequential run of a set of interrelated models according to a redefined procedure. Most importantly, the MBMS allows for flexibility in both input and output. The greatest range of resources developed specifically for DSS is in the software area. Ultimately, all DSS software is built upon general purpose programming languages. While such languages can be used to develop specific DSS, they are not unique to them. We will concentrate on four major classes of software resources for DSS.

1. *Specific DSSs*—systems tailored to a specific decision situation of particular users. Whilc many such systems arc custom built, some can be bought off-the-shelf and put to use immediately. One such example is MYCIN a system designed to support medical diagnosis. Few systems have become commercially available for microcomputers, though there are many proprietary microbased systems within organizations.

2. *DSS tool*—Software packages that can be used to construct DSS. A tool can address only one of the DSS subsystems, not all three. There is quite a number of DBMSs and dialog management packages. There has been relatively little work on tools for model management.

3. *Dss generators*—Collections of DSS tools. These are software packages that can be used to construct SDSS tailored to support specific decision situations. All generators have a model management capability and all address, to some extent, the data and dialog management function. For example, Louts 1-2-3 is a modeling package that provides data and dialog management facilities; FRAMEWORK provides an integration of spreadsheet, data base, word processing, graphics, and communications facilities.

4. *Generalized DSSs*- Software packages that provide support for a large class of problems, typically used by many individuals within an organization who face decision problems in that general class. Unlike SDSS, generalized DSSs are not tailored to specific problems. They differ from DSS generators in that their capabilities can be directly applied to the decision situation, rather than being used like a generator to develop an SDSS that can then be applied to the problem. The modeling facility of these software resources leans heavily on statistical processing.

Like DSS generators, these generalized DSSs vary in the degree of data and dialog management facilities. For example, there are packages that provide some data management and extensive dialog management; other packages provide good dialog management, nut no data management. The hardware resources include processors (mainframes, minicomputers, micro-computers), terminals, storage devices, and communications networks. We have already mentioned the possible three-tiered structure of a DSS hardware configuration. None of these resources is unique to DSS and all are applicable to other systems as well. The choice among these resources depends on the DSS environment. For example, different hardware configurations will be required for a personal support system, for an organizational support system, or for a DSS supporting both.

Certain characteristics of a decision support system dictate specific hardware requirements. Decisions made using a DSS need timely data. Often a quick model must be run several times, with a slight modification each time, before the decision maker is prepared to reach a decision. Any delay in receipt of the necessary information would impair the effectiveness of the DSS. This implies a fast response-usually through an online system-that can provide the user with the best means for performing many interactions of the decision-making process. The greatest benefits of a decision support system are derived from a manager's ability to obtain instant feedback through direct access to the computer. This can be accomplished by placing a terminal within easy reach of the manager.

A menu-driven system can be employed to provide the decision maker with even greater ease of use. All the user would have to do is move the cursor to the desired application to begin the chain of events that will lead to the final decision. The CRT can be used to present graphic displays, often in full color, to delineate and accentuate certain relationships of particular importance. For example, a graphic display of sales trends for a given consumer product may help the manger conceptualize the problem at hand. A plotter is another peripheral device that can serve this purpose.

Reliability of the system hardware is just as important as fast response. The trade-offs between an in-house mainframe and subscription to a time-sharing service must be examined. In selecting a time-sharing service, the amount of down time is of critical importance. Another consideration, particularly in regard to the selection of in-house hardware, is the size of the computer needed. Sophisticated software components of a decision support system may require extensive hardware capabilities.

The type of data base and DBMS chosen will affect the size of main storage needed. Direct access storage devices will also be needed. All this many imply a heavy initial investment in hardware, which should be considered before a DSS is implemented. A trend to significantly increase the computing power delegated to end-user equipment. This will enable users to perform most of the computing needs of a DSS at the front end. The mainframe computers will then serve as hosts for large corporate data bases and "switch-boards" for communications networks.

Only very heavy computational tasks will be performed by mainframes. This trend is a blessing for end users since most of them prefer to rely on local equipment supported by powerful central machines rather than being connected directly to a central computer shared by thousands of users.

Many DSSs used in organizations were described in detail in published books or articles. Most reflect the components and tools of DSS discussed in this chapter. Successful applications of DSS include portfolio management; merger and acquisition analysis; the design of police force beats; the redesign of school districts; market planning; corporate planning; personnel planning; policy analysis in state government; management of research and development; product planning media selection; and budgeting.

It is extremely difficult to evaluate the success of these systems. A DSS is not a package that can be bought off the shelf and plugged into the organization. It is implemented gradually and evolves over time with the organization. In general, DSS cannot be justified in terms of costs an benefits. We have already seen in chapter 3 how difficult it is to measure the dollar benefits resulting form correct or improved decisions. Keen concludes that the benefits of a DSS can be hard to quantify but not necessarily to recognize.

A DSS seems to be of direct value to managers, often providing intangible benefits and in many instances costing comparatively little. There were probably numerous microcomputer-based DSSs in the late 1980s. Their proliferation is due to the advances in DSS resources (microcomputers, micro-based software generators and tools, storage and communication technologies, and computer literacy of organizational users). Following is a brief survey of several maniframe-based DSSs. The references mentioned describe each system in more detail.

PMS is a DSS developed by Gerrity to support a portfolio manager. It is based on graphic display with integration of simple models and a complex data base. The system, in use in several major banks in the U.S. is considered to be a success for the following reasons: it enables the portfolio manager to concentrate on the important parts of a decision; the effectiveness of decisions and of the decision-making process increased; and it improved the thinking process of portfolio managers.

Brandaid is a DSS developed by Little to support market planning. It aids brand mangers in determining prices promotion and advertising budgets, and sales price allocation for a product. The system was designed with the following principles in mind: simplicity; ease of control and use: ease of updating and communications; and marketing managers. It is considered a success for its ability to support managers in thinking in an orderly fashion.

GADS is a DSS developed from 1970 to 1974 at IBM. It constructs and displays computerized maps that can aid in geographic distribution of resources and people. It can describe the geographic allocation of crimes and thus help design police beats. Also, it was used by IBM to determine how many representatives to put where, when, and how. One of the impressive aspects of GADS was its flexibility and ease of use; over 200 noncomputer people at 17 different organizations have used it.

The system developers emphasized the importance of the human interface element of the system by incorporating a special interactive terminal and a special management language. MAPP is a system designed to support financial planning, cost assignment, and budget preparation. It deals with a spectrum of activities, ranging from structured to unstructured: it establishes a discipline for defining banking products; it identifies the costs incurred in producing these products; it allows for analysis to determine how resources might be shifted among products; it helps to prepare the budgets for the departments that product these products. The system is conversational, with extensive multilevel prompts to lead the user through the required steps.

Group decision support systems

In large organizations, organizational decision making inevitably involves groups of people. This has given rise to requirements for new decision support systems that can accommodate a multi-user environment. With the advancement in computer technology, particularly in the area of distributed electronic workstations, the concept of DSS has been applied to support organizational decision making. As result, the concept of a group decision support system has been proposed by several management information systems researchers.

Empirical findings suggest that the technology of GDSS significantly influences idea generation in group decision-making processes. A group decision support system can be defined as a computer-based system that is used to support collective problem solving. A collective decision-making process can be viewed as a problem-solving situation in which

1. there are tow or more persons, each of them characterized by his/her own perceptions, attitudes, motivations, and personalities;
2. participants recognize the existence of common problems and goals; and
3. participants attempt to reach a collective decision.

Decisions may take many forms: rendering an opinion, finding a solution for a problem, making a specific recommendation, defining alternative courses of action, handing down a verdict, or stating a general policy. Two aspects are present in any decision making. One is the content, which has to be valid and meaningful. The other is how the decision is made.

A decision that disregards these two aspects frequently leads to unenthusiastic participation of those who must implement it. Calling for a vote when the issue has not been well-discussed gives a bare majority decision, which can result in hostile feelings among those who have been defeated. Because of too little regard for the *how* side of making decisions, they frequently have to be remade.

Communication is a very important factor in group decision-making process. Moreover, it has emerged as the core issue in designing and implementing an effective group decision support system. Three types of participants use a GDSS while in session. The first type is the meeting chairperson, the person who presides over the discussion. However, the chairperson does not necessarily have to possess strong computer competence. Therefore, he or she is aided by a chauffeur: a technical expert who is proficient in operating the hardware and software features of the GDSS.

Typical activities of a chauffeur would include: transferring data from an individual's screen to the public screen, data retrieval from corporate data base, activating a certain software package, producing hard copies of reports, and the like. The chauffeur does not have to be a participant in the meeting but may act as a "shadow operator" that facilitates the process. The third type is a regular participant who may come to the meeting with some ideas and preparatory work already recorded in a diskette. He or she may wish to operate a microcomputer and at a time impart some of the data to the public screen. Here again, the chauffeur may be of help.

As the ease of use of end-user workstations improves and the availability of local and wide area networks increases, the extension of DSS to GDSS becomes more common. It is likely that many board meeting rooms of large organizations will be equipped with microcomputer networks in the near future.

All of the examples used so far in this chapter had to do with applications that involved processing of data that was mostly numeric in nature, and with models that manipulated such data by using mathematical algorithms. Thus we have described customer order transactions, inventory reordering transactions, accounts receivable file update, and support of sales decisions.

It may seem from the preceding sections that the three-tiered structure of information systems in organizations pertains only to operators, mangers, and operations that are directly related to the activities that produce the outputs of the organization. Indeed, we have discussed transactions and decisions that are part of marketing information systems, manufacturing in formation systems, accounting information systems, and like. Neglected were people and operations that only indirectly contribute to the final outputs, but nonetheless are vital to the organization. Organizations often require the services not only of drivers, lathe operators, cashiers, and salespersons, but also of office personnel-typists, receptionists, telephone operator, technical writers, and secretaries. In fact, managers at all levels spend more time in the office writing and reading reports, drafting letters and memos, participating in meetings, than they spend on actually making decisions assisted by the conventional TPS, SDS, or DSS.

Office information systems are the combination of hardware, software and people are in information systems that process office transactions and support office activities at all levels of the organization. It is basically the lack of office information technologies in the past that made the office one of the least efficient segments of contemporary organizations. The most unproductive workers in many organizations are office employees and executives.

Office information system is thus a concept involving a number of current and future technologies that are introduced into the office to improve office productivity, to facilitate organizational communications, and also to provide more stimulating and intellectually rewarding work for people in the office. These technologies, which are briefly reviewed in the following sections, include microelectronics, telecommunications, main storage, micrographics, image and voice processing, teleconferencing, videoconferencing, facsimile, and software technologies.

Classification of activities and information

The activities performed in the office can be classified into two main categories. These are:

1. Activities performed by clerical personnel (clerks, secretaries, typists, messengers)
2. Activities performed by an executive and professional personnel (mangers, staff, assistants, engineers, economists, and researchers)

Obviously there is some activity overflow between the two categories. Therefore, the characteristic activities discussed here are not necessarily exclusive to one category.

Stages of office computerization

It is rare for an organization to have the technological and organizational capability to simultaneously computerizes the number and variety of office activities. It is, therefore, necessary to set priorities. The order of priorities presented here is based on the degree of activity complexity and on the availability of technology. We are not taking economic consideration into account, since these must be examined for each case of computerization. The order of stages presented here assume; that since most of the work load in the office is performed by the clerical personnel, the greatest marginal savings will be obtained by computerizing these activities prior to computerizing activities of the executive/professional personnel.

A word processor is a configuration of hardware and software that provides typing, editing, production, reproduction, and document storage services. A word processor can operate as an independent *workstation* where the minimal configuration is a keyboard, a CPU with internal storage, a screen, a printer, and an external storage device. More complex configurations can include several workstations sharing common resources.

Since a word processor produces documents on a magnetic medium, its implementation is practically a prerequisite for computerizing an office. While its advantage is that it can be independently implemented in different office, it is necessary to retain the option to link such independent systems to a network that may be implemented in a subsequent stage.

Once a WP system is implemented, filing of outgoing mail on a magnetic medium is an almost immediate consequence. The implementation of this function relies on appropriate cataloging and retrieval software. Most of the work involved concerns conventional office and procedures analysis, and not technological issues. This immediate electronic filing pertains to outgoing mail and to other documents generated by the WP system, such as contracts and manuals. The electronic filing of incoming conventional mail and documents requires a much more complex technology.

Controlling performance is a managerial function pertaining to the recording of decisions and important dates in the sequence of implementing various organizational tasks. With appropriate software, the computer can be used as a memory aid to managers or other entities. Controlling performance is not usually a high-priority computerization function. It is noted here as stage 3 because it can be implemented on a stand-alone WP system. The functions described in the following stages require a communications network among the various offices.

Electronic mail involves the transfer to letters and documents through telecommunications lines, rather than through physical facilities. It speeds up mail deliveries and reduced the cost and time of paper mail. Electronic mail relies on facsimile transmissions equipment and on communicating word processors to transfer any type of document. An electronic mail system requires a telecommunications network and software that can identify addresses and temporarily store incoming and outgoing mail.

Terminals in the office workstations are tied to a computing and telecommunications net work. The workstations handle all internal correspondence by delivering letters and memos electronically; each piece is electronically read from any location and is then indexed, filed, retrieved, or disposed of automatically.

The linking of office workstations in a telecommunications network can provide for the transmission of message in the network in addition to electronic mailing. A message, as distinguished from mail, is information that is not filed or cataloged. A considerable amount of office time and a number of telephone conversations involve such memos and notes. A message keyed in form one workstation that is transmitted to another workstation reduces the load on telephone lines. It also involves a single activity-the sender and receiver of the message do not have to be in the office at the same time, since the message can be saved on an external storage device until it is retrieved by the receiver.

Scheduling of meetings and conferences can be facilitated with electronic calendars. When several office workstations are linked in a network, calendars can be stored on a magnetic medium. A person who wants to schedule a meeting can use the automated office system to find a meeting date that is convenient for all participants. A computer program will accept, in this case, such parameters as the duration of the meeting, the subject, and a range of dates for scheduling the meeting The program will review the various calendars, come up with a tentative meeting date, and display the date to the participants. If the participants approve, the program will finalize the date, enter the data on the calendars, and then announce the meeting date to the participants. If all do not approve, the program will come up with another tentative date and will again poll the participants.

The information relevant to office activities is classified into several patterns: textural data, numeric data, graphics, images, and voices. Stages 1 to 6 mainly deal with processing textual data, or with substituting a textual medium for another medium. Future office information systems will be able to process other patterns of information in an integrative way.

Currently, information patterns other than textural are processed independently using the following devices:

1. Numerical data—processed by electronic data processing systems
2. Graphic data—Processed manually by

draftspersons or by electronic devices such as plotters, graphic monitors, computer-aided design and computer-aided manufacturing systems, photocopiers, and facsimile transmission equipment.

3. Images—Processed by photocopying devices, facsimile equipment, TV and video devices

4. Voice-Processed by recording and playback devices, PABX systems, and dictating machines

Current trends indicate future integration of these distinct systems. For instance, a drawing could be transmitted from one workstation to another, filed on a digital magnetic medium, and then merged into a text handled by a word processing system. An other example of such integration is a videotex system involving telephone television, and computers.

The integration of the systems will enable integrated office activities such as teleconferencing or video-conferencing. Several people in different locations can conduct a joint meeting using telephones to converse, video monitors to watch facial expressions, and computer monitors to view numerical data displayed simultaneously on all screens and retrieved from a common data base. Another example of integrated systems is a voice message switching system. A person wishing to send a message will not have to key it in. Instead, he or she will dictate the message to the office workstation and key in the list of addressees. The computer will store the message in a digitalized form and send it to the addressees when each switches on the workstation.

Information system briefly presents the technological components needed to implement each stage of office system automation. While it does not deal with the technical specifications of the components or with their availability, it does specify what is needed to implement each stage listed in the previous section. The basic workstation required for word processing comprises a microcomputer a monitor, a keyboard, a printer, and an external storage device. This hardware configuration, together with appropriate software, constitutes a stand- along word processing system.

Electronic filing requires the same configuration, but with additional software for filing and retrieval. An office and procedures analyst is also needed to design filing and retrieval procedures. A more complex word processing and electronic filing system can contain several microcomputer-based workstations linked in a network and accessing a common data base. Or, alternatively, a number of "dumb" workstations can be linked to a central computer, thus enabling simultaneous work by a number of persons. The progression into controlling performance does not require a change in the hardware configuration, but does require appropriate software. Above all it requires a conceptual change since a workstation in this stage serves not only the clerical personnel but also the manger, either directly or through staff assistants.

The implementation of the next stages requires the technology of telecommunications. Telecommunications is the basic technology in advanced office information systems. The area of telecommunications encompasses a spectrum of topic covering optical communication, packet radio techniques, satellite communications, digital signal processing, fiber optics, and electronic switching. Where office computing was the most significant force for change in the 1960s and 1970s, office communications will probably be the most important force in the 1980s and 1990s. By the early 1990s, many of the large offices will probably have an in-house telecommunications branch exchange that will electronically connect all types- numeric, textual, audio, and visual- of interoffice data and information flows. Communications network technologies have led to the emergence of value-added networks and information utilities, which may incorporate various useful features into the communications network. For example, the network may provide teleconferencing, electronic mail, or computer power as basic utilities in addition to basic communications. The idea behind this is quite simple: since computers are already used for switching in communications networks, they can also be used to provide other services to the customer.

Generally we can distinguish between two types of telecommunications. These are

1. *A local area network* that links computers or workstations in an office building, in a campus, or in a cluster of buildings where distances are measured in hundreds of yards;
2. *A remote area network* that transmits numeric data, voices, and images over long distances

The implementation of an internal electronic mail system requires the installation of a local area network. An external electronic mail system requires subscription regular communication network. The same holds true for electronic mailing among offices of a single organization that are geographically dispersed. In addition to the network, the various workstations must be equipped with hardware devices, such as modems and controllers, and with software programs for controlling transmission, identifying addressees, filing, and retrieval.

The progression from the first three stages to the next three stages is not a linearly gradual one, but is more a stepwise change. After installing the hardware and telecommunications infrastructure, automating the functions of electronic mail, message switching, calendar keeping, and scheduling are achieved by the acquisition and use of appropriate software. The last stage of integration requires coordination among computer systems, photocopying machines, facsimile equipment, telephones, video an television systems, graphical display devices, dictating machines, audio devices, and the like.

Most objective experts agree that the first half of the 1980s have not yet offered fully integrated systems. However, high-tech companies have invested considerable funds in research and development of such systems. Hence, we can fairly assume that the typical office workstation of the early 1990s will encompass the following functions;

1. All hardware and software components support local WP
2. Linkage to a central computer for retrieving data from data processing systems, processing them at the workstation, and merging them with texts and other components of the workstation
3. Display and drawing of graphical data
4. Capability of entering, storing, and displaying images by linking to facsimile and photocopying equipment; also, capability of retrieving images and merging them with other components of the workstation
5. Capability to receive and send voice data and store it in a digitalized form

Before concluding this review of office information systems, a final note is in order. The integration and balance among automated office functions depend on the unique characteristics of each organization. We refer here to work loads, budgets, geographical dispersion of organizational units, nature of office work, size of the organization, organizational climate, and the like. When implementing the various stages of office automation, it makes economic sense to first automate backbone applications that could significantly raise productivity and then to automate more functions for relatively little extra cost.

DSS and office automation

The various MIS, DSS, and OA systems and technologies are converging to form an integrated organizational information system. These systems should not be treated as disjointed systems, but as subentities of the comprehensive information system plan of an organization. This plan develop from an overall corporate information system strategy, and be implemented by adherence to policies that are derived from the strategy. The policies relate to the various systems; thus an organization may have a DSS policy and an OA policy among other policies.

Organizations have been slow in defining a real policy for OA. Plenty of promises, expectations, buzz words, and ads exist, but very few companies have evolve a coherent, organizationwide OA policy. In many ways, OA succeeded only because it came in the wake of DSS, which acted as a dry run for office automation. DSS relied on a tremendous advantage in technology—the terminal; it bypassed the formal DP channels and went directly to users; and it focused on ease of use for people having no technical background. These DSS characteristics contributed to the goals of office automation—to diffuse computerized workstations throughout to the organization and to persuade people to use them for such key aspects of their work as text handling, communications, mail, scheduling, filing, and retrieval.

Access to external data bases is handled by the staging element of the DSS data management component. This element connects the DSS with multiple data sources and extracts subsets of data out of large external data based for immediate and direct DSS use. Obviously, some data communications facility is part of the staging element if data is to be accessed online. An information utility makes the PC-based DSS a powerful device. It can give national or international news, and provide not only information but also software for portfolio management, financial and marketing analysis, or even programming in languages that are not available for a given PC.

A user can communicate directly with, or transfer files to, other users whose computers would otherwise by incompatible. As of 1984, the three largest information utilities are Dow Jones News/Retrieval. The Source, and CompuServe. Each maintains many data bases covering a wide range of subjects and categories.

4

Strategic Planning

There is a natural tendency of the information system unit to control all activities and resources pertinent to the use of microcomputer in an organization. A lack of policy that explicitly sates the responsibility of that unit and its personnel in regard to microcomputers can easily lead to conflicts and clashes between the unit and functional user departments.

For instance, a microcomputer policy can involve the following responsibilities of information systems professionals: set procedures for the use of microcomputers; select hardware and software for users; train and assist in using microcomputers; maintain the data 4bases that are microcomputer accessible; point out areas in which users may be misled by vendors. Keen and Woodman cite a microcomputer policy statement of a large insurance company that clarifies the issues of who does what and defines an active role for both information systems and users. The statement can be broken down into three parts: the mission, the objectives and the strategies. Several conceptual frameworks are helpful to both general management and IS management in considering IS policies. Such frameworks are critical for understanding, considering, and comparing phenomena being observed and studied. Once such framework is nolan's "stages of growth" model. The major contribution of that framework is the concept that information technologies require different management approaches as they evolve through the stages of information systems growth in organizations.

A framework highly pertinent to the issues discussed in the chapter is the Strategic Impact of IS activities scheme suggested by McFarlan and McKenney and graphically summarized. The strategic grid framework is based on the notion that senior management must determine the current and future importance of information technologies to the organization before the right IS strategies can be chosen.

Organizations in which both current IS applications and future planned applications are significantly dependent upon IT are in the class labeled strategic; It has a strategic impact upon these organizations. Organizations in the class labeled turnaround are not totally dependent upon currently installed IT to function, but the organization has many new IE developments which are expected to give it significant competitive advantage in the future. Organization in the factory class are very dependent upon IT for theirs and products designed to attach the revenue side of the firm. This will move IS units from being cod centers to being profit centers. Another distinctive feature is that TPSs, MISs, and DSSs are internally-oriented, while SISs are externally-oriented, impacting the firm's relationships with its environment.

There are three levels of IT impact on a business organization: the industry level, the firm level, and the strategy level. At the industry level, IT impacts the nature of the industry's products, services, and markets, or the industry's economics of production and distribution. With IT, new services can be developed; the life cycle of a product, form the R&D phase to is marketing, can be shortened; distribution can be speeded up; the market can be expanded. Following are a few examples of industries that have undergone changes induced by IT:

Publishing-desktop publishing, electronic book ordering, Newspapers-electronic typesetting, computer-to-computer communication of news items and reports, Banking-Automatic Teller Machine (ATM) networks, cash management services, Distribution chains-electronic catalogs, computerized warehouses, Manufacturing-just-in-time inventories, computer-integrated manufacturing (CIM), Airline companies-booking flights from home or office, computerized reservation systems and Education-computer-literate students, computerized examinations, curricula changes.

At the firm level, the impact of IT is determined by the specific competitive forces facing the firm. These forces shape the industry structure and the competitive arena for each firm in the industry. Obviously, if I is expected o significantly impact the entire industry, it will impact a specific firm competing in that industry. This firm-level impact of IT is considered in the following section.

At the strategy level, IT can change the firm's execution of a generic corporate strategy, by supporting the implementation of one or more generic strategies. Such strategies are used by successful firms to position themselves relative to industry forces in the competitive arena. The strategy-level impact of IT will be discussed following the next section.

The the state of competition in an industry depends on five forces. The figure illustrates the interrelationships of a firm, which is the focus of analysis, with these five forces. The five forces are: (1) bargaining power of suppliers, (2) bargaining power of buyers, (3) threat of new entrants into the industry, (4) threat of substitute products or services, and (5) positioning of intraindustry rivals. IT can change the relationship between these forces and the firm.

The manifestation of each force for a specific industry will influence the profitability of a firm and will shape the strategies than the firm adopts. These forces are, in essence, the targets against which the firm deploys its competitive strategies. Such competitive strategies involve taking offensive or defensive actions to create a defensive actions to create a dependable position in an industry and to cope successfully with the competitive forces, and thereby increase the firm's profitability.

Following are a new examples of how IT can effect the competitive forces:

— Increase the number and mix of suppliers (e.g., by accessing commercial data bases that provide information on suppliers). Reduce the bargaining power of your suppliers by insisting on IT-based linkages

— Reduce the bargaining power of your buyers by increasing costs of switching to other suppliers (e.g., by using electronic bulletin boards)

— Create barriers to entry (e.g., mandatory heavy investments in hardware and software). Be the firs offering a new product or services. Speed up he life cycle of products.

— Intraindustry rivals. Join forces with rivals (e.g., ATM netwoproduct and manufacturing process (R&D)

Each activity adds value. There is a cost of adding a value in every level of the chain. If the total cost of added value is less than what the customer pays, there is profit. The value chain enables a company to analyze where and how it can add value to products or services and where it can reduce costs. It can thus help identify strategic opportunities.

The concept of value chain a useful framework for identify IT opportunities. IT is a structural way of looking a how, with IT, a firm can improve its profitability.

IT can be employed in all levels of the chain: product development-shorten product life cycle, develop unique product features, manufacturing-reduce manufacturing costs, improve quality control, distribution-move information instead of product, reduce cost of delivery and marketing-supply ordering terminals to customers, identity market niches

Since the value chain is a series of interdependent activities, IT can be used not only at each level of the chain, but also between levels. For example, IT can be used to lower transfer costs between players at two or more levels. Or, information resources that exist at one level can be used to improve performance at other levels that exist at one level can be used to improve performance at other levels.

Companies need to understand not only their own value chains, but also those of key customers and suppliers, inorder to uncover potential opportunities. Similarly, understanding competitors' value chains provide insight on the likely sources of competitive attack and defense. These value chains comprise a value system, illustrated in the figure.

The value system is the collection of the firm's value chain and individual value chains of suppliers, buyers, and competitors for each product or service. A company can analyze the value system to discover ways of lowering costs or enhancing values of products and services with IT. One way of doing his is to use the critical success factors method to determine the critical activities in the value system for each product or service, and then explore what IT can do for those CSFs.

Any IS development project carries with it operational risks that the project will be a failure when implemented. The implementation risks have to do with budget overruns, time slippages and/or the system no adequately meeting users' information requirements. IS project characteristics that lead to such risks are usually associated with project size, degree of inherent structuredness, and degree of absolute or relative newness of information technology used by the system.

The larger the project size , the more difficult o meet preestabilshed deadlines and cots estimates. Inherent structuredness has to do with how well-defined the project's outputs are and how close they are to the information requirements as defined by users at the outset of the project. The lower the degree of structuredness, the higher the project risks. An IT may be new to a given organization. An IT may be absolutely new to all firms in an industry. The newer and IT is, the higher the project risks.

SIS projects are likely to be large, reflecting the growing complexity of the business environment. They will often be the first in an application area, with little previous structure to draw on. Many of these systems will be based on an IT which is absolutely new, or new to the firm. This suggests that high operational risk will accompany in formation systems that are designed to provide competitive advantage.

However, a SIS may technically "succeed," thereby creating potential negative strategic impact to the company implementing it. We refer here no to the SIS project failing, but to the risks of strategic disadvantages arising from unanticipated effects of the SIS on industry structure and the competitive position of the firm. Vitale discusses such strategic IS risks and proposes a way of assessing them.

1. Once SISs are implemented, their use may require continued investment for sustainability. Organizations with limited resources may be incapable of staying in he race with competitors who have larger resources. Thus, an initial SIS success may turn into a competitive failure.

2. By making IS the major vehicle for producing or delivering its product, a company may risk opening is primary line of business to competitors who es of the firm's value chain, buyer's value chains, suppliers' value chains, and competitors' value chains. The analysis can pertain to a strategic business unit of the firm and not to the firm as a whole.

Stages 1 and 2 are conducted simultaneously, with feedback between them. They focus on a range of strategic targets and the corporate strategies supported by IT that can be used to impact the targets. The targets include buyers, suppliers, possible new entrance, existing rivals, and substitute products and services. The process should generate the largest possible list of strategic targets. I is from this list that the firm can select those that are deemed suitable for attack by strategic strategies supported or shaped by IT. These strategies comprise cost leadership, differentiation, focus, growth, alliances, innovation, and the like. A corporate strategy and its associated SIS can be used to attack multiple targets. A target can be impacted by more than one strategic SIS.

Once a given strategy aimed at a given target is selected, stage 3 deals withe the SIS posture. It can be used defensively, to reduce a competitive edge held by a target, or offensively, to increase an edge. The SIS selected can, for instance, create high switching cost for the firm's buyers to defend against a new entrant; alternatively, the firm can join an SIS alliance in order to expand the firm's market.

In stage 4, the firm has to consider whether the offensive or defensive SIS is to employ an IT to be used internally or externally, by providing it to the target. For example, for a buyers' target, with a niche strategy and an offensive posture, the direction of the SIS is external if terminals and an inventory management system are provided to the buyers in order to lock them in. For a cost leadership strategy, aimed at buyers, with a defensive posture, the SIS selected may use CAD/CAM technology internally, to reduce costs of product development and manufacturing.

Stage 5 deals with the assessment of operational and strategic risks. The operational risks are evaluated, focusing on the size of the selected SIS, to its degree of structuredness, and the familiarity of the firm with the relevant IT. Based on this evaluation, the firm can select tools to deal with such risks. In addition, assuming that the SIS is successfully implemented, the strategic implications of an initial success must be evaluated.

Finally, a decision has to be made whether to endorse the SIS being considered. The firm can decide to completely avoid the project or to modify it and then reemploy the SIS opportunity identification process to evaluate the modified SIS. A positive decision requires incorporation of the selected SIS into the master plan for IS and the ensuing annual IS plan.

Smart systems can be categorized to a variety of expert and neural systems applications, usually implemented in software, ranging from maintenance advisors, to decision support modules, to pattern understanding, and sometimes including natural language interfaces for the human operators. Network management systems, for which smart capabilities are contemplated, should be examined for compatibility with these characteristics.

The whole thrust of technological innovation from the industrial revolution onward has been to extend and improve upon the capacities and capabilities of the human operator. Intelligent systems, to be referred to here as smart systems, are merely another step in that logical extension of human abilities in the telecommunications arena. To be more exact, smart systems are aimed at the extension of our ability to reason and learn. In order to emulate the human abilities for reasoning, associating, discriminating, and interpreting, one must turn to the model from which the conclusions are drawn, i.e., the human brain. Smart systems are viewed as subsets of the total apparatus of the system that oversee some purposeful mission, in this case the telecommunications network operation and support.

These systems have the capability to draw conclusions and implement or recommend decisions based upon the inference of and reference to facts available to those systems. They, of necessity, must be able to generate, transmit, receive, and interpret communications between themselves and the controlling elements of the system, these controlling elements, many times, being human. In addition, they must be capable of some form of reasoning or logic process that allows them to reach their inferences or their recommended reference points. And, finally, smart systems must have access to real-time or external information sources and the reasoning framework, called by such names as rule base, frame base, etc., necessary to act upon these external data sources.

The importance of smart systems with regard to telecommunications technology developments, and in particular network management, cannot be over-emphasized. In today's competitive environments, coupled with differing communications options available to the buyer, such as wireless, broadband, etc., the availability of the telecommunications platforms their services is critical for ongoing customer satisfaction. This availability can only be realized through effective network management systems implemented using smart systems tools.

The system's knowledge should be coherent, i.e., it should be capable of being shared among all the modules within the system, be commonly available to these modules, and adhere to a common formatting structure, taxonomy, and lexicon. In conventional processing programs, information is segmented and parsed so as to be available to only one or a few processing modules. Distributed database systems, in a far-flung and complex network management system, provide this coherent knowledge reservoir by providing a consistency and accessibility of data.

All data available to the system should be accessible to all the intelligent modules regardless of the potential variety of data structures and access methods used in the individual database systems servicing the system. Conventional programs are usually constrained to interface with one database system because the interface driver software is designed for only one database system. Integrated access provides the capability to reformat and translate data files from one system environment to another. Thus, the subnetwork managers must be supported with data translators, so that access to needed data can be had. Integrated access also requires that a security system be established so as to provide appropriate levels of access privileges. To some greater or lesser extent, the reasoning and understanding used by the system should be made available to the user on demand through the use of informal-style questions that the user can pose to the system for resolution, or as part of a more lengthy dialogue with the system.

In conventional software, the algorithms used by the program are seldom made known to the user during module execution. At a minimum, these algorithms should be made available to the user, the logic used should be published, on demand, to the user, and decision criteria should be made available as required. This facility enhances the network manager and gives its decisions or recommendations credibility. The execution of decisions either reached by or supported through smart systems, is a more far-reaching proposition that will entail further research and incremental development work in this area.

However, as this time arrives, the affects of inteliigent systems can be hypothesized. Intelligent submodules should, eventually, be able to initiate appropriate actions on their own as conditions warrant. Execution of these modules depends upon external stimuli as opposed to user initiation. These smart sensors can also be integrated into a data *fision* module so that filtering and data integration can make decision support more accurate and timely.

The intelligent modules should be able to extend the expertise of the overall system and to identify inconsistencies. Because these programs are dealing with a view of the entire system, they are in a position to determine the limits and extent of the system's capabilities as well as identify analytical inconsistencies. Knowledge is currently acquired through information input by way of rules, or through references to desired results.

In such circumstances, the rules involved are updated from outside sources as well. Research and some limited development efforts to date have attempted to train systems to acquire and use acquired knowledge to reach new conclusions.

These systems are known as neural networks, and are based upon a human-interpreted emulation of the operation of the vertebrate brain. The acquisition and use of knowledge in network management, such as that provided through neural networks, makes the operation more stable, and system reports more believable and accurate. Further down the product development road yet is the ability for the smart system to solve problems outside the realm of the intended application. This is known as non-domain-specific problem solving. The intelligent system should be capable of solving problems not anticipated by the developer. Sometimes the smart system leads to a point of departure not anticipated by the developer by identifying a condition that requires further investigation. These requirements are best handled through a system capable of learning on its own, such as neural networks. The technologies of network management are constantly crossing into areas not anticipated by the developers. This tool, if properly implemented, could be a great time saver and problem solver for the system administrator.

Data sorting

Here we will begin to survey and explore the various elements of the network management system that can be implemented with smart features. To begin with, there are several areas in the network system into which smart systems technology can begin to be infused, as a result of architectural design. These areas include front-end monitoring, and data fusion, which is closely aligned with the overall data collection process.

Data fusion is the physical and logical integration of temporally and spatially dispersed reports. Data fusion, although not always explicitly stated in discussions on network management, is also an integral task in any network management system even though it may not be implemented to any detailed level.

The first area is the front-end monitoring of system components. Sensors monitor, evaluate, and report on component performance, and status. Sensors, as a general category of performance monitoring, have been around since the advent of electronics. Up until recent times, they have been relegated to the position of reporting on such problems as framing errors, transmission errors, and the like. Since the system sensors, as we will characterize them, are operating as elements within the network components in locations remote from the monitoring and control points, we would like for them to be somewhat autonomous in their roles and actions.

The various functioning components and elements of the telecommunications network are usually the sources of status information about the network that is needed for the assessment of the total system. Each is a sensor of sorts that collects and reports on the status of its environment. The second area into which smart systems technology can be infused into the network is that point at which the sensor data are brought together, and typed, sorted, and categorized. This is the data fusion function, and comes in two varieties, these being direct fusion and indirect fusion.

Direct fusion is an integration of sensor data in a local environment, e.g., among the various equipments within a communications node. Here certain problems of distance, communications relay, and so forth, are minimized or negated due to the localization involved. Indirect fusion is the integration of widely dispersed sensor data collected in, and through, many nodes and transmission paths. Information flowing into these areas must be continually evaluated both individually and in relation to other data in order to track the status and performance of the system.

It is interesting to note that the very act of data integration has an impact upon the conclusions of system and subsystem health, and when added to the fact that synergistic data can be derived from multiple inputs and/or confirmations, the whole issue of data fusion becomes even more powerful. Unfortunately, data fusion requires additional effort to implement and even more effort to take full advantage of it. Thus, like everything else, there is a trade-off to be considered when considering its relative advantages versus its disadvantages.

There are six main tasks associated with data fusion. Association is especially critical, since it is the point at which reports from seemingly divergent areas, but concerned with the same objects, are matched. Correlation is then invoked to determine the extent to which these initially matched reports are actually related. These data fusion tasks are:

Collection: This task is performed by the sensors at the collection sites specifically, or as part of the relay process of data from the collection sites to the fusion site(s). The collection process is critical for the data fusion activity, because the data reports have to be separable and definable for later correlation and collation. The number of incoming reports can be staggering, so a network management system must be provided that meets these data rate needs. The collection task can help mitigate the number of incoming reports by examining reports for redundancies, duplications and repeats, and eliminating such reports.

Alignment: This is the point at which filtering occurs. Filtering consists of clearing up ambiguity, as much as possible, about the individual incoming reports. Additionally, alignment means to assign credibility to individual reports, so that such reports can be given even more confidence as the data fusion process continues to the next steps.

Association: This task involves updating and composition of report states. The task of associating reports, either the same reports over multiple time periods, or different reports relating to the same circumstances is handled in this task. The object here is to match different reports with the same object or event, and to single out redundant and/or unnecessary reports, either from the same or different sources

Correlation: This is the point at which ambiguity resolution occurs when the association process cannot resolve ambiguous reports. Correlation is of its nature a chance situation; thus, techniques suitable to the specific network management situations must be employed to minimize the probabilities of errors.

Classification: This task is directed at the identification of a class of problems from which more specific elemental identification can be made later. The integration of several sensors is usually involved accompanied by some form of decision process to specify class I.D. and confidence level. In a network management environment, classification may involve categorizing reports into different levels of alarm, different levels of maintenance attention, different levels of operational alerts and so on. Thus, a multi-level, multi-category set of needs arise.

Control: This task is involved in the allocation of direct sensor systems, their optimization, and their prioriti-zation. Control encompasses a range of tasks and functions too vast to address here. In essence, the control subject involves the acts of delivering the right information to the right point at the right time. Decision support/executive information systems are all about the problem of control and its ongoing resolution. Because of the increasing complexities of equipment, functions, and sizes of networks, the various smart systems technologies to be addressed here are critical to the effective control of telecommunications networks.

Data fusion is a more complex subject than it may appear. The network data involved are many times from vastly different environments and from different vendor equipment arrays. The formats vary from each other and the correct interpretation of data contents can be very different. Data fusion is also the point in the data collection and analysis functions which the confidence of incoming status data is confirmed or calculated. As a at matter of fact, the major reason for implementing data fusion is to verify network status indicators, and to assess confidence in the ensemble of incoming data elements.

Data fission is the opposite of data fusion. Data fission is the process of finding an object of interest in an array of previously collected objects. Data fusion involves the act of sorting individual objects, locating, then labeling them for future fission operations at which point they are split out for usage. Clearly these two processes are mutually dependent, because the efficacy of the fused data makes searching very dependent upon the time element which in turn determines the usefulness of the total process.

The last area of smart systems infusion into the network management scheme is the point of decision making. This point is often referred to, in the defense sector, as decision support, and, in the commercial sector, as the executive information support function. Decision support involves the use of categorized and sorted data from the data fusion function, coupled with decision criteria, frames of reference, decision criteria, and the decision maker's preferences, to arrive at a rational course of action.

Each of these topics will be briefly addressed and associated with each other before a more thorough examination is made in the ensuing chapters. The smart system concept is broken down into three main segments, namely, sensors, data fusion and decision support. The primary operational segments of the communications system, its data converters and transmitters, its switches and relays, and its monitoring and control units are each roughly equated to each of the smart systems segments, e.g., sensors are associated with the data converters and transmitters, and so forth.

The selection of an architecture that provides the system coverage, responsiveness, and diagnosis capabilities is always difficult, partly because no two telecommunications systems are the same, and partly because these systems lack homogeneity. The typical approach has been to integrate individual network management subsystems using an additional network manager that recognizes the attributes and characteristics of each of those subsystems with which it interfaces.

Another approach is to bypass the subsystem network managers, and to route each of the equipment elements to a single network manager. Yet another approach has been to utilize the existing performance characteristics of the subsystems and to infer the maintenance and performance of each equipment on the basis of these characteristics. Smart systems greatly enhance this latter approach.

The intelligent features of each of these segments is infused into these segments via the main avenues defined, i.e., sensors, fusion, and decision support. Thus, the sensors associated with the data converters and transmitters are designed and implemented so as to incorporate Artificial Intelligence (AI) features and autonomous operational capabilities. Similarly, data fusion is associated with the switching and relay elements of the typical system, and its features are designed to incorporate expert systems capabilities. Likewise, the decision support function is akin to the monitoring and control elements, where their functions are incorporated into the design of decision support capabilities that reflect AI features.

The overall network management scheme is to monitor operating units for status and health, and to take action when and where necessary to continue the communications traffic flow. From such collected data, there is an assumption that all other needed information can be derived. This information is periodically or continuously relayed to a point where it is analyzed or in some way organized. From there it is evaluated and decisions are made based upon the logic used for such decisions, the criteria established for decisions, and the efficacy and accuracy of the data categorization. Until now, the thinking was that the various data organizational and evaluation parameters would be found or derived in the data fusion and decision support functions. Now, however, processing power makes it possible for these capabilities to be off loaded into the sensor function. Hence, intelligent systems technology can possibly be imparted to the front end of the system using very high scale integrated circuits (VHSIC) or very large scale integrated (VLSI) circuits.

5

Computer Management

In light of the importance of information in the decision-making process, it would be logical to assume that top executives have always actively participated in the planning and implementation of new systems which would influence their future decisions. Such leadership has often been lacking. A study conducted a few years ago by the management consulting firm of McKinsey & Company concluded that no company achieved above-average results without the active participation of top executives. The study further pointed out that 18 of 27 of the nation's largest computer users obtained results which, at best, could only be described as marginal. Other studies conducted in the past have arrived at similar conclusions.

Many executive apparently felt that the introduction of a computer was primarily a technical problem. They were content to define the goals of the new system vaguely and then to turn the entire project over to data-processing specialists. Such abdication ignored the far-reaching personnel and organizational implications of the undertaking. Without precisely defined managerial information needs and without the backing at the top echelons which is often required to secure cooperation and overcome resistance to procedural and organizational change, the specialists could be excused if their efforts resulted in marginal results.

Top managers should realize that their serious involvement in planning for computers is perhaps the most important single factor determining the success or failure of a computer installation. They should also be aware of the magnitude of the problems which will have to be overcome. Firms which have been successful in making computers pay off have been through in the initial planning stages. A careful feasibility study is required to answer such questions as:

1. What data-processing improvements are needed—i.e., what are the data-processing objectives of the firm?
2. Has proper attention been given to systems review and redesign?
3. Is a computer usage the best way to achieve all of the objectives? Have noncomputer alternatives been evaluated?
4. Have all computer alternatives been considered?
5. If an in-house installation is justified, have all feasible machines and vendors been considered?
6. Have different acquisition methods been studied?

If, as a result of careful study and planning, a decision is made to order a computer, then the following additional plans must be developed:

1. *Technical preparation plans*: Prior to the delivery of hardware, the computer site must be laid out and prepared; initial programs must be written and tested.

2. *Organizing plans*: It is important that adequate attention be given to the composition and location of the computer department.

3. *Personnel preparation plans*: Staffing plans should be made to fill the new jobs which will be created. For example, the selection and training of programmers should take place without delay so that they may begin preparing the initial programs. Plans should also be made to alleviate the hardships brought about by the elimination of jobs.

4. *Control plans*: The quality of the information produced must be controlled. The accuracy of input data must be considered. And internal controls should be created to minimize error and disclose fraud when and if it occurs.

Information played an important part in he successful completion of each of the steps in the planning procedure which was presented earlier. Generally speaking, computer usage can improve planning by providing effective information which (1) leads to problem awareness, (2) supports problem analysis and selection of alternatives, (3) influences the choice of the most appropriate option, and (4) permits feedback on the implementation of decisions. More specifically, the use of computers can have an impact on the planning function by:

1. *Causing faster awareness of problems and opportunities*: Computers can quickly signal out-of-control conditions requiring corrective action when actual performance deviates from what was planned. Masses of current and historical internal and external data can be analyzed by the use of statistical methods including trends analyses and correlation techniques in order to detect opportunities and

challenges. Planning data stored online may permit managers to probe and query files and receive quick replies to their questions.

2. *Enabling managers to devote more time to planning*: Use of the computer can free the manager of clerical data-gathering tasks and permit him to concentrate more attention on analytical and intellectual matters. The computer is an intelligence amplifier which broadens man's time dimension.

3. *Permitting managers to give timely consideration to more complex relationships*: The computer gives the manager the ability to evaluate more possible alternatives. It makes it possible for managers to do a better job of identifying and assessing the probable economic and social effects of different courses of action. Awareness of such effects, of course, influences the ultimate decision. In the past, oversimplified assumptions would have to be made if resulting decisions were to be timely. More complex relationships can now be considered and scheduled. In addition to broadening man's time dimension, the computer can furnish him with planning information which could not have been produced at all a few years ago, or which could not have been produced in time to be of any value.

4. *Assisting in decision implementation*:When decisions have been made, the computer can assist in the necessary development of subordinate plans which will be needed to implement these decisions. Computer-based techniques to schedule project activities have been developed and are now widely used. Through the use of such techniques, business

resources can be utilized and controlled effectively.

Computer usage can certainly improve the effectiveness of managerial planning. But before leaving the subject of planning with computers, it should be emphasized that computers *do not* "make decisions." Rather, they follow program decisions made earlier by managers and programmers. Although experiments are being conducted by extremely able researchers attempting to improve the machines' ability to solve ill-structured problems, it is man who defines problems, selects strategies to follow, and formulates hypotheses and hunches. Heuristic is a word which means "serving to discover." Much of planning is judgmental or heuristic in nature, and man is far superior to machine in the heuristic area of intellectual work.

Decision-producing analyses

A number of quantitative managerial aids have been introduced which utilize computers to provide the framework for decision-producing analyses. These techniques can be used to (1) speed up problem or opportunity awareness, (2) permit more timely considera-tion of increasingly complex relationships, and (3) assist in decision implementation. In particular, the computer-based techniques of network analyses, mathematical programming, and simulation have managerial implications.

Network analysis

Both PERT are network models which are used to plan, schedule, and control complex projects. The basic concepts of PERT and CPM are similar. The following procedure is used to set up a network model:

1. All the individuals activities to be performed in the project must be identified.

2. The sequence of each activity must be determined—i.e., it must be known what elements have to be completed prior to the start of a particular activity and what tasks cannot commence until after its completion.

3. The time interval required to complete each activity must be estimated.

4. The longest sequence of events in the project must be identified. The sum of the individual activity times in this sequence becomes the total project time, and this sequence of activities is known as the critical path.

Network models have gained widespread acceptance. The Department of Defense requires that they be used on all major defense contracts, and major construction projects employ them. They have proven quite effective in helping manage the transition to computer data-processing systems. The use of PERT and CPM improves the planning function because it forces managers to identify all of the project activities which must be performed. Control is also improved because attention can be focused on the sequence of activities in the critical path. Managers quickly become aware of potential problems. If a critical activity begins to slip behind schedule, steps can be quickly taken to correct the situation. By trading project cost against project time, several alternative paths can initially be computed to help in planning. By a greater commitment of resources, managers can often reduce the time required to complete certain activities in the critical path. The effect of a greater resource commitment, however, is often higher project cost. Network models can simulate the effects on time and cost of a varying resource mix. Computations for small networks can be produced manually, but a computer is needed with networks of any significant size. Most computer manufacturers have PERT and CPM packaged programs available.

Mathematical programming

The purpose of mathematical programming is to find the best strategy from among a large number of options. Most mathematical programming work involves the use of linear programming. Not to be confused with computer programming models are used to find the best combination of limited resources to achieve a specified objective. One important class of linear-programming applications is in blending operations, where the objective is often to minimize the cost involved in the production of a given amount of blended product. For example, cattle feed may be mixture of minerals, grains, and fish and meat products. The prices of these ingredients are subject to change, so the least expansive blend required to achieve specified nutritional requirements is subject to variation. Linear programming can help managers quickly determine the correct blend to use to minimize cost while meeting product specifications.

In addition to blending, linear programming is being used for such diverse purposes as scheduling manpower, selecting media for advertising purposes, determining minimum transportation costs from given supply points to specified points of delivery and determining the most profitable product mix that may be manufactured in a given plant with given equipment. Practically all linear-programming applications require the use of a computer. As a powerful planning tool, linear programming enables a manager to select the most appropriate alternative from a large number of options. It is also a technique which may aid the manager in carrying out his other functions. Its use in scheduling manpower, for example, has definite staffing implications.

Simulation

In the physical sciences, experiments may be performed in a laboratory using small models of a process or an operation. Many complex variations may be possible in these tests, and the results show the scientist what happens under certain controlled conditions. Simulation is similar to scientific experimentation in that managers may evaluate proposed strategies by constructing business models. They can then determine what happens to these models when certain conditions are given. Stimulation is thus a trial-and-error problem-solving approach; it is also a planning aid which may be of considerable value to executives.

Simulation models have helped managers decide, for example, whether or not to expand operations by acquiring a new plant. Among he dozens of complicating variables which would have to be incorporated into such models are facts and assumptions about (1) present and potential size of the total market, (2) present and potential company share of this total market, (3) product selling prices, and (4) investment required to achieve various production levels.

Simulation models are also used to improve inventory management. The problem of managing inventories is complicated because there are conflicting desires among organizational units, and what is best for one department may not be best for the entire firm. To illustrate, the purchasing department may prefer to buy large quantities of supplies and raw materials in order to get lower prices; the production department also likes to have large inventories on hand to eliminate shortages and to make possible long—and efficient—production runs; and the sales department prefers large finished-goods inventories so that sales will not be lost because of out-of-stock conditions. The finance department, on the other hand, views with concern large inventory levels since storage expense is increased, risk of spoilage and deterioration is increased, and funds are tied up for longer periods of time. Through the use of simulated inventory amounts and for longer periods of time. Through the use of simulated inventory amounts and simulated assumptions about such factors as reorder lead times and cost of being out of stock, managers can experiment with various approaches to arrive at more profitable inventory levels.

In short, we see from this brief summary of simulation that it can aid in planning by permitting managers to give timely consideration to complex relationships. Of course, in many respects there is nothing new about simulation.

As Franklin Lindsay points out:

> A corporate planner who sets forth half a dozen alternative investment schemes, together with the costs and expected return from each, is simulating each alternative so that his board of directors can judge their relative merits. But the new mathematical tools, together with high-speed computers, extend tremendously the capabilities of simulation processes.

Organizational implications

The organizational framework of a business is structured on the work to be done and on the human and physical resources to be committed. With the introduction of a computer, however, significant changes are likely to be made in data-processing activities and thus in those departments which are engaged in informational activities. When this happens, it is often desirable to restructure the organization in the interests of greater efficiency. Work groups may be realigned; tasks formerly assigned to a number of departments may be eliminated or consolidated in a single new computer department; and existing departments may be eliminated or the scope of their operations may be sharply curtailed. Basic changes of this nature require the attention of top executives.

We have seen earlier that broader information systems are now being designed and implemented. Related to this trend is an organizational issue of fundamental importance. The issue to be decided is to what extent the new systems should concentrate or centralize authority and control in the hands of the top-level managers. With a computer, a greater degree of centralized control can be supported in a business because top managers can be furnished with information from outlying divisions in time to decide on appropriate action. Without computers, such action must be determined by a a lower-level manager because of time, distance, and familiarity factors. But although greater centralized control can be supported with a computer, it is not necessarily a requirement. The defree of centralized authority and control which should exist in the new system is determined by managerial philosophy and judgment and not by computer usage. The impact of the path chosen on future organizational structure, basic company philosophy and policies, and managerial authority of managers below the top echelons will be great. Certainly, decisions of this magnitude require the serious consideration of top executives; they are just too fundamental to be left to data-processing specialists of lower-level managers.

Staffing implications

Data-processing changes often bring about organizational stress. The introduction of computer also requires employee adjustments. Staffing decisions are necessary (1) to select and train workers for new jobs and (2) to deal with employees whose jobs have been eliminated or reduced in content or appeal. REsistance may be expected from employees and managers because of significant changes occurring in the alignment of work groups, in the content of individual jobs, and in the methods of performing data-processing tasks. Proper planning and leadership can reduce this resistance.

In addition to considering the implications of filling new jobs and of coping with resistance to change top executives should also realize that it does no good to attempt to install sophisticated system if company managers at all levels are usable to (1) define their information needs, (2) develop analytical planning, decision-making, and control procedures, (3) state specifically these analytical procedures, and (4) interpret and make use of the output of the sophisticated systems. If the machines are to be effectively utilized, it will generally be necessary to undertake an educational effort to acquaint managers with computer capabilities and with the analytical tools which will make use of those capabilities.

Control implications

Several ways in which computer usage can affect the control function have already been pointed out, so we need not dwell long on the subject here.

The control implications of computer usage include the facts that:

1. Computers can quickly signal out-of-control conditions, thus bringing about faster awareness of problems. Going a step further, programmed analyses may be carried out by the computer to present recommended courses of action to managers.

2. Triggered control reports, based on the principle of exception, may be prepared only when actual performance varies from planned standards. Managers are thus relieved of much routine paper shuffling and are freed to concentrate on more important personnel and environmental matters.

3. Computer-based techniques such as PERT and CPM may permit more effective control of business resources.

4. Computer systems make it possible to centralize authority and control previously delegated to lower echelons because of time, distance, and familiarity factors.

5. Internal control and auditing techniques will generally have to be revised to accommodate computer systems.

Economic implications

From an economic standpoint, the acquisition of a computer cannot be taken lightly. An investment decision involving many thousands of dollars must be made. It is the duty of top executives to determine if a computer can be justified economically. A computer *can* improve the firm's economic position by reducing ratio of expenses to revenues in tangible and intangible ways. But there is no guarantee that profits will be improved merely because a computer is installed. On the contrary, many firms have invested large sums in computers and have received returns of less than a dollar for each dollar spent.

Computer acquisition is a difficult capital-investment decision; it must be recognized as such by the top officers in the company. They must also be aware that the level of expenditures initially required is frequently underestimated and that this level will probably continue to increase in the years after acquisition. Finally, they must consider the possible economic implications of not keeping pace with competitors in the development and use of new information systems.

There are a number of surveys available on the percentage of time spent in the different phases of a project. Each company should be able to develop its own average percentages according to the type of project it undertakes and its past history of projects. For those without such averages.

Depending upon the size of the project, we must plan it in a number of discrete phases. For each phase, we need two types of plan; a technical plan showing the tasks, resource and time allocation, and a financial plan which translates the resources into monetary terms. The technical plan is the main document for the Project Leader.

The financial plan is the communicating document between Project Leader and Project Board. Phase plans are produced prior to the start of a phase. An exception here is the plan for the very first phase which is done as one of the first tasks of that phase.A graphic plan is inadequate alone. It needs explanation to a reader.

A complete planning package should consist of:

— A graphic plan

— A description

— Assumptions on which the plan is based

— Potential problems

It will be too late to say to the contractor representative 'I thought I would have priority'. If we are making such assumptions when planning, we must make this clear to those who will approve our plan.

Before creating a technical plan for a phase, it is usually worthwhile to create a schedule showing the availability of the phase resources. This covers not only the Team Members, but also the other resources required. Such a plan will include data on when each resource becomes available, when its availability ceases, and when it is not available during the phase. The availability plan also notes holidays, training and allocation to other projects, thus providing a useful check of availability against the technical plan being created.

The user or customer is committed to a defined level of cost, but in turn expects the project to reach a certain point for that cost by a certain data and with a certain level of quality. If one of these factors should begin to vary beyond an agreed tolerance limit, it is the responsibility of the Project Leader to bring this to the attention of the Project Board. As described in the chapter on control, this is one at a meeting with the Project Board. At this meeting, the Project Leader will present a deviation plan.

The description part of this deviation planning package describes the problem, the reason, the impact, the possible alternatives and the Project

Leader's recommendation. The graphic plan will normally cover only the problem area and will extend until either the phase end or the recovery from the deviation, if this is sooner. It is not necessary for the deviation plan to go beyond the phase end. Any recovery work to be done after that will be incorporated in the next phase plan.

For those who like to approach planning in a methodical fashion, here is a general sequence of actions to follow.

— Complete the provisional 'duration' and 'end date' lines. This is achieved either by copying from the final estimate, or, if a project completion date is imposed by some external factor, by calculating the stage durations by working back from the end data.

— Remember that this is elapsed time, not manpower.

— Complete the resources section showing how much effort is available if the size of the Phase Team is already known.

— Examine the task checklists and mark any which are not applicable to the particular project.

— Identify any special tasks which are not in the checklists.

— Identify any necessary tasks on the checklists which have already been completed. For example, a description of the current product should normally be available.

— Consider the management of the project and allocate a percentage of manpower resource for this function throughout the plan.

- Identify, under applicable activities, those which can only be done by a certain Team Member.
- Calculate the length of time needed for each task.
- Allocate the time to produce each sub-product within the project. It is usually easiest to work backwards from the completion dates of the major tasks.
- Define which activities can be done on parallel and which must be serial
- Define quality control points
- Add to activities the time for quality control plus time for regular meetings.
- Total the resources required.
- Review the completed plan for individual workload balance, continuity of work for each Team Member, and re-cycle, where necessary, to smooth the workload.
- Determine whether any remaining time problems are best resolved by extra resources, the purchase of external products, stretching elapsed time, or reducing the facilities to be provided by the current project.
- Calculate the cost of the planned resources.
- Add the tolerance percentage
- Compare with the final estimate from the feasibility study.
- Write the plan description to provide an explanation of the graphic plan, and how it will be implemented. This description includes information on how the plan will be monitored, and the Project Leader's proposal of a suitable tolerance level.

- List the technical and business assumptions which have been made when developing the plan. It is important to document these assumptions, so that any changes to them can be quickly identified and appropriate action taken.
- Identify potential problems and the likely impact on the plan should they occur.

Developing a project plan

Staffing: The anticipated project leader and his or her manager should work closely to develop the documents required for completion. calling on technical expertise as needed. External assistant may be required.

Problem definition: Entry into assumes that user requirements or a market study provide general project justification, or at lease Phase justification. The first step in initiating any project must be describing the general problem to be solved. The result should be a brief but formal problem definition.

Initial project plan: After the user (marketing management) agrees with the written problem definition, the next step is to develop an overall project plan showing critical path developments and a brief description of each research and development (R and D) problem that must be solved. Reasonably detailed cost estimates on must be prepared, possibly with minimum and maximum limits.

Review: It is necessary to conduct a formal review of the general project definition and plan as well as required changes by developer and user. Copies for reading and time for commenting should be provided before scheduled meetings. If the effort is justified, changes should be incorporated and the project should proceed. Review should not terminate without countersignatures representing user and developer management agreement.

Functional analysis and specification

Staffing: Requires the experience of people knowledgeable with the probiem of user/costomer interface. User personnel must be dealt with carefully at all levels, and the analysis team must be groomed for marketing purposes. This is not the time to show off individual technical expertise or cleverness. The user must believe that his or her problems are in the hands of people who sincerely want to help. The use of outside expertise knowledgeable in the particular application area can be vital.

Analysis of overall system functional requirements: Unless the user constrains particular hardware specifications (for example, a particular printer, modem, and so forth), hardware should remain unspecified. At this time the user should be encouraged to be completely open as to what is desired ideally as well as realistically. Obviously, the final system must lie between the present system and the ideal system.

System functional specification

This specification, in conjunction with the initial documentation set, should completely define the user functional requirements. No reference should be made to specific hardware types unless constrained. This must be a joint development effort with user personnel who will be involved in operating and using the existing system.

Continuation plan: With the functional specifications completed, the overall project plan should be revised or refined, along with cost estimates and a detailed plan.

Review: The last step of Phase is to review specifications, plans, changes, and cost estimates with user/management, ensuring that total functional requirements are well defined and explained and that the plan is acceptable. If the effort is justified, changes should be incorporated, and the project should proceed to Phase Incremental movements from each phase to another through a formal review "gate," enable potential project problems to be adjusted.

Environment analysis/specification

Staffing: Emphasis during this phase must be on the enlistment of highly qualified technical personnel, particularly in the advanced systems area. At least one person should be aware of the latest technology available. Real-world experience in a similar application area is also vital.

Technology analysis: Existing hardware/software technology, applicability, and trade-offs should be analyzed to meet overall system functional specifications.

Hardware environment synthesis: The system hardware environment should be synthesized, on a building-block basis. For example, computer processors and peripherals for both the development and field environments should be selected.

Software environment synthesis: The system software environment should be synthesized, on a building-block basis. For example, operating system, language, and support software should be, selected for both the development and field environments.

Hardware/Software System Specifications: These specifications should reflect the hardware/soft ware synthesis requirements as stated above.

Preliminary documentation set: A detailed user's manual should be completed, along with the remaining detailed functional documentation, including system outline, output formats, database descriptions, and input formats.

Continuation plan: A more detailed project plan should be developed, nailing down any unresolved R and D elements along the critical path. A more detailed cost estimate should be developed, particularly for Phase.

Review: Specifications, documentation, changes, and estimates should be reviewed with user/ management, ensuring a clear understanding of approach. If the effort is justified, changes should be incorporated and the project should proceed to Phase.

System design

Staffing: Programmers who are expected to write code for subprograms called for in the system outline should be selected to help write the corresponding detailed program documentation. In addition, particular staff members should be given specific responsibility for coordinating each of the following areas: total system documentation, detailed test procedures and full cycle test implementation plan, and quality control standards and procedures.

Detailed Program Documentation: The detailed design and corresponding documentation of each program module must include detailed narratives on each subprogram and specifications of all references, both internal and external to each module.

Detailed test plan: This must include detailed test schedules and a description of the required data sets needed to test each subprogram as part of a regression test set.

Quality control plan: Procedures should be developed for maintaining, refining, and enhancing the system, ensuring system identity and integrity of the product libraries as changes are developed and implemented.

Continuation plan: The final detailed continuation plan should include formal specifications, documentation, and cost estimates for the critical design review.

Critical design review: The critical design review evaluates the continuation plan and required changes. At this point the user must be made to understand the potential level of difficulty of incorporating changes once program development (Phase) is under way. A reasonable amount of time should be allowed for this review/revision period because of

1) level of complexity of the decisions at this time,
2) volume of documentation and corresponding effort for changes, and
3) fermentation period to allow review of how changes propagate through the system.

Program development

Staffing: After the written, detailed system software documentation is reviewed, it may be desirable to shift personnel assignments. This is a critical decision step. It is most desirable that those designers who have written satisfactory documentation remain to supervise writing of the corresponding code. Poor documentation will generally indicate lack of understanding or the inability to supervise or write good code. Also, the personnel resources required to produce an adequate test set should not be underestimated.

Program development/integration: It will be necessary to coordinate emphasis on the development of critical path programs to facilitate proper test plan implementation. For example, it is necessary, to ensure construction of input edit and database update programs before accessing the database for processing and output.

Hardware facility coordination: Scheduling of required hardware facilities for compilation and testing may be crucial, depending on the environment for this phase. It is easy to accumulate day-by-day slippage owing to improper coordination of hardware test facilities, conversions, and so forth.

Test set development: As compilation gets underway, programming personnel should have gained sufficient knowledge and should have been provided sufficient time to develop detailed test procedures. In any event this time period must be planned in advance, with emphasis on input interface and database maintenance programs to ensure database integrity. It is imperative at this time to isolate personnel responsibility for the coordination of detailed test procedures and materials for a regression test set to be used in whole or part each time the system is modified.

Continuation plan: A detailed plan should be developed for operational testing (Phase), and plans for future phases should be refined. A detailed cost estimate should be developed for operational testing and for future phases. Sufficient resources should be included to ensure integrity of specifications and documentation for project intracommunications as well as user review. Plans for long-term system/ product support and distribution should be developed at this time.

Review: Specifications, documentation, changes, plan, and estimates should be reviewed with user/ management, ensuring clear understanding of system operation and the approach to projected effectiveness of the operational testing plan.

Operational testing

Staffing: Direct management responsibility for coordination of operational testing should be assigned to a specific individual. The objective is the development of a set of full system tests with effectiveness that is satisfactory to both user and developer management. The responsibility for operational testing must be kept separate from completion of final documentation and coordination of user requests for review and modification.

User personnel training: The user personnel training period provides the opportunity to "shake down" the documentation--for example, the user's manual and the operations manual--as well as the system itself. This period usually generates requests for modifications that should not be introduced without following formal procedures.

Full-Cycle acceptance testing: Final full-cycle acceptance testing must be performed with user personnel (or the equivalent) under simulated real-world conditions in order to be effective. For software products, initial versions usually can be given out at no cost to friendly users to accomplish real-life operational testing. Such user installations generally are known as alpha and beta test sites.

Quality control procedures: Formal distribution and support procedures should be implemented. Finalized procedures for processing requests for corrections, refinements, and enhancements, must ensure a thorough understanding of both user and developer management regarding the generation of new versions and releases.

Final documentation: Additions to the documentation set that depend on final program construction must be incorporated at this time. Assignment of this function to someone other than the originating programmer can be an effective method for review of internal documentation, programming practices, and skill, as well as the detailed external documentation.

Continuation plan: A detailed plan should be developed for cutover to installation and support (Phase 7), and any future plans should be outlined. Cost estimates should be included for steady-state operation as well as for the initial period. Allowances for formal modification procedures should be included as should recovery procedures to cover (1) on-site restart and (2) abort and return to operational testing phase.

Review and acceptance: This is the final review and acceptance of documentation, changes, plan, and estimates for installation and support with user and developer management. Emphasis is on recovery, maintenance, and modification procedures. Written approval and schedule to proceed should be obtained.

Installation and support

Staffing: Staff considerations during Phase VII include users in selecting any additional personnel required beyond those participating in operational testing, shifting present personnel where desirable, and selecting personnel for user training. The developer should assist the user in selecting user interface as well as on-site or on-call personnel for system support and in evaluating requirements for implementing and controlling product library changes. Ample time should be allowed for this step and the next before system production begins.

User personnel training/guidance: Off-site as well as on-site classroom sessions should be provided for all personnel, both user and support. Ongoing training for new and backup personnel should be considered.

Full operation implementation/product release: Timing and coordination usually are critical. Plans must include abort timing and corresponding personnel activity or nonactivity. Revovery procedures should be well documented and understood.

Quality control implementation: Formal support procedures are required to determine responsibility for system errors and the corresponding correction process. Notification for correction requests can be initiated by the system support agent as well as the user. The divergence of identity of multiple fielded systems can prove catastrophic in most applications; its avoidance depends on well-disciplined support procedures to ensure congruence.

Formal procedures for processing requests for system refinements and enhancements are necessary to ensure that required resources are scoped properly and that allowance is included for preserving system identity and integrity of the product libraries. Accumulating modification requests is desirable as long as the system remains operable so that total documentation and program modification efforts can be grouped into new releases.

Quality control procedures should be strictly followed for all modifications that are under direct management responsibility for process and approval. The objective is to ensure reliable operation within an effective test bed, simulating real-world conditions before each new release.

Control of project

This section considers the need to control various aspects of a project, and covers the control requirements of the various groups involved in a project. It is also deals with the problem of written and verbal communications in a team and project environment. We shall consider two ways of interpreting the information and passing it on; the use of meetings and of reports. As far as our project management standards go, the collection of data will be considered from the bottom upwards. That is, gathering data from the working level and passing it upwards to Project Leader and Project Board. The interested parties are

— Project board

— Project management team

— Project team

Requirements

Consider the type of information each of the parties needs.

The Project Board numbers represent user and contractor management. They are not involved on a day-to-day basis. If possible, they want to manage by objectives and by exception. As management, they are mainly concerned with the status of the budget. On technical matters, they are only concerned with schedule status and knowing if the customer will get what he wants at the end of the project.

They therefore do not want too much technical detail, but brief status information until things begin to go wrong. Then they need early advice of what is going wrong, together with a means of collecting all the relevant details plus technical solution proposals. The Project Leader needs both technical and financial information regularity. The Team Leader needs up-to-date technical progress and quality information.

Team Members need to be able to measure their own progress against objectives, and know the status of any interfaces within the team. They need to be able to identify with the total product.

We can provide a simple recording and reporting structure to suit large and small projects. Below is a brief description of the recording and reporting activities, plus the proposed forms

Time Sheet

By: Team Members

For: Team Leader

Frequency: Daily

Team Members record efforts against tasks on time sheets.

By: Team Leader

For: Project Leader

Frequency: Weekly

Effort is recorded against the phase plan from the time sheets. Completed tasks and slippages are noted.

The phase summary is in graphic form to allow summarized information to be passed in a very brief document. Its main purpose is to pass financial information to the Project Board.

1 The costs of the resources consumed are recorded. A report is sent to the project Board in graphic form, comparing current phase cumulative costs and completed tasks with the plan.

2 In certain recording systems, one trap into which it is easy to fall at this time is that the team are asked to estimate 'percentage complete' for their current unfinished tasks. The danger is that this is a subjective estimate, normally optimistic, and therefore misleading. The Project Leader also has the problem of assessing all the team's estimates on different sizes of task and turning these into a single percentage complete' for the phase. A much better idea is the one incorporated by BP in their plan. Having produced the phase technical plan, each task in the plan is calculated as a percentage of the total phase plan. This is done by taking the total man days needed as 100% and calculating each task's effort as a percentage of that. When reporting against the plan, completed tasks are noted and their percentage totalled to give the 'percentage complete'. In reporting this figure, we ignore any tasks which have started but are not yet complete. In order for this approach to be really effective, no task in our plan should be greater than 10% of the total phase effort, or 10 man days for a small project. Any task larger than this can always be broken down.

3 The 'Work Planned Completed' is calculated by adding up the percentages of the total phase effort of those tasks which have completed so far.

Modification requests

By: Usually a user

For: Review by the Project Board

Frequency: As required

There is one other type of report which is vital if a project is to be kept under control. There must be a document produced for every major change proposed after the feasibility study, and for every major or minor change proposed after the user specification has been signed. The implementation of such changes without proper control and authority has been responsible for many project failures to meet schedule and/or budget.

Let us make this point. Having accepted the feasibility estimate, approved the user specification, and committed resources against those documents, only the Project Board has the authority to agree to any changes. Only the customer has the authority to agree to more expenditure, and this must be done at Project Board level.

The procedure should be that anyone requesting a modification should document it. The request should be assessed for its impact on the project and its likely cost. All outstanding requests should be reviewed by the Project Board at the next project review meeting. Where agreement is reached to implement certain requests, the Project Board must approve the necessary extra resources and time.

Meetings

Only two types of meeting are described here; the Phase Review Meeting and the Walkthrough. The first is the formal meeting of Project Board and Team Leader at defined times during the project. The definition of these times relates to the size of the project. The second is a quality control meeting. These are the types of meeting for which must define very clear standards. There my be other types of meeting during the projects lifetime, but normally they will not require such rigorous standards

Phase review meeting

The purposes of this meeting are as follows.

1 For the Project Board and Project Leader to meet;

2 For the Project Board to hear a more detailed report of progress and have the opportunity to ask questions;

3 For the presentation of plan to the Project Board for their approval;

4 For the Project Board to consider changes of direction for the project;

5 For commitment of resources to the project by the Project Board;

6 To terminate the project, either at its completion, or earlier if the Project Board considers that a valid business case for the project has ceased to exist.

Walkthrough

This is the second type of meeting which will be useful in project control. Its main function is not the imparting of knowledge by one person to a group, but the imparting of an evaluation by a group to one person.

It should be stressed that although there may be a number of roles to be taken, one person may often take several roles, especially in a small project. Most practical Walkthroughs will be carried out by two people, but it is still important for the to know how they have shared the various roles between them, so that they can check that they have fulfilled their obligations.

Preparation

Objective

1 To become familiar with product under review

Roles

1 Error-finding.

2 Check for completeness.

3 Check against standards.

4 Education

Documentation

1 Request to attend a Walkthrough

2 Checklist of questions to ask for this type of product

3 The piece of work to be reviewed

4 Minor errors list.

Activities

1 Distribution of the work to be reviewed.

2 Review of the product.

3 Compilation of list of minor errors

4 Noting points for discussion

Review

Objective

1 To review the product and produce a list of any corrections needed.

Roles

1 Chairman.
2 Secretary.
3 Review.
4 Reviewer(s).

Documentation

1 Product.
2 Lists of minor errors.
3 Action list.

Activities

1 Collection of minor errors.
2 Chairman's introduction.
3 Listing of problems.
4 Step-by-step review. It is up to the Chairman to:

sense consensus,

stop repetition,

take a problem off-line if no agreement can be reached,

maintain impetus.

5 Secretary notes actions.

6 Action list read-back.

7 Who will take action to correct the identified errors?

8 Who will check the corrective actions?

9 Go to follow-up or re-schedule?

Objectives

1 To ensure that all errors notified during the review are corrected.

Role

1 Actioner

2 Checker

Documentation

1 Completed action list.

2 Revised product.

3 Notification to management.

Activities

1 Resolution of errors.

2 Sign-off by nominated reviewers of the individual action items.

3 Sign off by the Chairman at the foot of the action list, confirming that all items have been corrected and approved.

4 Notification to Project Leader.

We have now described the formal procedure for a Walkthrough. Not all Walkthroughs in a project will be formal meetings with four or more attendees. Were this the case, we should be spending far too much time and resource in Walkthroughs. To avoid this, there are a number of options open to the Project Leader and Team Leader when making their decisions on how many Walkthroughs to hold.

1 What are the key points in the project? Where are critical decisions made from where a lot of work will stem? Where is it most important to check that we are right?

2 What is known about the quality of work of individual Team Members? Can some members be allocated just a few Walkthroughs, with more for trainees?

3 Which Walkthrough can be handled by only two people? In practice, most Walkthroughs will be of this informal type, with two people sharing the roles between them. For example, in the reviewer might also take the role of chairman, leaving the reviewee to be also the secretary.

6

Networking

The network layer is the primary layer for host-to-host communication. The network layer makes use of services from the link and physical layers; it also provides an end-to-end service to the transport layer. The network layer can utilise a number of physical networks to provide its services. The two services provided by the network layer are the connectionless services, and the connection-orientated service. This chapter begins by looking at the connection orientated service provided by the X.25 protocol. This protocol is important as it is being used on all public packet-switched networks operated by the PTTs.

The X.25 protocol defines the necessary operation of layers one, two and three. Within any layer, a connection orientated protocol has two common tasks: error control and flow control. Error control is concerned with detecting, and correcting, errors that may have occurred in the information being transferred. Flow control is concerned with managing the resources of bandwidth and storage so that no single user can monopolise these resources, and the two endpoints are kept in step with each other. This is usually achieved by keeping the sending and receiving rates of information transfer approximately in step. The X.25 protocol covers the three lower layers of the protocol hierarchy. X.25 is defined as an access protocol, which means that it is used between a host and a node (in most X.25 networks the nodes are called 'exchanges') for the host to access the network so that communication between remote hosts is possible.

The X.25 protocol has been adopted by the CCITT as a standard, which means that nearly all future networks will use it. The latest version of X.25 will be adopted by ISO as an international standard. As well as describing the particulars of X.25, the principles of error and flow control will be shown and the mechanisms used to implement them in each layer explained. The description of level 2 is very detailed, as this is the first consequential level to be met in the bottom-up approach.

The discussion of level 2 examines a number of problems which occur at many other protocol layers. For instance, the mechanisms used at level 3 for flow control and protocol synchronisation are very similar to those of level 2, so less detail is given in the level 3 explanation and references are made to the level 2 mechanisms.

In the X.25 parlance a host is called a DTE (Data Terminating Equipment) and a node is called a DCE (Data Communications Equipment). X.25 provides a standard mechanism for a DTE to access and use a DCE to transport data across a network to a remote DTE via its remote DCE. X.25 level 1—the physical circuit level provides the physical communication by specifying the electrical signals, voltages, plug shape and pin assignment that the DTE needs to connect physically to the DCE.

The DTE/DCE boundary is shown on the host side of the MODEM at the host site. This would be the normal arrangement, as the supplier of the network (usually the PTT) will provide the MODEM link to the node (DCE) from the user's premises. The actual specification of level I is contained in the CCITT X.21 recommendation. For practical purposes the user will order a computer interface to this standard which plugs straight into the computer at one end and into the MODEM at the other.

The user will normally also be able to buy the software necessary to handle the interface. As the level 1 hardware is bought as a ready-made unit, no further discussion of it is necessary. The important information needed about level 1 is the type of interface it presents to level 2, and the functions it must perform. The level 1 will provide transport for a bit stream from the DTE to a (remote) DCE.

The level 2 will present the level 1 with the bits which are then delivered to a level 2 at the DCE. The hardware of level 1 will also indicate if the physical circuit is working correctly, that is whether the MODEMs are switched on and able to exchange synchronised data. So the interface has two parts

1. the sending and receiving of a serial bit stream
2. the control signals indicating the status of the physical circuit.

The purpose of level 2 is to control the physical link between the two ends of the level 1 circuit to provide a reliable transfer of information for level 3 between the DTE and DCE. X.25 level 2 uses a link control protocol based on the ISO HDLC (Higher Data Link Control) protocol. The advantages of using an existing protocol are greater than those to be gained from designing a new one. For instance, a new protocol would have to be adopted by a large number of people wishing to communicate; adoption of the protocol would then require a lot of effort. Other link protocols have been designed: IBM use one called SDLC (Synchronous Data Link Control) on their SNA network, which is not dissimilar to HDLC; DEC have their own as well. Information is passed from level 2 to level 1 in blocks called 'frames'.

The use of frames enables easier management of storage and error control. Each frame consists of some protocol information added by level 2, and possibly an information packet from level 3. 1 will use the convention of calling level 2 blocks frames and level 3 blocks *packets. The* functions performed by level 2 are:

1. To establish the link connection to a level 2 at a remote site.
2. To transfer packets for level 3 securely, and in sequence.
3. To disconnect the link without loss of level 3 information.

To carry out these functions, the X. 25 level 2 uses three types of frame format. The uses of each format are shown in the next section, but first the fields in the frames are detailed

Flag field

This is a unique 8 bit pattern (01111110) which marks the beginning and end of each frame. The use of the flag as a delimiter presents a problem: to ensure that the end of the frame is correctly interpreted by the receiver, the flag pattern must not appear anywhere within the data in the frame. This means that the frame must be transparent to the hardware looking for a flag to mark the beginning or ending of a frame. The problem of transparency occurs in all link level protocols as they all use special bit patterns for synchronisation and for marking various parts of the frame. In X. 25 level 2 the flag is used as the level 1 synchronisation character. To ensure that the flag pattern does not occur within the frame, X.25 uses a technique called 'bit stuffing'.

The bit stuffing technique involves the sender in inspecting the frame contents prior to transfer to level 1. Whenever a sequence of five Is occurs a 0 is inserted. Notice that the 0 is inserted regardless of the value of the sixth bit. Bit stuffing in this way is easily implemented by hardware and only increases the length of the frame by 1 bit for every sequence of five Is. As the receiving hardware scans the incoming frame, a 0 following a sequence of five Is is removed. If the sequence of five Is is followed by a further 1, then the flag may have been found.

The seventh bit is then inspected: if it is a 0 the flag has been found (01111110), whereas if the seventh bit is another 1 (01111111) then the frame is in error. Thus a sequence of seven Is is used to abort the frame. There are other ways of providing transparency, such as using escape characters, or bit counts, but none is quite so efficient and flexible as bit stuffing.

This is really redundant in a point-to-point link. The intention in the HDLC protocol was to use this as an address for multipoint lines, but the present X. 25 recommendation does not include multipoint lines. However, X.25 uses the field as an additional check in the protocol, as well as having the field ready should multipoint lines be considered in the future. The addresses used in this field allow commands and responses to be separated. The level 2 link can be thought of as two separate channels.

Channel A for transferring data from the network (DCE) to the host (DTE) and

Channel B for transferring data from the host (DTE) to the network (DCE).

Any frames relating to information flow from the DCE to the DTE carry the address A (11000000) including any frames from the DTE to the DCE relating to information transfer from the network to the host; similarly for channel B (10000000). To help separate the channels, frames are divided into two classes: *commands* and *responses*, Commands always flow in the direction of information on a channel; responses flow in the opposite direction. Responses are obviously the receiver's replies to various commands.

This 8 bit pattern determines the type of the frame, as well as being used for sequence numbering and acknowledgement. The command field has a different meaning for the three types of frame (information, supervisory, unnumbered). A 0 in bit 1 indicates that this is an information frame. An information frame is the only type that carries a level 3 packet in the information field. Bits 2, 3 and 4 contain the sequence number of this frame, bits 6, 7 and 8 contain the acknowledgement number.

The sequence number and acknowledgement number are used in the ARQ techniques explained in chapter 6 for error correction and flow control. Level 2 uses a stop-go flow control. Bit 5 is the poll/final (P/F) bit. This is set in a command frame as a poll bit and the receiver will set the final bit in any response frame that is a reply to a command frame with the poll bit set. The use of the poll/final bit enables the sender of a command to recognise the corresponding response frame. Bits 1 and 2 set to 10 indicate a supervisory frame. Bits 3 and 4 indicate which type of supervisory frame, Supervisory frames are not given sequence numbers as they do not contain any level 3 information, but they may be used to acknowledge information frames and so bits 6, 7 and 8 contain an acknowledgement number. Bit 5 is the poll/final bit which is the same as before. The command field format for the unnumbered frame, so called because it contains neither sequence number nor acknowledgement number.

Bits 1 and 2 set to 11 indicate an unnumbered frame and bit 5 is the poll/final bit. The remainder of the bits are used to indicate the type of unnumbered frame.

This field only occurs in information frames; it is the position in the frame where the whole level 3 packet is placed. The other level 2 fields provide an envelope for the level 3 packet during the level 2 transfer.

Frame check sequence

The FCS field is found by counting 16 bits back from the terminating flag. This is a 16 bit field to contain the CRC remainder used in error checking. The remainder is calculated using the CCITT recommended generating polynomial of $X^{16} + X^{12} + X^5 + 1$. It is interesting to note that all the fields of the X.25 level 2 header and the CRC are multiples of 8 bits.

This makes transmission easier, because the 8 bit byte is the lowest common multiple of most modern computer word sizes, as well as being the character frame size for synchronous transfer. However the information field and the CRC may be increased by bit stuffing for level 1 transmission.

This section describes the semantics of level 2, with the various commands and responses being explained in context. The level 2 at the DTE (host) end of the connection performs the protocol functions with the level 2 at the DCE, using the HDLC protocol over the level 1 physical connection.

An earlier specification of the X.25 protocol included a lever 2 initialisation procedure called LAP (Link Access Protocol) This procedure has been superseded by a simpler *balanced* procedure called LAPB. The LAPB method of initialisation sets up both channels simultaneously.

Data transfer

Level 2 should provide a sequenced, error-free transport of lever 3 packers from the DTE to the DCE and vice versa. As only 3 bits are allowed for the sequence number and acknowledgement number in the C field, the maximum window size is 7. In X. 25 the link level window size is fixed when the subscriber first applies to use the network.

The operation of the data transfer allows the use of limited buffers at the sender (no more than 7) and no requirement for extra buffers to handle out-of-sequence frames at the receiver. The cost of the small buffer requirement is extra channel capacity taken up with retransmission. The use of X.25 to connect hosts to networks would normally involve a fairly high-speed circuit between the DTE and DCE The limiting factor in performance is more likely to be the network and level 3, so a superefficient level 2 is not necessary; thus simpler techniques, such as Go-Back-N, can be used. The transfer of sequenced frames of information is straightforward but what makes the operation complex (and this applies to every protocol) is the handling of exceptions and errors. There are two basic errors that can occur during data transfer.

1. The frame check sequence indicates an error in the packet.
2. The packet appears to contain no transmission errors but the contents of the A and C fields are not those expected.

In case 1 above the frame is thrown away and no further action is taken by the receiver. Obviously when a frame is discarded the next frame received is not the one expected. In case 2 there are a number of inconsistencies that can be classed as errors. The most common would be a sequence error where a previous packet had been lost or discarded. To ensure that the frame sequence is maintained at the receiver, any frame that does not contain a sequence number matching that of the next expected frame variable, V(R), is an error.

If the sequence number of the error frame is within the window, the receiver returns an REJ response to indicate, in the N(R) field, the frame from which the sender should retransmit. If the frame sequence number is not within the window then the sequence numbers of the two ends have become unsynchronised. The only way to recover from a synchronisation problem is to reset the sender and receiver to a known state. The CMDR (command reject) frame initiates a reset which is completed by going through the link establishment exchange. After a reset, the two end-stations will be in a known, initial state.

The reset procedure is used to recover from all errors other than the loss of an information frame. A reset may be caused by the receipt of a command or response that is not expected; for instance, a UA if the data transfer is in progress, or the setting of the P/F bit in a response when no command has been sent with that bit set. The RNR (receiver not ready) frame tells the data sender that the receiver will ignore any further information frames (flow control stop). Once the receiver has returned an RNR response to an information frame, no more information frames are accepted, but the *N(R)* field in the header of any further information frames is inspected so that information frames in the opposite direction are properly acknowledged. The RNR response only stops information on one channel; the other channel is unaffected.

When the receiver has more buffer space, an RR (receiver ready) frame is sent to inform the information sender on that channel that more information frames may be transmitted (flow control go), starting at *N(R)*. Note that both RNR and RR have acknowledgement numbers, *N(R)*. The RR frame has another use: if the receiving station does not have any information frames to be sent on the opposite channel, the acknowledgements cannot be piggybacked, and the RR frame is then used to acknowledge the information frames.

A receiver, especially a DCE (node), may not have enough buffers to take a full window for every level 2 link to which it is connected. Instead a statistical allocation could be used which assumes that not all links will be fully active at the same time and that the data is forwarded within a given time. When the network becomes busy this allocation means that a receiver may run out of buffers and need to use some technique to stop the flow of data from one or more links.

Every frame, whether it is data or control, needs some buffer space for its receipt. If all the buffers are used up by one link then none of the other links will be able to continue transferring information. Also, if every buffer is allocated, there may be no more buffers to receive a control frame acknowledging a data frame and releasing buffer space! To avoid these problems, complex buffer allocation methods may be used. Normally, enough free buffers are always kept to receive at least one frame on each link so that control information can be exchanged even if data cannot.

An information frame would be received, the control information used (for example N(R)), and then the frame discarded so that the buffer may be used again. The loss of information frames as a result of buffer starvation means that information is lost not only because of errors in transmission, but also because of the internal operation of the nodes of a network, especially when the network becomes heavily loaded.

The LAPB procedure for closing a link requires an exchange of a DISC command and a UA response. The poll/final bit is used to obtain synchronisation between the DCE and DTE.

X.25: the network level

The function of level 2 is to carry a level 3 packet across a link. The function of the network level is to carry a piece of information from one host (DTE) to another via intermediate network nodes. The transfer of the level 3 information will involve a number of level 2 links. The X. 25 specification only covers the link between the DTE and DCE, but we will assume a similar protocol is used between each node of the network as well. Each level 3 packet contains a certain amount of level 3 protocol information in a header, and possibly some user data (from the transport level). The major differences between levels 2 and 3 are the use of addresses and logical channel numbers. Most hosts will be connected to the network by one level 2 link. This link then has to be used to enable the host to communicate with several other hosts by multiplexing logical channels on to the one physical link. Level 3 is used to achieve this multiple connection via a single link. Using level 3 a host establishes a logical channel to another host by making a connection request using the full address of the remote host. When the connection is established it becomes a logical channel with a unique number, the logical channel number.

The logical channel number is unique only for each link. Using the logical channel concept, packets for several calls may pass across the same level 2 link as they are all identified by the unique channel number. At the DCE the channel number is used to decide which route the packet will take. The logical channel is in fact a virtual circuit.

The network level has the same basic functions to perform as the link level.

1. Connection establishment.
2. Data transfer.
3. Connection disconnection.

The difference for the network level is that these functions are now carried out (apparently) between two hosts.

Packet format

The X.25 level 3 headers are used to contain a variety of information, so they are not of uniform size like the level 2 frame headers. The level 3 headers are different for every type of packet, which makes the format quite complex. The general format identifier (GFI) field indicates which format of level 3 header follows. The logical channel group number and logical channel number provide a 12 bit channel-numbering field. Splitting the field may allow subdivisions to be used for, say, different services. Call request and incoming call packets contain the address of the remote host (DTE). The addresses may contain fields indicating a particular process on a host as well as identifying a host. The address fields are of variable length, preceded by a byte count.

To begin a call, a host uses the full address of the remote host in a call request packet sent from the DTE to the DCE. The DCE will respond with either a call accepted packet if the request was successful, or a clear indication packet if the call was refused. At the remote host the DCE will send an incoming call packet to the host to indicate that a remote call has been requested.

The DTE receiving an incoming call packet will inspect the header to decide if the call is to be established or not. If the call is accepted a call accept packet is sent to the DCE; if the call is rejected a clear request is sent to the DCE. The channel number chosen for a new outgoing call by the DTE is the lowest available number. The channel number for an incoming call is chosen by the DCE as the highest available number. If the DTE and DCE agree on the channel numbers, and the DCE will accept the call, all subsequent packets on that call will only use that channel number, not the full address.

A call has been established to a remote DTE when a host receives a call accepted packet having the same channel number as the call request packet. The call is established at the remote DTE when the call accepted packet is sent to the remote DCE.

Level 3 transfers data to the network in a sequenced stream using Go-Back-N ARQ. The techniques of sequence numbers, piggybacked acknowledgements, RNR, RR and REJ responses are the same as for level 2, but they control the data flow across the network and into the remote host for each, independent logical channel. The use of windows and sequence numbers was for error control in level 2 as the level 1 link was prone to errors. At level 3 the level 2 link is assumed to be error free so. the emphasis is different.

The windows and sequence numbers are now used primarily for end-to-end flow control. The receipt of acknowledgements allows more information into the network, while the window limits the number of data packets in flight at any one time. Complete suspension of the data flow can be achieved by using a level 3 RNR, but the flow can be partially adjusted by the rate of acknowledgement.

An extra mechanism is used at level 3 to handle what is known as *out-of-band* transmission. Normal user data on an X.25 virtual call is kept in strict sequence; this is called *in band* transmission. However, a user application often requires a special signal which is not subject to the normal flow control. Such a signal is the abort character which a terminal user would type to stop a runaway program. X.25 level 3 uses an interrupt packet to carry this out-of-band signal.

The interrupt is not subject to the normal information flow control, the idea being that the interrupt could overtake information packets already in the network. The interrupt packet contains a field to indicate the cause of the interrupt; it is up to the application to decide what to do both with the interrupt and any subsequent data. When the DTE sends an interrupt packet the DCE responds with an interrupt confirmation.

Resets and restarts

In level 2 the reset was introduced as a mechanism for recovering from a protocol error where the two ends in the link became unsynchronised. The same thing can happen between the DTE and DCE at level 3, except that there are two areas where problems may occur. The first problem is due to the information frames and sequence numbers becoming out of synchronisation on a single call. This may be detected by receiving a sequence number outside the window or an acknowledgement for a packet that was not sent.

An error may also have been detected by a higher-level protocol, perhaps because of a network failure. In these cases only the one logical channel is affected so a *reset* is used. This sets the level 3 sequence numbers to 0 at the DTE and DCE. The reset will also be propagated to the remote DTE-DCE pair. The reset can be initiated from either the DTE or DCE and requires the usual request-confirmation exchange. A reset may cause the loss of any information packets within the network so a higher-level protocol will need to recover any lost data.

More drastic action is needed if the DTE and DCE become unsynchronised over global level 3 operation. An example is the choice of a channel number for a call request. If the DCE does not agree with the DTE over the chosen channel number (it should be the lowest free number) it means one of them thinks it has more logical calls opened than the other! The freeing of logical channel numbers correctly is the reason for the clear-request and clear-confirmation pair. When the whole level 3 needs resynchronisation a restart is initiated. This affects all the logical channels on the DTE-DCE link. A reset on the level 2 link is propagated as a restart at level 3.

A DTE wishing to terminate a call issues a clear request packet, to which the DCE will respond with a clear confirmation packet when the call has been cleared in the DCE. This may involve waiting for the forwarding of any information packets still held there. When the clear confirmation is received the channel number is freed for further use. At the remote end the DCE wit send a clear indication packet indicating that the remote host has closed, and no more information packets will follow. The remote DTE will respond with a clear confirmation packet when all outstanding information packets have been acknowledged.

The level 3 transport mechanism requires the data from the higher-level protocols to be broken into packets for transfer across the DTE-DCE interface. The X.25 recommendation specifies possible data lengths of 128 256, 512 and 1024 bytes, where 128 is the preferred maximum. It is probable that the PTT networks will guarantee 128 byte data packets. This means a user message must be broken into 128 byte sequences, the last one being perhaps less than 128 bytes. To enable the receiver to reassemble a message from multiple packets, level 3 uses a *more data bit* (M) in the information packet header to indicate that the current packet is not the last one of a message.

Just as the level 2 and level 3 need to include control information in the frames and packets as well as information from the next higher level, it is likely that a higher-level protocol would like to send control and data over level 3. The higher-level protocol may decide to add the control bits to the front of messages it passes to level 3. However, level 3 provides a mechanism that allows a higher-level protocol to multiplex data and control information on to the level 3 packet stream, thus maintaining the sequence of data and control across the network. This mechanism is the Q *bit.* The Q bit is set when the packet contains control information, and is clear when the packet contains data. Thus the higher-level protocol can quickly separate control and data information when receiving level 3 packets.

X.25 implementation

An advantage claimed for X.25 is that it only describes the host-to-node (DTE-to-DCE) interface. The network itself (internode) can use any convenient protocols, even completely different protocols, and the user would be unaware of them. In fact the proposed PTT networks are all planning to use X.25, or variations, within the networks for node-to-node transfer. The problem considered here is the implications of two methods of implementing an X.25 interface in a DCE that produce quite different results for the user. The discussion will show that even standards have complex problems of meaning (or semantics).

The two methods of implementation involve the mechanism for generating responses to various DTE packets at level 3. From the above description it can be seen that a command response sequence is used throughout level 3. The X.25 specification indicates quite clearly what responses are required, but leaves it up to the implementer to decide when, and under what criteria, the responses are made.

Consider the implementation that produces the DCE response as soon as the DTE's packet has been processed at the (local) DCE. This means the DCE's answer is sent to the DTE at the same time as the original request is forwarded across the network and well in advance of its arrival at the remote DTE. Such an implementation would give a very quick response to the user host. For instance, as data is passed to the DCE it is acknowledged immediately, even before it has crossed the network. The DCE-DTE flow control would ensure the DCE was not flooded with data, but large amounts could be in transit within the network before the call has been established at the remote end. This implementation would give the host the appearance of high throughput, as the DCE-DTE flow control would be the only restraint.

If the DTE receives a level 3 acknowledgement for a data packet, does this mean that the remote DTE has received it, or only that the local DCE has? To be consistent in this implementation it would have to be the latter, so the DCE has taken on the responsibility for delivery of that data. A higher-level protocol would be needed, with its own flow control, to handle the host-to-host transfer. This implementation has the effect, mentioned above, of apparently providing a fast throughput.

A host may be able to open a call (to the local DCE), send data, and close the call, before the remote DTE has received any data. The network, however, will contain a large amount of unacknowledged packets as the DTE-DCE flow control will accept packets as fast as the DCE can forward them into the network. This makes end-to-end flow control in the network difficult and can quickly lead to congestion.

In the second implementation we only allow the DCE to respond to the DTE when the response from the remote DTE has been received by the local DCE. Data sent from the DTE is not acknowledged until the remote DTE has accepted the packet. This gives the host an impression of a long delay. In fact the delay is the round trip to the remote host, plus processing. This end-to-end use of the level 3 protocol reduces the amount of processing required from higher-level protocols. The sending DTE will only be able to have a window of packets outstanding which will represent the maximum number of data buffers which the whole network will need for the call. This makes the resource management within the network easier and is less likely to produce congestion.

The cost is the lower performance seen by the user. Each packet takes longer to be acknowledged, thus reducing the throughput. There is also the problem of gaps which occurs when a window full of packets is sent rapidly, which is followed by a delay until the first acknowledgement comes back. This *bursty* mode of operation gives the network an uneven response and is difficult for both the host and DCE to manage.

The current X.25 recommendation allows a subscriber (DTE) to set a D bit in a data packet at level 3. This bit requires the acknowledgement to have end-to-end significance, as in the second example above. The D bit is an option, which means a network does not have to implement it.

The communications techniques covered so far have been concerned with centralised systems. Terminal networks are all built around a central computer; similarly remote job entry stations are usually connected to a single computer. In the remaining chapters some of the problems and techniques of a network of intercommunicating devices are discussed.

The devices at present connected to networks are usually generalpurpose computers, with their own terminal networks. One reason for networking multiaccess computers, rather than terminals or smaller devices, is that these computer systems already existed when networking was proposed. A second reason is that the protocols used in computer networks are very complex so that only a large computer system would have sufficient spare computing power to implement them. However, terminals can be directly attached to a network, by using a dedicated computer. In the near future computer networks will become as widespread as the telephone network, and large scale integration will enable cheap processors to handle the protocols. The result will be the networking of every sort of computing device. The current trends indicate that powerful, single user, workstations will replace terminals for network use. The workstations will be directly connected to a local area network and use the resources of larger computers via the network.

This chapter is primarily concerned with the technology used to connect the computers and devices that make up a computer network. For the purposes of description the range of technology has been divided into three areas

1. wide area networks
2. Radio and satellite broadcast networks
3. Local networks

The network technology includes the techniques used to interconnect the computing devices and physically transfer information from one computing device to another.

Wide area networks

The term 'wide area network' is applied to a network that covers a large physical area, say a whole country or large area under one administration. Such an area may be worldwide where a multinational organisation owns the network. The basic communication media used are dedicated circuits, usually of about 50 kHz bandwidth. Where digital circuits are available the bandwidth would be 64K bps. The recent introduction of fibre optics in longdistance trunks has make link bandwidth of 2-3M bps available. Wide area networks will be using these links over the next few years. Examples of such networks are PSS, ARPANET, Tymnet, Telenet, etc.; details of some of these networks are given at the end of this section. The physical circuits are usually provided by a PTT, although in the case of PSS the whole network is also run by the PTT.

Although 50 kHz bandwidth seems to be a lot compared with the 3 kHz nominal bandwidth of the voice telephone line, it is not very much when highspeed or large-volume transfers of information are required. Even at these high speeds the channel capacity is a resource that needs to be used efficiently.

It is now necessary to see how information can be transferred from one computer to any other on the network. The problem falls into two parts. The first is that of transferring information via a medium, such as a wire. The second part is concerned with addressing and routing. If there were only two computers on a network, then they could be connected by two channels, one for each direction, and whatever one computer transmitted the other would be bound to receive. When more computers are added, the bidirectional connection solution can be extended by having each computer connected to every other computer by a full duplex connection. To send a message to a particular computer the appropriate connection is selected; thus the routing of a message is carried out by the sender. Using a dedicated connection between every computer on the network is very expensive. If there are n computers on the network then $n(n-1)/2$ lines are needed, and have to be paid for! As a single computer would not normally be communicating with every other computer on the network at the same time, most of the lines would be unused in a fully connected network. Therefore to increase the utilisation of the connection circuits, their number is reduced, and switching is introduced within the network.

There are three forms of switching that can be used in communications: circuit switching, message switching, and packet switching.

Circuit switching

Circuit switching is used on the PSTN to connect telephone subscribers. To use it for a computer network each computer would have a private circuit to a local exchange, and the exchanges would be connected to form a network.

Whenever two computers wish to exchange information, a physical path is established between them via the exchanges. The path is then disconnected when the connection is closed. The circuit has been switched by the exchanges. This method of connection is not used on established computer networks. The major disadvantages of circuit switching are

1. The cost of the equipment is very high, whereas the resulting circuit is not necessarily of high enough quality for computer communications.
2. The resulting circuit can only be used by the two computers on the call, thus the equipment is dedicated to the circuit. In particular the connection from the computer to the exchange is dedicated. To enable a single computer to communicate with more than one other computer at the same time, extra equipment is needed for each simultaneous call. If there are no connections all the equipment is idle but being paid for.

3. The time taken to set up the physical path can be very long in computer terms.

As high-speed connection using good-quality circuits is important for efficient computer networks, circuit switching is discounted in favour of the other methods. Circuit switching is used for some networks connecting computers-for instance, the Nordic Data Network.

Circuit switching has two advantages

1. Charges are made only for the time that a call is connected. If infrequent and short connections are all that is required, then circuit switching may be advantageous to the customer. It is expected that many slower devices, such as terminals, will be connected to national computer networks via the PSTN to gain this advantage.

2. Where a single device is used for long periods, such as a facsimile machine, circuit switching is economically advantageous. This is particularly true where digital facilities, such as X.21, are available.

The above discussion is based on the existing PSTN services offered by the PTTs. When the ISDN service is widely available, then it will be an attractive mechanism for some computer networks. Each host will be able to set up calls, use the 64K bps bandwidth, and quickly close the call, as required. The circuits will still carry packets for the end-to-end data transfer; but circuit switching will be the main link-switching mechanism. In the UK it is intended to bring all the PTT communications together into Integrated Digital Access (IDA). This will combine ISDN, X.25 networking and special digital services into a common access interface.

Message switching

To overcome problems in setting up and taking down physical circuits via exchanges, computer networks use permanent circuits and switch the data, A partially connected network is used in which each computer has a permanent circuit to a number of its neighbours, but not to all computers on the network. An example will illustrate the basic operation of information switching where the unit of information is a message.

If the computer at A wishes to send a message to B, the message must pass through either D or C. The points on the network are called *nodes. A will* address the message to B by placing the address of B in the message header. The message and address are then sent on the circuit to D. At D the node inspects the address; if the address is 'D' the message is given to the computer; if the address is not D the message is forwarded on a circuit that the node believes will enable the message to be delivered, In this case D will forward the message to B. Thus the node at D has switched the message on to the appropriate output circuit. In this example two major characteristics of a computer network can be seen.

The message is addressed to a remote destination and sent on the next stage of its route.

Store and forward

Each message is received into the node storage so that it can be processed as a whole unit. Usually an error check is carried out and the whole message has to be received before this can be completed. The message is then inspected for routing information so that the node can decide which output circuit to use to forward the message.

The nodes have been introduced in the network to carry out the functions of routing and store and forward, so the host computer is separated from the network operation as much as possible. The 'hosts' are the user computers which wish to use the network. Often a number of hosts will be attached to a single node.

The node computers are usually minicomputers chosen for their ability to respond in real time to the communications devices. Each node receives incoming messages and stores them. When a complete message has been received the destination address is inspected so that the message can be placed on the output queue of a circuit to forward the message. If the message is for a host attached to the node, the output circuit will be the one connected to the host. If the message is for a distant host the node must forward the message to another node on the route to the distant host. While the message is in the node store, waiting to be processed or waiting for output, it is, of course, being delayed.

The link into any one node may be used to carry messages from several different computers, as may the connection between the node and host. The physical equipment involved is used more efficiently than in circuit switching as a result of this multiplexing. Message multiplexing is the most important advantage of message and packet switching computer networks.

To distinguish between message and packet switching it is necessary to understand what a message is. This has already been introduced in earlier chapters, but a more detailed discussion is given here. The easiest way of defining a message is to say that it is a unit of information which is exchanged by users of a network. This means the characteristics of a message are only dependent on the user or the application. A message could be a few bits or a file, or even a whole database. In a message-switching network the whole message is passed from one node to another as a complete entity. Compared with circuit switching, a message-switching network has the following characteristics.

1. Any computer can communicate with any other computer without having a direct physical connection.
2. Any computer can communicate with several others using the same equipment by multiplexing messages.
3. There is no delay arising from circuit set up, but messages are delayed when they pass through a node enroute.

The messages can be transferred between nodes, and nodes and hosts, using an *ARQ* protocol. Characteristic 3 implies that there is no delay arising from the use of a network other than the store and forward operation of the nodes. This is true in some networks using pure datagram techniques. However, in most networks the internode protocol used within the network introduces some delays.

Any network using a virtual circuit protocol, at any level, will introduce a delay when the message or packet is given to the network. In many networks the local node negotiates for resources within the network before actually forwarding a message. This is true of an X.25 network when the call is first set up, and is true of every message on the ARPA network. A user of a message-switching network will pass the network a message, together with a destination address, and the user will receive messages as single units.

Advantages and disadvantages

The advantages of message switching, over circuit switching are:

- The sender may dispatch the message when convenient, even if the receiver is not ready, as the network will store the message for delivery, However, if network resources run out, an undelivered message may be deleted and thus lost; this depends on the network protocols.
- Computers can exchange information at different speeds, as the network will buffer the message.
- Broadcasting of a message may be possible.
- Equipment is used more efficiently.
- Messages may be handled by priority.

Each message is treated as a single unit. However, there are also some disadvantages.

- A very long message will hold up other, perhaps more urgent, messages as it monopolises a circuit for the duration of its transmission.
- As a message may be very large, the node computer may not have enough memory to store it before forwarding it; in this case the message is lost. Further, this message will never be delivered as the network does not have the required resources.
- A very large message may monopolise the storage of a node, because it cannot be delivered, so that other messages cannot be received by this node.

Packet switching

The disadvantages of message switching relate to the possible occurrence of large messages, where the exact value of 'large' will depend on the network. If a network could be certain of only handling small messages, the disadvantages would disappear. The transfer of messages is a user requirement, so a network that meets user needs must be able to handle very large messages as well as small messages.

The solution to these two conflicting requirements is to break the user's message into small *packets* for transfer through the network and have the packets reassembled into the message by the receiver. Note that the message header is included as the data in the first packet and that each packet has its own header. This refinement produces packet switching, which is the most widely used switching technique for computer networks.

The physical organisation of a packet-switching network is the same as for message switching. The network is a partially connected mesh of nodes. For practical reasons most wide area networks use special node computers to perform the switching, with the user computers being attached to the nodes. The term 'host' is now widely used to mean a user computer system attached to a network.

The nodes are part of the network, so the hosts use a well-defined interface for accessing the node to enable data transfer across the network. By using a node separated from the host, all of the packet-switching functions, such as storage and routing, are removed from the host. However, the host still needs considerable software to handle the protocols used to access the node and to transfer data to other computers on the network.

The advantages that packet switching has over message switching are:

— The small maximum packet size makes storage allocation and management easier in the switching nodes, sufficiently so for minicomputers to be used.

— The multiplexing of packets enables several messages to be interleaved on one circuit, reducing the delay seen by the user.

— The total transmission time through the network is reduced. It shows a message passing from A to B which would normally require 6k + d seconds to reach B, where 3k is the transmission time of the whole message on one link and d is the node delay. If the message is broken into three packets, each taking k seconds to transmit, the whole message arrives at B in 4k + d seconds. The difference increases with the number of links traversed and the size of the message.

It would appear that packet switching solves all the problems of wide area network organisation: it uses fixed highspeed lines and minicomputers for nodes; it is also more efficient and responsive than message switching. However, although packet switching is a better technique with which to implement a computer network, users still want to transfer messages. Packet switching introduces another layer of complexity and translation between the user and the physical network transporting the bits. Fortunately, the cost of processing is falling so the extra cost is outweighed by the practical advantages. A second cost, not so easily overcome, is that each packet will have its own overheads as well as those used by each message; this will reduce the efficiency of the physical circuits.

The conclusion drawn from consideration of these three switching techniques is that packet switching, especially used in a partially connected mesh of nodes with wideband circuits, is currently the best technique for wide area computer networks. Packet switching is also used in other network technologies, rather than message switching, for the same reasons. Wide area networks have been in existence since the early 1970s.

The best known example is the ARPA network in the United States. This network was established by a government research agency to link together computer centres that had contracts for government research so that research workers could share the available computing resources. The network itself also forms part of a research project to evaluate the feasibility of a large computer network, and to investigate techniques that could be used in such a network.

The ARPA network has been very successful in showing that the concept of resource sharing by use of a network is feasible. One of the most noticeable advantages that the network has introduced is a mail facility. This allows each user with access to a computer on the network to exchange mail with all the other network users. The mail facility is probably one of the main sources of traffic on the ARPA network and has certainly improved the amount of communication between researchers at different sites. The basic techniques used within the ARPA network have been influenced by the defence aspects of the research, particularly the need for a fast response and resilience to the failure of any part.

The network consists of a mesh of partially connected nodes called Interface Message Processors (IMPs). Each IMP can have up to eight hosts connected to it and may be connected to up to eight other IMPs. Each IMP accepts messages from the hosts of up to 8K bits in length. The IMP breaks the message into IK bit packets which are then forwarded through the network of IMPs to the IMP attached to the destination host. This destination IMP reassembles the message before delivering it to the destination host. If a host wishes to send a message of more than 8K bits it must break the message up itself, into 8K packets, and the destination host must reassemble the message from the 8K packets. Thus the translation between messages and packets takes place at two levels.

Within the network of IMPs, packets (1K) are sent individually along whichever route is best at the time, so that packets in a single message may use different routes and may arrive at the destination IMP out of sequence. The destination IMP has to reassemble the message from the packets as they arrive. However, messages passed from the host to the IMP are delivered in the same sequence to the destination host. The technology developed for the ARPANET is now used in a number of commercial wide area networks all over the world. The British Telecom network PSS (Packet Switching Stream) is an example of a network provided by a PTT as a public service.

The design requirements for such a network are different from those of the ARPA network so they have resulted in a network with different characteristics. The network topology consists of a number of *exchanges* which are also partially connected. Each exchange is connected to a number of host computers in its area. The exchanges contain the node computers, the number of node computers in each exchange depending on the number of hosts attached to the exchange.

The hosts use an access protocol called X.25 to enable them to make virtual calls to other hosts. A host will give the local exchange the destination address of the host with which it wishes to communicate. The network will route the call to the destination exchange which will then complete the call to the destination host. The call is represented by information kept at all the exchanges on the route. The information is then used to forward the packets transferred on the call. Once the call has been established the hosts may exchange their own information. This is very similar to circuit switching on the PSTN although it is provided using packet-switching techniques. The PSS network techniques are different from those on the ARPA network, where each message is addressed and transferred separately. The hosts can use a single link to the PSS exchange to carry a number of virtual calls to other hosts, thus the link is used to multiplex the calls.

These networks differ from wide area networks in the way in which the channel is used for communication between users. Broadcast networks use a channel to which all the users are connected, so all the users receive any transmission made on the channel. At present the two types of channel in use are local radio, covering up to a few hundred kilometres, and satellite channels which are used to span very large distances.

Networks using radio and satellite channels have special problems because noise in the channel can cause errors. There is also the problem of allocating the channel for transmission. The first operational broadcast computer network was built at the University of Hawaii using local radio transmission; many of the techniques and much of the terminology derive from this first network.

Every node receives all packets transmitted on the broadcast channel. When the received packet is complete, the node checks the packet for errors and then checks the destination address. If the address of the receiver matches the packet destination address, it is accepted; otherwise it is discarded. The problems particular to a broadcast network occur in the allocation of the channel to a node for transmitting a packet. Different solutions are used for radio and satellite links. Each node is only able to communicate with each other node via the common channel, so some scheme is needed to coordinate transmission. The schemes that have been proposed and used are discussed here in increasing complexity and are compared for channel efficiency. The simplest transmission technique is called pure aloha; when a node has a packet to transmit it does so immediately. Having transmitted the packet, the node waits for an acknowledgement.

This is therefore a positive acknowledgement protocol. If an acknowled-gement is not received within a time out period, the packet is assumed lost. Transmission collisions, which occur when two nodes transmit at the same time and thus interfere with each other's transmission, are detected by the time out mechanism. When a collision is detected, each node waits a period of time of random length before retransmitting the packet to of traffic increases, the rate of collision will increase and more re-transmissions will be needed.

As the older packets are re-transmitted, more stations will have newer packets to transmit, causing more collisions, etc. Analysis has shown that a pure aloha scheme can only use a maximum of about 18% of the channel bandwidth. A node may transmit at any time, thus the maximum length of time the channel is wasted as a result of a collision is 2t, where t is the transmission time for one packet. The 2t period is the worst case, where one node begins transmitting just before the previous transmission is complete. An improvement on pure aloha is *slotted aloha* in which the transmission channel time is divided into time slots of *t*. Each node is then only allowed to begin transmitting a packet at the start of a time slot. The nodes are kept in synchronisation by a time signal on the channel. Now if a collision occurs only one slot *is* wasted, so the maximum efficiency rises to about 34% of the channel capacity. When a collision is detected, a transmitter must wait for a random number of time slots before retransmitting. When the traffic is light the wait can be quite short, but as the traffic load increases the waiting period should be increased. From the aloha schemes it can be seen that it is collisions that cause problems, so a collision avoidance mechanism should improve efficiency.

In packet radio networks a scheme known as Carrier Sense Multiple Access (CSMA) is used. When a node is transmitting all other nodes can receive the transmission, so they can avoid a collision by not transmitting themselves until the channel is free. A transmission is detected by the presence of the carrier signal in the medium. When a node has a packet to transmit it looks for the carrier; if there is no carrier the packet is transmitted. If the carrier is detected the node waits for a random length delay and tries again. Even in a radio broadcast the signal from a transmitter takes a finite amount of time to reach all the receivers in the network.

When two nodes find the channel free, they may both begin transmission because neither has heard the other one. This case is most likely to happen when two stations are waiting for the channel to become free. The length of time it takes to propagate the signal to all receivers is the time band in which collisions may occur, but it is less than the total packet transmission time. As with the aloha technique, the CSMA technique can be improved by dividing the channel time into slots and only allowing the transmission of packets to begin at the start of a time slot. The slot length is set to the propagation delay, not the packet transmission time. The CSMA technique has been further refined by modifying the action of the node when the channel is busy. When the node samples the channel again and finds it free, it transmits its packet with a probability p, or waits for a further delay of random length, with a probability (1-p).

This is called persistent CSMA or p-persistent transmission. If p is high then the delay before transmission occurs is lower, but the possibility of collision increases if two stations are waiting for another station to finish. In persistent CSMA a trade off is made between channel efficiency and delay with the value of p. Channel efficiencies of about 80% may be achieved using these techniques. Packet radio networks have a small delay between the start of a transmission and the detection of the transmission by all stations on the network. On a satellite broadcast network there is a very long delay between transmission and receiving, of the order of a quarter of a second.

A satellite network operates by each transmitter sending its signal to the satellite. The satellite then broadcasts the signal to all of the Earth stations, which may be spread over a very large area. One satellite system currently used for packet switching connects nodes in England, Norway and North America using a satellite in stationary orbit over the North Atlantic. A different channel allocation technique is used on satellite broadcast networks because of the long propagation delay. This satellite channel allocation technique involves making reservations for the future use of slots in the channel. The channel is divided into frames consisting of a number of reservation slots and a number of packet slots. Each reservation slot represents a packet slot in the second part of the frame. All ground stations are synchronised to the frame timing by the satellite transmission. During the first part of the frame the ground stations reserve slots for the packets they have ready by transmitting a marker during the reservation slot time. When the reservation slot is heard on the satellite down channel, the ground station inspects the slot to see if it contains its own marker. If so it can transmit a packet in the corresponding packet slot in the second part of the frame. This scheme uses some of the channel capacity to avoid the collisions which could reduce the network to a pure aloha scheme. Obviously more than one ground station may attempt to reserve a particular packet slot by transmitting during the reservation slot time. There are a number of algorithms to overcome this, including allocating some slots to busy stations.

Thus if a station successfully obtained a packet slot in the last frame, the same slot is allocated to that station in the next frame without competition. If an allocated slot is not used then the slot is open for competition in the following frame. Usually there are some slots that all stations can compete for in every frame. Another mechanism involves using a central allocation station to which each station sends its requirements and the central station allocates the slots. This has two disadvantages: firstly, the central station becomes a weakness in the network reliability, and secondly, the delay between requesting an allocation and receiving the allocation may be of the order of 1 or 2 seconds before the packet can be transmitted. A chapter in the book by Kuo is dedicated to broadcast satellite protocols.

Local area networks

A local, or private, network is a communication system connecting computers in a small geographical area, say less than a few kilometres between the furthest points. The network is wholly owned and run by one administration. There are currently two basic types of technology used on such a network: these are cable, or bus, technology and ring technology. Whereas wide area networks and satellite networks use nodes to separate the internal network switching from the user hosts, local networks are meant to be as cheap as possible and so the separate node computer is omitted. In both local network technologies all the computers are directly attached to the transmission medium by a special interface, and all the interfaces receive all the packets.

The difference between a ring and a bus system is the way in which the channel is allocated. Local networks are designed for use in local computing by allowing the interconnection of very small computers, such as microprocessors, personal workstations and peripheral devices. If the local network is to be useful, the cost of the computer interfaces into the network channel has to be low compared with the cost of the computer or peripheral, and microprocessors are very cheap in computer terms. A widely forecast use of local networks is connecting word processors within a set of offices for the exchange of information and electronic mail.

The cost constraints, the limited processing power of the small computers and the protocols used on a local network are different from those used in wide area networks. A local network usually has a very high bandwidth channel of between I and 10 MHz and a very low error rate say one bit in several million might be corrupted. These characteristics permit the use of simple protocols. The lowest level protocol for using the transmission medium is built into the computer interface.

Cable or bus networks

These networks usually use a length of coaxial cable, or an existing cable such as that used for closed circuit television (CCTV). The medium is used in a broadcast fashion, exactly as described in the previous section on broadcast networks. The channel allocation techniques vary slightly on the theme of the CSMA techniques, or on a centralised slot allocation. The most popular broadcast local network is the Ethernet system developed by Xerox.

The Ethernet principles can be used on any broadcast medium: radio, telephone lines, coaxial cable and optical fibres have all been used successfully. The Ethernet uses a base band signal, rather than a modulated signal, to simplify the broadcast transmitter and receiver, with a modified CSMA channel access technique. To obtain the maximum efficiency from the broadcast medium an Ethernet transmitter can listen to its own broadcast to detect a collision and abort the transmission. This extra complexity is known as CSMACD (CD = collision detection) or listen-while-talk. As with the other CSMA techniques a station does not begin transmitting until the broadcast medium is free.

Two stations waiting for another station to finish a transmission will begin transmitting together, and thus interfere with each other. The collision is detected by the stations and they both abort the transmission immediately. To enforce the protocol a station that aborts a transfer then jams the ether. After a collision each station waits for a random time before trying again. The CSMA-CD technique enables the Ethernet system to obtain up to 95% of the broadcast channel bandwidth. The improvement in performance over ordinary CSMA is due to the stopping of transmission as soon as a collision is detected. Note that no slots are used so a network-wide timing signal is not required. The transceiver handles all of the CSMACD access, including the retries and delay calculation which is varied with the traffic load. Thus only complete, and checked, packets are passed up to the station interface and only one request is made for a packet to be sent. The checksum generation and checking are carried out within the hardware: bad packets are discarded. A time out mechanism is used to retransmit packets that may have been lost as a result of errors.

Ring networks

The ring technique originated in the USA. The idea was then developed in parallel at Cambridge University in the UK and at two research centres in the USA. The version developed at Cambridge is known as the Cambridge ring in the UK. The computer interface is divided into two parts: the repeater and the interface proper. A ring uses a twisted pair of wires as the transmission medium. However, to improve reliability, the repeater is powered from the ring and electrically isolated from the computer interface, so four wires are used to connect the repeaters.

The four wires are used as two pairs for signalling and carry sufficient power for the repeaters. In this way the computer can be switched off and removed from the ring without switching off the repeater. With the ring the medium is terminated at each station, whereas in the cable network it is not. Each station is represented by a repeater, several of which are then connected together into a ring. The repeater is a simple device containing a shift register and some logic to detect certain conditions in the information being passed around the ring. The repeater normally passes any information received on to the next repeater, so transmission only occurs in one direction. When a station transmits data, the repeater transmits the information from the station instead of the information received from the previous repeater.

Slotted ring

There are slight differences in the channel allocation mechanism used in the Cambridge ring and in those rings developed in the USA. In the Cambridge ring a fixed-size mini-packet is used which constantly circulates in the ring, and a special station called a monitor is used to generate and maintain the mini-packet and provide the power for the repeaters. In the American versions a variable-size packet is used which may be lost and regenerated as required by each repeater.

The current format of the Cambridge mini-packet. Note that only 16 bits of information are carried in a ring mini-packet whereas the broadcast network packet may contain several hundred bytes. The assembly of information into a block has to be done by the computer. The monitor station also provides a buffer if the ring is not physically long enough to hold a complete mini-packet. The monitor performs a check on the mini-packet each time it passes to ensure that it is intact, and to replace it if not.

The monitor is an obvious weakness in the Cambridge ring design so far as reliability is concerned; however, experience so far has shown that monitor failures are rare. The advantage of the monitor is that the repeaters can be very simple as well as cheap, which is the purpose of a local network. To use the ring to send a packet of information, the station will wait until an empty mini-packet is detected by the repeater. When the full/empty bit in the mini-packet passes the repeater it is set to one. If the packet was already full no change has been made to the bit; if the packet was empty (full/empty bit = 0) the mini-packet is now reserved by this station, The repeater will use this mini-packet if the full/empty bit was received as 0.

The addresses of the source and destination stations are placed in the address fields followed by the next 16 bits of the information that the station wishes to send; these are placed in the data field from the station buffer. The reserved mini-packet then travels round to all the other stations on the ring. Each station has a source select register in which an address is placed. If the source address in a mini-packet matches the contents of the source select register, and the destination address matches the station address, the data field is copied into the station receive buffer and the accept status is set at the end of the packet. If the packet is refused, or the destination station is busy, the destination repeater will set the appropriate value in the status bits at the end of the mini-packet. No other change is made by the receiving repeater, and all other repeaters will pass on the mini-packet unchanged. Special values which can be used in the source select register are: all ones, which means accept any source station address, and all zeros, which means do not accept the data from any mini-packets.

When the mini-packet returns to the sending station the full/empty bit is reset to 0 and the status bits are checked to see if the information was accepted. As an error check, the station also reads back the 16 data bits and checks them against the data in its buffer. Having reset the full/empty bit, the station must now wait for another empty mini-packet before it can send the next 16 bits of information. In this way the now empty packet becomes available to successive stations around the ring and the packet slot is allocated in a round robin fashion.

The variable nature of packet traffic in a local network makes it difficult to design a system that will provide a very fast response, especially when there is little traffic, and yet not become overloaded or unfair when the traffic becomes heavy. The broadcast techniques provide a low delay, especially in low-volume traffic, as the transmitter can usually send a packet as soon as one is available. However, as the volume of traffic increases, the broadcast system suffers from collisions and longer delays which can eventually lead to an unstable situation. In the slotted ring the channel is allocated by means of a round robin mechanism so collisions never occur, and during a burst of traffic each station is able to continue transmitting with only a larger delay. During periods of low traffic volume the ring does introduce a delay while a station waits for the empty packet to come round.

Proponents of both systems argue that because of the very high bandwidth available on the channel, and the low processing power of the computers attached to the local network, the volume of traffic is nearly always low in a broadcast network and the delay is negligible in a ring.

Token Ring

The token ring attempts to provide the advantages of broadcast access in low-volume traffic periods, with the inherent sharing of the slotted ring during high-volume traffic periods. The physical topology of the ring is the same, but instead of a circulating mini-packet there is a circulating token. Any host requiring access to the ring waits for the token to arrive; it then changes the token to indicate that a packet is following. The modified token is then followed immediately by the data packet, which can be of any size up to some system maximum. All hosts detect the modified token and examine the packet to see if it is addressed to them; if it is the packet is copied off the ring.

The receiving host still sends the packet on though, so the data packet goes all the way round the ring to the sender. The sender takes the packet off the ring. Normally the sender receives the front of the data packet before it has finished transmitting the rest of the packet, owing to the short length of the ring. When the receiver detects the end of the data packet it marks its status by changing the last few bits, as in the Cambridge ring mini-packet; thus the sender knows if the packet was accepted or not. Immediately the sender has finished the packet it puts a token on the ring so another host may have a go. The token ring is a simple idea, but it is more complex than the Cambridge ring and the interfaces are more expensive.

The initialise sequence which is required to start the ring is quite complex as the token has to be put on the ring to start data transfer; of course there can only be one token. The mechanisms for detecting duplicate tokens and lost tokens, without the use of a monitor station, add to the cost of the computer interfaces.

7

Process Evaluation

The concept of the electronically-aided executive will be explored as well as the growth of decision support systems. Alvin Toffler, categorizes the development of a society into three waves. During the first wave, the majority of people worked the earth as farmers, living primarily off what they produced and trading or purchasing the few items they didn't produce or make themselves. The second wave, the industrial age, changed all that with the introduction of different forms of energy and machinery. The second wave brought with it bureaucracy and the hierarchical management style that still predominates: standardization, specialization, and synchronization; concentration, maximization, and centralization. Order, discipline, and assembly-line mentality are the foundation of the second wave. The third wave, is built around four clusters of industries that Toffier thinks will be the backbone of what he calls the new technosphere: (1) Electronics and computers. (2) Space industries. Toffler projects that we can accomplish things in space not possible on earth. For example, with no gravity in space, there is no need for containers nor is there any problem in handling highly poisonous or reactive substances. TRW has identified 400 alloys we cannot manufacture on earth because of gravity. (3) The oceans will become the source of much-needed food, of minerals, and of phosphate ores for land-based agriculture. We will have the aquavillage under the oceans and floating factory in space. (4) The biological industry. Toffler feels this area could be the most important of all. Metal-hungry microbes will mine valuable trace metals from ocean water while genetic engineering will employed to develop people, for example, with cowlike stomachs to digest grass and hay, thus alleviating the food shortage.

We will use bacteria to turn sunlight into electromechanical energy and use microorganisms to eliminate the need for oil in plastics, paint, and so on. The cloning of mice and the test-tube conception of babies are actual examples of what is to follow. The technosphere will be blended with the *infosphere*, which will have an equally profound effect on society. Information in the new infosphere will be damassified with the advent of more local newspapers, regional newscasts, the additional selectivity of cable TV and its myriad of channels, and personalized computer-based information for working a prescribed shift to a more flexible, individually tailored work pattern and style.

The epitome of this trend is the previously mentioned electronic cottage, where because of home computers and terminal links to corporate and other data bases, activity can again center on the home as it did in the agriculture or first wave. The words are flexibility, diversity, and personalization with the accent on flexible working hours, individually customized compensation packages, participative management, matrix management, and the like. Second-wave leaders today are like passengers on the Titanic squabbling for deck chairs, the dying order trying to hold onto their position and power while their world sinks under them. In another vein he remarks that no corporate president would run a large company with a table of organization first sketched by the quill pen of some eighteenth-century ancestor whose sole managerial experience consisted or designed in a pre-Marx, pre-Darwin, pre-Freud, and pre-Einstein era, and before the airplane, automobile, factory, computer, nuclear bomb, and birth control pill.

We are ready now to compare second-and third-wave thinking about MIS impact on (1) higher-level management decision making, (2) higher-level management information style, (3) company organization, and (4) overall job structure and content. This will set the framework for the discussion that follows. Second-wave managers feel business will be run much as in the past. They see the prime role of middle management as motivating and directing the workers under them to achieve prescribed goals. Second-wavers feel that the computer can do little to aid in this process. They observe also that for over 20 years now the seers have been claiming that computers will replace managers, and little if any headway has been made.

The responsibilities of top management are to plan the long-range activities of the firm and to ensure that the necessary resources are available to reach long-term revenue and profit objectives. With this longer-range outlook, the idea of a top executive needing to have instantaneous real-time data on current operations and to be hooked on-line to the computer represents faddism rather than the result of a careful business cost/benefit analysis. The on-line, real-time executive is a business anachronism. The two professors projected an on-line management world in which middle management would be eroded as to managers with information models and an information elite corps at their side would plot the strategy of the company. These strategies would then be translated into structured decision rules and actions that could be implemented directly by machines and operating personnel, thus eliminating the need for middle-level management.

Second-wavers still believe in a centralized, hierarchical form of organization. They point to the failures of matrix management, where an individual has two or more bosses, and suggest that this runs counter to the natural order of things where one works for a single boss who in turn reports to a single boss. MIS, they conclude, is a central service provide to the corporation and should be run centrally. As MIS users, they want to prescribe what they want, but they don't want to be involved in developing applications and running computers. That's for the professionals. The second let the MIS people do what they do best, providing the technical leadership for keeping the technology under control.

Second-wave managers feel that information technology will have an impact on their job but not a major one. They take more of a defensive than an offensive role. They feel they should have a fundamental understanding so that MIS people cannot pull the wool over their eyes and not charge them an extraordinary amount for mediocre services. They are aware of the growth in MIS budgets and rare concerned that the charge-out of these costs will impact their ability to meet department expense goals and affect their yearly bonuses. Thus the position is a reactive rather than a proactive one. The key is that they are not convinced that MIS will have a significant influence in the way they conduct their business.

Third-waves managers, the other extreme, feel MIS can have a major influence on their decision making. They see an evolving innovative and highly individualistic management style being abetted by personalized executive decision support systems. They see computerized decisions models to which they will supply parameters in the form of "what if" questions, with the models spilling out the results of various options, thus enabling the executive to select from among them while adding the subjective and intuitive elements that only he or she can.

The third-waver envisions the ability to personally browse through a data base for specific performance data and projections of future performance based on a variety of selective factors. The third-wave manager is an on-line executive in that his style is consistent with the personal use of an executive terminal. He sees office automation in the broad sense not only as a help to his secretary in typing memos and reports and communicating them electronically to predefined distribution lists, but also as a personal productivity tool. He is the electronically aided executive who runs a nearly paperless of office because his correspondence, departmental instructions, meeting schedules, and the like are computer produced through the use of electronic filing and communication systems. He believes in a team management style in conjunction with MIS. His company has organized around market segment or niches, wherein products and markets have been pinpointed and selected because of the company's particular expertise and desire to penetrate and dominate. No longer does competing across the board make sense.

The successful companies are those that specialize in growing and profitable segments and subsegments of a specific market place. Third-wave management views decentralization as essential in achieving the necessary entrepreneurial thrust and motivation. Thus means the manager must control as much of the information flow and support for his department as it logically makes sense to control. Highly defined and distinct into the business world the political viewpoint that the government that governs best, governs least.

Finally, the third-wave manager feels MIS will have a major impact on his future job, probably more than any other single force in his company or in society. He senses that if a manager does not recognize this, he will probably be obsolete in five years. With this mind, it behooves the executive to be heavily involved in MIS projects that affect his operation. Not only will he become involved when asked to, he will be taking greater leadership in directing the MIS efforts. He sees the impact on his job not just in the operation and control areas but in the strategic area as well. The future third-wave manager will be an on-line executive tapping his personal as well as the company data base for information. He will need to have this capability to compete against companies whose executives operate in this mode.

Before speculating on what future influence MIS might have on management, let us take a look at the situation as it appears today. Which is based on several computer surveys and verified by own experience, indicates that MIS has had less impact at the top management level than at the middle or operating management level. MIS has had moderate influence on the decision-making process, little impact on job content, and no influence on the decision-making process, little impact on job content, and no influence on reducing or increasing the number of top managers required. The major responsibilities of top management involve long-and short-range planning, resource and capacity analysis, setting of profit and budget goals, and, in general, establishing the business objectives of the company. There is a heavy planning content as opposed to a heavy control content at the lower management levels. Information systems have been more effective in the control than in the planning area. However, the harbingers of potentially significant changes in this area are leading-edge executives such as the president of Northwest Industries. Control functions tend to be more structured, more programmable,. more straightforward, and, therefore, more receptive to automated information systems.

There are a host of potential solutions to improve the areas that are identified. This step in decision making analyzes the situation in more depth in order to develop the scope and range of possible solutions and to give priority to the solutions in accordance with predetermined criteria, such as resource availability and time to resolve. In the preceding example, the introduction of a new product could be focused on filling a gap in the existing product line or could open up an entirely new market. Possible alternatives to the competitive price weakness could be the development of new pricing contracts or a heightened merchandising program that stresses specific product features and advantages.

Each of the potential solutions must now be developed. The specifications of each solution are identified so that they may be evaluated in the next step. If a new product is to be introduced, its characteristics must be determined, specific market targets for the new product described, and the necessary marketing support, training, and sales plans developed.

Alternate solution involves projecting the potential profitability and company impact of each of the alternatives. Although there are many quantitative factors in the analysis, many factors will be qualitative in nature and will involve an analysis and weighing of relative risk. For example, the introduction of a new product may be two to three years away, such that the marketplace at the time of product introduction is the significant element. This may be difficult to prediction a rapidly changing industry.

Although carried out after the decision is made, implementation considerations must be a strong element in the decision. In some instance, a pilot or test model is necessary to validate the final decision. Thus the implementation effort serves as a feedback loop to the decision-making process. In reviewing several studies on this subject and through my own personal contact with executives of medium and large companies utilizing computers, the impact of MIS and computers on top-management decision making. Since top management does not regularly receive computer printout directly, the effect of MIS on decision making is scant. However, this is not to say that decisions have not been influenced by MIS through the intercession of middle management and that they wont' be further influenced in the future.

Although computerized performance reports may indicate areas of improvement, these areas are usually pertinent to a specific operational entity. For example, reports may show that production variances of material and labour are reaching alarming proportions or that the order backlog is growing because of inability to fill orders from inventory. The areas for improvement are generally not of the scope that require top-management decision. Similarly, the areas of improvement that represent new opportunities do not come from computerized reports. News opportunities evolve from a variety of sources, including staff-planning departments, executive committee meetings, "brainstorming" sessions, attendance at seminars and trade shows, outside consultants, and just recently from strategic and financial computer modeling.

The step most influenced by computer systems are the development and evaluation of alternate solutions. The degree "moderate" does not indicate that the majority of companies are utilizing computers for this purpose; it indicates that a good number represent the leading edge in the use of techniques such as simulation that are required to develop and evaluate solutions to problems. Although a few top managers utilize these techniques directly and review computer output, most often the middle managers and/or staff department act as the information middlemen between the computer and top management.

The writers who state that computers are making decisions for top management usually are referring to operating decisions that happen to be made by top management. These decisions should rightfully be delegated to middle management and even to operating management. Important elements that are subjective or nonquantifiable in nature bear heavily on decisions of this type. Therefore, although the computer may have accomplished a good deal of the analysis and testing of alternatives, the final decision was not tied directly to the automated information system.

Automated management information systems can make decisions on lot sizes and length of production runs, but they as yet ate not utilized to any major degree in making final decisions on the introducing of a new product, the site of a new warehouse, or the need for an additional factory. Decision support systems, which are becoming more prevalent and which show great promise in upgrading the "scants" to at lest "moderate" and in some cases "heavy", will be discussed later in the chapter.

MIS plays a prominent role in the implementation of decisions once made. For example, the entire introduction cycle of a product from initial design to its availability in the marketplace is materially aided by automated information systems. Indeed, the overall schedule and resource allocation for the new product can be controlled by a computerized PERT or critical-path system. There are some basic reasons for the relatively limited effect of MIS on decision making to date. They are presented here as an indication of what areas must be further studied and what obstacles overcome to increase the successful employment of MIS in decision making.

The data required by top management is unstructured, nonprogrammed, future oriented, inexact, and external. Such data is the most difficult to acquire, update, and process, and therefore not many computerized systems exist in this area. Another factor restricting the development of MIS for top management is the lack of definite cause-and-effect relationships of data. An example is a sales forecast for a new item that is planned by a company in a future period. In order to project a reasonable forecast, the company must know such factors as the marker in which the product will compete, the market saturation for the particular product, and the impact on existing products in the line.

Whether the most reasonable forecast is an extrapolation of how similar items have behaved in the past or a competitive share of market analysis, is open to question. The basis is available-for example, past sales history by item-there may be no proven or logical basis by which to show the effect on sales of the introduction of a new item. There are many other examples where management decisions must be made in the absence of quantified cause-and-effect relationship of data. This is not to say that these relationships will never be known. However, the problem of obtaining the type of data required for top-management decisions when combined with the questionable decision rules of how to analyze the data meaningfully presents a formidable obstacle for computerized information systems directed at the strategic planning area.

In many cases these types of methods have been used with a good deal of success in aiding top-management decision making, the companies that utilize management science are still in the minority. Assuming that the proper technique has been selected for tackling a particular problem, there re still some major barriers to overcome. A communication gap exist between management and the operation research analyst who is responsible for preparing the set of liner equations if, for example, the problem is one that can be handled by liner programming. Management is skeptical of making a decision based on a set of linear equations if, for example, the problem is one that can be handled by linear programming.

Management is skeptical of making a decision based on a set of ill-understood equations, and often the *or* specialist is incapable of explaining in management terms just what the mathematical processing will accomplish. Furthermore, if a manager realize that the data used as input to the model does not have a high degree of accuracy, he is suspicious of the results. Although the only alternative may be a complete "seat of the pants" decision, the manager somehow feels more secure doing so than depending on the model. At least it is cheaper, he rationalizes. What he fails to realize is that, although perhaps neither the *or* solution nor the "seat of the pants" solution will prove accurate, the odds on the *or* solution are a good deal better.

Many top managers feel that good strategic decisions are made more by intuition than by a quantitative analysis of the available data. They do not ignore the data completely but believe that there is a strong intuitive factor, particularly when little or no data is available. It has been observed that the higher a man is in the organization, the more incomplete is that data on which he bases decisions and the more he relies on something called intuition, hunches, or instinct. We may be putting too much faith in machines and data, in the logical decision maker versus the so-called nonlogical decision maker.

Studies suggest that some managers have more "precognitive" ability than others and that this ability gives them a better batting average in making decisions intuitively as opposed to logically. A particular study involved dividing 25 chief executives into two classes on the basis of their proven performance based on profitability. The tests included things like matching a series of numbers printed out randomly by a computer. An average score is 10 percent.

The successful executives outscored the nonperformers in 22 out of 27 tests. Statistically the changes of this happening by accident are fewer than 5 in 1,000. This study does not claim to define the role of intuition in decision making, but it does raise some interesting questions. If there is such a thing as intuitive ability and if the ability can be tested, to what degree should the intuitive decision be valued in contrast to the logical decision based on advanced management science techniques? Granting that the logical decision is the preferable one when the data is known and quantifiable, what degree of data reliability is the breakeven point where the logical decision becomes the preferred one? One need not answer these questions to realize that management is well aware of the somewhat illusive quality called intuition or precognitive power. Many have extended the thesis and used it as a rationale for ignoring quantitative and logical approaches to management decision making.

Effective tools are still lacking to define problems: Data processing developments have not focused on the area of problems definition. Despite the advances in hardware and software, there have not been major advances in basic systems methodology. We talk about the "system approach" to solving problems, but we really haven't made significant advances in the tools for defining the problem to be solved. For example, how does one go about analyzing the determinants of profitability so that the resultant formula can be modeled on a computer? This is not a trivial job when one has to consider both the short and long range. It seems obvious that before a computer can help, the problem must be defined and the cause-and-effect relationships determined.

The "bottoms-up" approach has predominated: Computers have been put to work on those things that are best understood, easily structured, and which require little management involvement. While it is true that are is a necessary application foundation for management information systems in the basic operational areas, it doesn't necessarily follow that an MIS will spring forth as a by-product of the data gathered at the lower levels.

The bottoms-up applications often are fragmented and are not built around an integrated data base required for management control and strategic planning applications. The findings are that a "top-down" approach or at least a simultaneous tops-down and bottoms-up approach is required at the outset to ensure that the necessary framework and plans are established to evolve an MIS.

Business conditions are always changing: Many well-intentioned MIS designers have discovered that dramatic changes in business strategy coupled with changes in top management personnel as well as organizational structure have muddled the systems approach they had planned. While computer systems handling the operational functions such as order processing and inventory control remain handling the operational functions such as order processing and inventory control remail relatively stable in times of organizational changes, management systems are geared to individual management temperament and style and can be impacted dramatically by personnel changes at the top.

The management/systems gap still exists: Information systems that impact management require a greater degree of interaction and involvement between the systems function and the management function and the management function. Coming from different worlds with different backgrounds and different motivation, this contact has often resulted in confrontation rather than communication. Systems personnel often are enamored more by the purity and sophistication of the approach than the satisfaction of seeing a less sophisticated approach succeed. Although it is lessening, this is management/systems gap is still a major cause of the slow evolution of systems aimed at improving the management decision-making process.

MIS requires long-range panning Because it is so sensitive to organizational and business strategy changes, the MIS planning focus must be longer range than has been the case for more conventional information systems. Effective long-range planning is never easy, particularly in the data processing field where technological change of investors. It is obvious that a good deal of professional judgment and expertise is needed to establish the key stock indicators in stage one and the classification scheme ins stage two.

Stage three involves the categorization of the investor based on a predetermined classification scheme. The salient elements of such a categorization include current and anticipated income level, current cash position, investment objectives, and so on. There may be some seemingly intangible but necessary personal criteria: for example, the stocks must be in certain industries and the companies must not be doing work for the military defense effort. These criteria must be considered beforehand so that the necessary information is contained within the system to make this classification possible.

With the completion of the three developmental stages, the resulting model is now able to aid the decision-making process of the investment counselor in selecting a portfolio individually suited to his client. The model permits the counselor to develop a wider range of alternative solutions and to test them out under a wider variety of circumstances.

The computerized system widens the scope of potential stocks and minimizes quick and premature decisions, which are often resorted to because the counselor lacks the time or the knowledge and which are unfavorable to his client. The example illustrated here aids steps 3 and 4 in the decision-making process operation. A direct parallel is an investment decision when many alternative choices are available. Market models and revenue models are extensions of this technique. It is obvious that the type of information analysis does not give the complete answer and thus allow the decision to be made by the computer system. Certain subjective, external factors must also be reflected quantitatively or, if this is not possible, qualitatively. However, the development of this programmed type of analysis in an ever expanding variety of business operations will give the manager more time to explore the intangible subtleties of problem solving and thus reach better man-machine-based decisions.

The preceding discussion has assumed a "black-and-white" world; that is, either something is known or it is not. In actual business operation, however, obviously there are certain risks or probabilities that a certain course of action will be successful. The technique of risk analysis is called *decision theory* and is being linked to a computer system in a growing but still selective circle of companies. A basic example of the technique and its benefits to decision making may help qualify its future use. The problem to be solved by the use of decision theory is the evaluation of prospects for the purchase of a high-value durable goods item that entails a good deal of presale effort. The selection of prospects that hold great profit potential is of prime significance in order to focus a limited sales force on an expanding marketplace.

The profit potential is based on the revenue that can be expected over a five-year period. A five-year period is selected because a customer can be expected to contribute add-on business after the initial sale. If installation is not anticipated before twelve months, the profit potential must reflect this factor. For example, a multidivision company expecting to sign a contract for one machine to be installed in twelve months with two similar machines to be installed two year after the first would have five-year revenue potential of $880,000. The revenue potential must then be viewed in light of its profit contribution and must be discounted in light of the fact that revenue does not all accrue the first year. The resultant discounted contribution margin for the above sale might be $170,000.

What presale effort must be expended in an attempt to sign the account? This figure covers the cost of special engineering, system analysis, special training courses, demonstration programs, proposal preparation, and other support needed to bid for the business. The next step is the determination of the betting odds or the probability that the sale can be closed. This is a rather subjective evaluation, but an analysis of competitive factors, plus past experience, can be used to establish the odds. The result is stated in terms of a percentage probability.

To see how decision theory works, assume that there are two prospects and that it is desired to rank them according to priority, for it is not possible to expend a major sales effort on each. The decision table on page 304 indicates that prospect B holds the greater profit potential. It brings this out by comparing the expected monetary value of the two accounts. Prospect A has higher potential but with less probability of realizing it and with a greater selling expense. If prospects A is signed, a profit return of $ 170,000 will result, whereas a loss of $29,000 will be incurred if the prospect is lost. If prospect B is signed, a croft return of 90,000 will result, whereas a loss of $6,000 will be incurred if the prospect is lost. The expected monetary value of B is $32,400 as compared to $10,800 for A. These figures are obtained by multiplying the probability of getting the sale times the profit if the sale is made and subtracting the amount obtained by multiplying the probability of losing the sale times the sales cost or loss if the sale is lost.

Decision theory is a systematic method of facilitating decision making under conditions of uncertainty. The example used here has but a few variables and there are only two alternate course of action. As the variables and alternatives are multiplied severalfold, as is the case in most business decisions, the need for techniques such as decision theory becomes more apparent. Decision theory analyzes the factors underlying a decision and allows the decision maker to quantify the major parts of the problem so that he is free to concentrate on those factors that cannot be readily quantified. The human mind has a difficult time handling multidimensional problems.

Decision theory divides a problem into its logical parts, analyzes each part separately, and then puts the parts back together in their proper prospective in order to reach a decision. Decision theory follows the philosophy of "divide and conquer"—that is, divide a problem into its logical components, analyze and quantify each component, and thereby conquer the overall problem.

The management process was published in 1969, the basic management process has not changed a great deal and that MacKenzie's analysis of the management process remains quite valid today. The manager basically deals with three elements ideas, things, and people. The elements are reflected in the task of conceptual thinking, where one formulates new business ideas and opportunities, administration, where the details of the management process are handled, and leadership, where people are motivated to accomplish business objectives.

The functions of analyzing problems, where facts are gathered and alternate solutions are evaluated, making decisions, and communicating the decisions to the people who must implement them are termed continuous functions for they occurs repeatedly throughout the management process rather than sequentially. The sequential functions consists of plan, where a course of action is selected, organize, where the work is arranged for accomplishing the plan, staff, or the selection and allocation of the work to the people who will perform it, direct, the commencement of purposeful action on the work at hand and control, where the plan is carried out and satisfactorily completed.

The activities indicate what constitutes the five sequential functions of the management process. In order to develop a plan, one must forecast or determine the effect on future sales, costs, or profit; set objectives, the end results; and develop strategies on how to achieve the end results. One must program or establish a priority and sequence of the strategy budget or allocate resources, set procedures or arrive at standardized methods, and finally, develop policies ensuring that rules and regulations exist to govern significant recurring matters.

An example might serve to bring the plan function into perspective. In planning the introduction of a new item, a forecast of the future marketplace and impact of the product in the marketplace and impact of the product in the market are important starting points. Then objectives, such as desired market share and revenue and profit goals, are established.

The strategies of how to achieve these goals involve statements such as following: we will go after new markets, we will offer the lowest-price products, we will offer the best-quality product, or any combination thereof. The programming involved is to indicate what products, or any combination thereof. The programming involved is to indicate what product with what features will be offered first and why. The budget for the project must be established at this point, and it must be consistent with what it will take to carry out the objectives and strategies, and yet it must not affect on-going programs to any great degree. The procedures and policies begin in to the *organize* function because they involve statements stating, for example, that PERT will be used as a project control technique with monthly status reports prepared for top management.

The organize function is more straightforward and, following the example above, includes establish the organizational structure for the production of the new product. If the product is to be produced by the existing line organization, this point will be determined, or it may be that a new operational unit is organized to design and produce the new product. If a new organization is set up, too management must delineate relationships between the new and the existing structure and define communication and liaison points.

The *creation* of position descriptions and the establishment of position qualifications will indicate whether the plan can be carried out by the existing organization or whether additional people with specifically required skills are needed. This leads into the staff function, where the qualified people selected, oriented to the plan objectives, strategies, policies, and so on, trained in the necessary tasks to be performed, and developed to the extent of making them feel a part of the company and the project on which they are working.

The direct function involves the steps that are normally associated with "getting things done through people". These steps include delegating or assigning responsibility and accountability, motivating to persuade and inspire, coordinating to ensure that the efforts of one group are consistent with the efforts of others, and stimulating change when differences occur, conflicts arise, and it is necessary to resolve these differences before proceeding with the task. The control function completes the cycle and involves the establishment of a reporting system that is consistent with the total reporting structure but that reflects pertinent milestones and progress against a schedule, the development of performance standards, to set the conditions that will determine if the job properly completed, a technique to measure results to ascertain if the desired quality was attained and the extent of variance from the goal or standard, the taking of corrective action to get the task back on schedule and up to standard when deviation occur, and, finally, to reward, whether by praise or remuneration for the accomplishment of the job and the meeting or goals.

Having analyzed the management process, it is appropriate to assess the relative impact of management information systems on the various functions and then to overlay the categorization of top, middle, and operating management that was developed to get a clear idea of how MIS can be expected to influence management.

MIS can be expected to influence the five sequential functions in the next five to ten years in accordance with the following percentages.

Plan	40%
Organize	30%
Staff	50%
Direct	10%
Control	90%

It has been shown that the plan function can be materially influenced by MIS; the 40 percent reflects this. MIS will not have a great of influence on the organize function, although job and skills inventories will assist in the process. The computerized skills and job inventories can materially assist the staff function, but a strong qualitative element will remain. The direct function is people and motivation oriented. The big area for MIS is in the control function; here, more experience in analyzing business operations and in experimenting with programmed decision rules will bring more functions under automatic programmed control. It is obvious that the categorization of management into three levels is an oversimplification, because the nature of the work within the same category differs greatly and no definite line separates the top from the middle and the middle from operating management.

For example, a job of management a group of forecasters whose job it is to project the sales, shipments, returns, and so on, differs dramatically, depending on the nature of the product. If the product is a stable one that is influenced by competitive and other external factors to only a minor extent, the job of forecasting is much more receptive to computerization than if the product is hi

A job manufacturer dealing in one-of-a-kind specials has a different problem than a repetitive, assembly-line operation. In order to ascertain the impact of MIS on a management job, the percentage of time devoted to the five functions described can serve as a general indication. This approach has many subjective factors, but I think the exercise is a good one. The message to be gleaned is that before assessing the future impact of MIS on management, we need to know exactly what functions management people perform and what responsibilities they have. The computerization quotient is a thought process that does that.

We have divided management activities into three general categories: (1) administrative, (2) leadership, and (3) conceptual thinking. The first and second categories can be aided by electronic means as an extension of office automation, the third by executive decision support systems. We now discuss these areas.

The first application in automating the office is usually word processing, and this is no surprise. Typewriting has been with us for decades, and word processing, which provides functions such as automatic paragraph insertion, simplified editing, spelling verification, and the like, is a natural extension. Also there is a fairly well-defined cost/ benefit resulting from either pooling the typing or increasing the productivity of typists. However, there is potentially a bigger payoff in automating the office-and that centers on automating the managers as well as the secretaries. As much as 30 percent of a managers's job can be spent on administrative matters, such as letters, memos, reports, expense accounts, meeting, travel, and telephone calls. If electronics can reduce the time it takes to carry out these administrative duties, it is obvious that more time can be spent on the conceptual-thinking portion of the job, where the real payoff is.

Builds in stages the accoutrements of the electronically aided executive. The terminals device can be used either directly by the executive or by a secretary or aide. The first stage is to be able to write letters and memos and store them on electronic media. The first stage is to be able to write letters and memos and store them on electronic media.

The terminal can be a typewriter, a dictating device linked to a telephone line, or even, in the future, voice message electronically interpreted directly into electronic storage, thus bypassing the typing or keying by an intermediate. Because of communications lines and networks, the origination point can be any site where a communication linkage exists. Thus the executive is freed from his office. He can initiate a memo or a letter from his home, at the airport, or in his hotel room. The inputted data is transmitted to his personal file, where it can be accessed by his secretary for further processing or can be sent directly to individuals at various destination points.

Letters and reports are maintained in indexed storage for retrieval at a later date. The key element is a proper indexing system, usually involving cross-indexing so that the executive can retrieve, for example, the Jones letter, or the letter on chemical waste, or the letter he wrote last Wednesday. The file can include graphic material and even digitized pictures and illustrations. Thus the executive begins to build an electronic file system than can be accessed directly via a communication link.

The next stage of automating the executive is the addition of the personal calendar and schedule processing. A personal time calendar is maintained on the file with meetings, appointments, and the like noted. The executive's subordinates, peers, and superiors do the same. It is akin to a schedule board in a sales office; in this case, however, the schedule board is electronic and can be changed or updated on-line from the home, the airport, or the hotel room. Reminders, memory joggers, and the like can be part of the file. It works this way. You want to call a meeting of the plant steering committee on July 8 from 1 to 3 P. M.

The personal files of those on the steering committee are checked for availability, the appropriate meeting room for the size of the steering committee group selected and reserved, and a list of the preparatory materials necessary for the meeting indicated. Once scheduled, the personal calendars of each of the participants would be so reserved. At this point a particular management style and work ethic come into play. A workaholic executive can have a field day with this type of system. He has an idea at 3 A. M. and has orders in Jones' file when Jones arrives at 8:30 A. M. that day. He can easily stay in the act while traveling or on vacation. This can be both positive and negative. The real benefit, as always, comes from judicious use of the new media. When one realizes how long it takes to personally contact six people, the productivity benefits of this type of communication are evident. Many companies now have teleconferencing rooms for "many-to-many" communication to and from remote locations. A meetings is convened in Boston, but there are neck microphones and an audio links so that voices can travel to and from the Los Angeles area where the other half of the meeting attendees reside.

Charts and other visual exhibits can be transmitted and displayed when necessary to clarify a point. Also access to electronic files can be made. Though this form of communication may not be as effective as face-to-face, it saves so much time and cost that it becomes a viable substitute in many instances. Freeze-frame television pictures are also being employed to give a video impression to the conference. It is likely that satellite transmission will make continuous videoconferencing a cost-effective medium. Whether tele-or video-conferencing, it is apparent that productivity of executives can be increased dramatically by the reduction of travel and the ability to hold meetings without the delay of travel.

The final stage extends the effectiveness of the systems, since, for example, market data bases or competitive market-share statistics from data service companies can be accessed. The executive can also add his personal file to the media, thus maintaining his bank accounts, assets, stock records, reminders or birthdays, physical exams, and the like. This is an alternate to having his own personal computer in the home. He would be the only one to have the password for access to this portion of the file. It is interesting to speculate on the ramifications of this mode of operation, aside from the obvious productivity improvements and the impact on work style, motivation, and the work ethic. Currently the office is the locus for the executive. He spends perhaps the majority of his working hours there. He writes, phones, meets people, reads, looks up things in his files, and so on. But if the scenario described here comes to pass, the locus can change to wherever there is terminal access-and this could almost be anywhere.

The executive decision support systems are geared for an individual executive or a group of executives. These systems may link to the integrated data base of the company but for the most part they involve a separate personal data file, part of which can be stripped from the main file or created apart from the main file, but geared to the needs of the individual executive. Professor John Rockart of MIT has devoted a good deal of time to studying and analyzing such systems.

An experimental support system was at first designed to allow executives to retrieve more than 70 predefined reports and to perform limited analyses such as compound-growth calculations, variance analysis, and trend projections. In January of 1977 the six top executives were given access to this system. By February, Mr. Heineman had stretched the limits of its analytic capabilities and was demanding more. The additional capabilities came in the form of a new access and analysis language called EXPRESS. EXPRESS includes not only simple file-handling and data-aggregation facilities but also much more extensive capabilities which facilitate extensive modeling and statistical analyses of data series. To complement this access facility, Northwest Industries has continually expanded its "Executive Data Base" to currently include:

1. 350 financial and operational data items of actual, budgeted, forecast, and planned monthly results for each operating company for the past eight years.
2. 45 economic and key-ratio time series.
3. Several externally subscribed data base, including Standard & Poor's Compustat and DRI services.

Northwest Industries' system is truly a corporate-level executive support system. It is now used by almost all managers and executives in the corporate office to perform their monitoring and analytical functions.

The corporate controller's department, the planning department, and the top line executives all use the data base independently to service their particular information needs. As a result, the data base is more all-inclusive and extensive than any other we have seen to data. It is constantly growing as new data items and series are added by various managers as they are found to be of use. The driving force behind the system, and its most significant user, is Heineman. Use of the system is an everyday thing for him, a natural part of the job. He programs using the EXPRESS language and a full ten-finger typing approach to the terminal keyboard. He believes that the knowledge he can bring to the analytic process from his viewpoint makes personal analysis preferable, in many situations, to handling assignments to staff personnel. What is more, instant access to the data base, to try out a thought he might have, is very useful. For this reason, terminals are present at home and available during vacations. Supporting Heineman and others in their development and use of the data base is an information systems group whose capabilities and tasks are quite unlike those of the data processing personnel found in the operating divisions of most companies. The corporate I/S personnel rarely design or program any reporting systems. Rather they function as "coaches" to the various managers at the corporate level. Their primary function is the training of the users, not the provision of service. They aid in helping a user determine whether the data he needs is already available, and whether any additional data needed can be obtained. They further assist by getting the data into the data base, coaching the users in access methods, and helping the users to understand what sort of best fitted to the particular types of analyses which are desired.

Only for major "modelling" applications do they take part in the system design and programming process. EDSS requires a different approach or at least a modification of the approach used in more conventional MIS development. First, the concept requires an interested executive who really sees benefit in pursuing this type of system. He is usually a reflective type who is willing to spend time and sees the payoff in analyzing the critical success factors for him and his company. The EDSS executive will be demanding but understanding of the weaknesses as well as the strengths of the systems that support him. He will realize that the system has to be more regimented and disciplined than he may be accustomed to and cannot possess infinite flexibility. He will be willing to make trade-offs and compromises, sometimes setting for what he thinks fulfils 80 percent of his needs rather than wait another year to get the 100 percent.

Second EDSS requires a user-oriented data base and a user-oriented data-base language. Many of the data base and data-base languages purport to be user friendly, but their "user" is the professional whose background has made him or her familiar with computers and information systems. The executive is a different breed and needs an executive-friendly system-and this doesn't mean typewriters or highly structured languages.

The executive interface features simple function keys and, if a language is needed, it is English or pseudo English. Heineman's willingness to type is a rarity among executives. Another requirement of an EDSS is MIS people with consultant skills. These consultants must bridge the gap between the technical world and the world of the executive. They must view the executive as a valued client and work with him or her in order to understand and be able to express the executive's information needs. They must assist him in translating these needs into a system that the executive can use directly, if that is his style, or use through an aide or accountant. This calls for skills of listening, probing, analyzing, and conceptualizing. It means understanding the elements of the business and the executives who run it.

Finally, the focus of EDSS is on effectiveness as opposed to efficiency. MIS applications aimed at performing repetitive operational tasks must have a high degree of efficiency. Since they are executed often, they must avoid elements such as data storage redundancy and excessive hardware and software overhead. Executives do not operate their EDSS's around the clock; in fact the usage is sporadic and may even be on a weekly rather than a daily or hourly basis. For this reason, the system should be optimized around effectiveness. It is perfectly permissible to waste a bit of file storage or a bit of operating overhead in order to make the system design criteria. The once-a-week use may have greater payoff than the around-the-clock use of an operational control system.

This, then, is the concept of the executive decision support system. The electronic office aids referred to earlier go hand-in-hand with EDSS. The former allow greater productivity in administrative duties, thus freeing up the executive to do the job he is being paid to do-conceptual thinking. Effect of an mis on operating management i ndicate that the impact of MIS on operating management is far greater than the impact on top and middle management in all three listed categories. This is true because the operating managers' job is directed more at the control functions. This discussion will focus on the nature of the change in job content caused by computerization, which is the reason for predicating the need for fewer operating managers to accomplish the same amount of work. An analogy to automated factory machinery will be used to illustrate the changes in job content occurring because of computerized management information systems.

There are lessons to learn by analyzing the accelerating trend toward numerically controlled machines. In numerical control, or CAM a machine such as a drill press or lathe is controlled by a computer. The software program in the computer generates the necessary impulses to control the drilling of a hole in a specific spot in a piece of metal. The reason that the process is called numerical control is that the movements of the drill and the work to be drilled are controlled by numbers representing the shape of the desired finished part. It is more accurately called symbolic control, because the actual machining process is described by symbols, some of which happen to be numbers.

It is interesting to analyze the ramifications of numerical control. It can be considered an evolutionary stage in automation in which the machine assumes a job previously performed by man. In this instance, the machine usually can accomplish the work more economically and accurately than man. Before the advent of the drill press, the worker drilled holes in metal by hammering a boringlike device of prescribed size through the metal. Later he used a hand drill with an adjustable bit. Then he used a drill press to position the work piece under the drill and pressed a button to lower the drill through the work piece. These evolutionary drilling developments removed the physical portion of the job from the worker and reduced his direct contact with the machine.

The advent of numerical control removes him still further from the machine, indeed almost all the way. However, one should not overlook the counting human involvement; the significance is that it occurs at a different part of the work cycle and the type of involvement has been changed markedly. It is appropriate now to discuss the job of the operating manager in an information system, keeping in mind the parallel to the effect of numerical control on the drill press operator.

The inventory control manager has reporting to him two assistant managers, who in turn have buyers reporting to them. The buyer controls a number of inventory items and supervises a clerical staff that prepares stock requisitions and purchase orders. For illustrative purposes, we shall analyze the effect of a computerized inventory control system on the job content of the buyers and assistant managers. Although it may be stretching things to call a buyer a manager, he is in effect because he supervises a group of people and manages the procurement and stock control of a group of inventory items. The buyer is an example of an operating manager.

Operating management has an initial advantage because it has been dealing in symbols for quite some time. The assistant inventory manager or buyer looks at an inventory status report, sees that there are 25 gauges in inventory, and orders 50 more even though he has not seen a fuel gauge in some time or perhaps ever. The buyer is dealing in a symbolic world. There is no earthshaking revelation. Of more significance is the level of symbolism being employed-to what extent the buyer uses symbols to control his operation. A computer system that merely records the status of inventory for the buyer is one level. Here it is using internal reported information. But when the computer automatically produces a purchase order or schedules a new lot of an item when it reaches a predetermined minimum, then we have another level.

8

Systems Management

Management Information System (MIS) today is a valid and meaningful term, placing emphasis on the elements that are the most significant. Information resource management, a subtle but important shift in the way MIS is viewed within a company. This change is characterized by the progression of titles under which the MIS function has operated. In the fifties the department head of MIS was called a computer manager or computer center manager. This implied that the central focus was the computer and that the manager was the custodian of this new electronic device.

In the sixties the term data processing came into vogue, and the manager was called the manager of data processing or manager of electronic data processing: now the department was called by the function it performed rather than the principal device that performed it. The late sixties brought increasing use of the world system, an acknowledgment that and EDP department was comprised of more than a computer and that indeed the principal tool being managed was a system. A system consisted of a computer, but also a host of input and output equipment, storage devices, software, applications, and the people that make the whole thing work. The emphasis shifted from the computer to the system. The seventies ushered in the term information as apposed to data. Data is defined as raw numbers and files; thus, to be useful to management, data must be processed into meaningful information.

The eighties brought a further shift to a new and imposing term-information resource management. Management and information remain, but system has been replaced by resource. The concept is that information should be treated as a resource the same as the more traditional ones of money, material, facilities, and people.

MIS, powered by sophisticated computer hardware and software with responsive communication to and form a variety of remote terminals to an integrated data base, has reached the stage where information has become a valuable-or perhaps invaluable-resource in a maintaining a competitive business. Whether the head of the IRM function is called an MIS director, an IRM director, or just the CIO, the concept is the same: that of viewing information as a valuable company resource and planning and controlling that resource with the same concern as cash and facilities.

Along with the evolutionary title change of MIS, the role of MIS within the organizational hierarchy has been elevated. Starting from a reporting position within the controller's function, the MIS operation now reports to the financial or administrative vice-president, or directly to the president. The title, too, has gradually evolved from manager to director to vice-president. The realization that information is a resource has brought the acknowledgment that its manager should be on the same level as managers of other equivalent resources.

Richard Nolan, the head of a successful consulting firm, has developed a staging theory to explain how companies have evolved their MIS function over the years. The premise is that companies progress through six stages of growth, each stage being characterized by unique elements. Adapted over the years, the stages theory now provides a framework that works surprisingly well for most companies. The first element of growth refers to the MIS resources a particular company employs. In the early stages, the principal storage device is tape and secondary storage disk, but even with disk the prevailing mode is sequential.

The computer system co-operates on one application at a time, starting with a single-shift operation, but as applications grow in stage 2, round-the-clock operation is more the norm. In stages 3 and 4, the major resource is a large, centrally based computer system. Stage 3 still employs large tape files, but as the need for fast response increases, on-line disk files become the predominant storage vehicle. Stages 5 and 6 usher in the concept of distributed data processing , where the processing work is off-loaded from the central mainframe to a bevy of off-site mini-and microcomputer systems and terminals.

DDP represents one of the most significant industry trends. Generally speaking, computing resources, the major concern and focus of early stages thinking, give way to the other growth elements in later stages. One of the principal benchmarks of the stage a company is in is its application portfolio. During the early stages, applications are batch oriented; that is, transactions are collected and grouped before they are processed. In stages 3 and 4, the evolution is most definitely toward on-line applications built around an integrated data base. Transactions are processed as they occur rather than being batched and processed after the transaction. Stages 5 and 6 still maintain some batch applications, but the predominant mode is on-line.

Another dimension of the application portfolio is activity focus. During stages 1 and 2, applications are developed from the bottom up and focus on operational control activities, the basic lower-level operational tasks. During stages 3 and 4 the focus shifts to management control applications, as on-line data from an integrated data base permits applications that aid management in controlling the operationally, in stages 5 and 6, data external to he company is combined with internal historical data to provide application assistance to upper and strategic management levels.

The third element of growth is the planning focus, where the stages are characterized by a progressively longer-term, planning focus, whether the stages are characterized by a progressively longer-term planning horizon. During stages 1 and 2, applications are developed one at a time on the basis of short-term opportunity, rather than that to relative priority and fit with an overall, longer-term strategy.

The planning perspective shifts from a three-to a nine-month horizon during stages 1 and 2, to twelve to 24 months during stages 3 and 4, to three to five years in stages 5 and 6 Also, stages 5 and 6 mark the beginning of the change of emphasis from the computer as a resource to information as a resource. This latter concept will be elaborated on throughout the chapter.

The fourth growth element refers to the organizational positioning of the MIS function. In the early stages the function resided under the accounting or financial arm. The computer was considered an adjunct to existing accounting and bookkeeping machines and as such became part of the controller's bailiwick. This rather a natural but shortsighted view is changed in stage 3 and 4, where MIS spins off from the controller, evolves into an independent activity, and is given full department status. The function is highly centralized, with systems analysts, programmers, and operators reporting directly to the MIS director. They may be doing work for specific operating departments, but they are part of the MIS department. In stages 5 and 6 a shift to a decentralized, matrix style of organization occurs. With the trend to distributed data processing, operating departments become much more involved in MIS. At this stage, it makes sense to assign systems analysis to specific operating departments, reporting on either a straight-or doted-line basis. It may be that control of MIS operations remains under the MIS director; more often than not, however, application development becomes the responsibility of the department employing the application.

The fifth growth element refers to leadership style. During stages 1 and 2, technical leadership is prevalent. Computers are complex, highly technical devices and must be managed by people with the requisite technical skills. However, concomitant with the other change elements, users and top management become more aware of MIS impact tans seek more involvement in managing it. MIS directors realize they can't completely manage the expanding scope of activity and take on a consultant role rather than direct management. Often the initial involvement by users is a reactive one, fueled by disappointment with the service or response level and the increasing application backlog built up by the central MIS organization.

During stages 5 and 6, however, team leadership evolves to a point where users, top management, and MIS management jointly determine strategy and establish implementation priorities; the we and they is replaced by us. Finally, the sixth growth elements portrays the change in the principal users of MIS. This element is natural by-product of the other growth factors. As data is integrated and applications focus on management control and strategic areas of the business, progressively higher-level managers become interested and dependent on system output.

At this stage, the upper levels of management not only are receiving the results of MIS but are actively higher-level managers become interested and dependent on system output. At this stage, the upper levels of management not only are receiving the results of MIS but are actively engaged in specifying their individual information needs-in many instances initiating and directing a particular system themselves.

Dick Nolan's stages theory presents a useful perspective by which to synthesize the change that have been and are taking place in MIS. Some professional MIS observers see the stages a company goes through not as six, but as two alternating cycles of growth and control or ingestion and digestion. In whatever way the cycle is viewed, it is generally agree that those companies employing the style and practices of the later stages will have the more effective MIS operation.

A key lesson to follow is to build in a greater degree of planning and control during periods of rapid growth, so that integration and repositioning can evolve more naturally and effectively. The greater the fragmentation, the more difficult it will be to achieve control and integration-elements that are necessary prerequisite to information resource management.

Though this book focuses on MIS from the user or developer viewpoint, we should also consider the characteristics of the MIS director's job, the MIS organization, and the people who work in the MIS department. It has been said that the growing demands on the MIS director have created an impossible job description that only a superperson can fulfill. The MIS director thus finds himself in a challenging, if not precarious, position within his company. He must understand the challenge and tackle it effectively in order to survive.

The prominent writer son this subject-Withington of A.d. Little, "Coping With Computer Proliferation," Nolan of Nolan, Norton & Company, "Managing The Crisis In Data Processing," and Rockart of MIT, "Critical Success Factors For The Information Systems Executive, " have all focused on this topic. It is a survival issue, with MIS directors facing the most crucial crossroad of their careers. The reason is that most MIS directors have exploited their technical and professional MIS skills in arriving where thy are.

What they need at this point are managerial, organizational, and strategic skills. The user coalition, often supported by top management, have been waiting in the wings, repressing their hostility; and now they have reemerged, waving the industry-accepted banner of distributed data processing. It is a bit uncomfortable to be forced away from one's strengths to deal with the opposition on unfamiliar terrain. But that is exactly the challenge for the MIS director. The issues are not technical; they involve strategy, planning, organization, human communication, and leadership.

Snow, an Englishman trained in physics with a doctorate form Cambridge, was a scientist and worked in a variety of government agencies; he also was a prolific author, writing more than a dozen novels. He was kinghted in 1957 and died in 1980. He was a man for many seasons. A continued confrontation between the scientist and the humanist. He referred, for example, to the decision on strategic bombing in World War II, wherein the thinking was that bombing a city's population centers as well as its military and support centers would remove the will of the people to resist. This thinking proved to be incorrect. Snow used this issue to show the danger inherent when a prime minister relies almost completely on a single scientific source on which to base a complex technical decision with such far-reaching effects. Snow elaborated on the necessity for the humanist and scientist to reach the proper level of communication and under standing.

The two-culture milieu is most appropriate in discussing the role of the MIS director versus that of the general manager. Often, the MIS group develops a culture of its own that is inconsistent with that of the company in which the function resides. This can prove most dangerous, because it is the generalist who must make the final decision. An MIS director, proceeding without management awareness and concurrence, particularly on major strategic issues, can run blindly into disaster. Pursuing a course of innovation and risk taking in a company that is in a cash blind and a cost cutting modem for example, will soon lead to the confrontation suggested in the figure. In accordance with the C.P. Snow philosophy, the outcome will be far from desirable.

At this point it is pertinent to look at the type of people who form the MIS culture. The MIS director must be aware of the types of people he or she is dealing with and must apply leadership and direction to blend that culture with the culture of the company.

Several studies suggest that MIS people are a bit difference from the operating people whom they serve.

Gerry Richardson, an industrial psychologist from Denver, administered a test to 6000 people over an eight-year period. The general profile of MISers indicates they are more cool and impersonal, more serious and reserved, more preserving, more dogmatic, and more perceptive. Other generalizations drawn form the profile show the MISer as preferring to be aloof, accustomed to dealing in precise and exact terms, and preoccupied with detail.

The question arises as to he MISer's loyalty to his company versus that to his profession; evidence points to a greater loyalty to the profession. Also the MISer likes to work on things he considers and advanced in nature. A study reported by J. Daniel Couger of the University of Colorado brings out that MISers have a low social need strength and a high growth need strength. The implications of the low SNS is that MISers do not feel the need to meet or communicate with their fellow MISers and particularly the users whom they serve. They may not be prone to develop the important interfaces and relationships that are so important to successful systems development and implementation.

The high GNS implies a need for strong personal accomplishment 5 and the avoidance of anything that gets in the way. This develops a low tolerance level for meetings and discussion with users. Attending meetings is a good way of fill social needs, but since MISers have a low social need, they have a dual barrier against meetings.

One of the best remedies is the interchange of people within the MIS and operating areas of a company. It makes good sense to staff the MIS department with personnel from operating departments who show an aptitude and interest for systems work.

Systems analysts should receive a tour of duty outside of MIS, in order to appreciate the problems of the actual business world and understand he difficulties of putting an advanced new system into productive operation. This rotation of people must not become a way of dumping the marginal performers within a department. Management should recognize the long-term benefit of transferring proven performers in key support departments such as MIS. Many companies have filled key MIS management positions with individuals with records of success in operating departments who possess a system outlook but lack direct computer experience. Transfer of people form MIS to key operating department positions should also be encouraged.

The SNS and GNS factors can be balanced by larger doses of human and organizational behaviour courses in the MIS curriculum in colleges and universities. He suggests a program stressing the importance of interpersonal and group behaviour skills and also the development of courses or laboratories where students majoring in human and organizational behaviour would interact and have joint projects with MIS students. We suggest that this approach also be followed within a company. MIS people should be trained in organizational behaviour and should attend the same courses with users. They should also be trained in specific business areas outside the MIS functions, as users should be trained in MIS subjects.

Whenever possible, MIS and operating personnel should be assimilated in everyday business activities. At conferences, work sessions, or business get-togethers, the groups should be encouraged to work together and to take every opportunity to discuss and explore things together. If possible MIS people and operating people should travel together, engage in social activities together, and develop an awareness of each other's standpoint on business matters.

Most people are prone to say with employees of their own department and to discuss matters with people of similar background. Following this tendency does nothing to facilitate the understanding and resolution of problems; it merely reinforces one's predetermined judgements. Another opportunity to work together is presented by special projects that require interdisciplinary participation. Mutual confidence and respect are built up when a task is accomplished by such a group.

John Diebold coined the term information resource management (IRM) in explaining the concept that information is a valuable and costly asset that must be preserved, protected, controlled, and planned as are other valuable assets within the corporation, such as money, material, facilities, and people. This may no seem like anything new, but the fact is that companies have not treated information with this perspective.

The Diebold Research Program report on the Administration of Information Resources states that "The ultimate goal of IRM is to put in place mechanisms to enable the company to acquire or produce the data and information it needs, of sufficient quality, accuracy and timeliness, and with minimum cost.

This is accomplished by creating conditions whereby all levels of the organization come to look upon information not as a free good, but rather as a costly and valued asset that must be treated with the same management discipline as is currently afforded financial assets, human resources, material assets and other resources the company utilizes to achieve its aims. In so doing, a major shift from a preoccupation and focus on the power of the technologies, to a focus on the power of the information content, must occur. The Diebold report goes on to point out the similarities between information as a resource and other corporate assets or resources.

— It possesses fundamental value, as does money, capital goods, labour, or raw materials.

— It is identifiable and measurable characteristics such as method, difficulty, and cost of acquisition; purpose for which used; and different forms and media by which generated, handled, and processed.

— It comes in various degrees of "purity" and utility.

— It must be refined and pressed in order to enhance its value.

— It passes through many hands that transport and exchange it from point of collection, to point of enhancement, to point of use.

— Synthetic substitutes are available-some cheaper, some more expensive.

— Information functions can be integrated vertically by buying and processing raw materials. Alternately, costs can be cut by buying processes materials.

— Consumption of the resource can be either expensed or capitalized, depending on management's goals.

— It is an expenditure for which standard costs can be developed and cost accounting techniques employed to help control outlays.

— A cost-benefit equation is possible at each point

in collection, handling, enhancement, dissemination, and so forth, which helps manage the efficiency and effectiveness of utilization.

— A variety of deployment choices are available to management in making trade-offs between different "grades.," types, and prices.

Policies would include a statement of the company's attitude and view of the information it collects, processes, and produces, a procedure to indicate who should have access to different classes of information, the methods of safeguarding and protecting the confidentiality of information against physical disaster, sabotage, or fraud, and an expression of the rights of different groups to information, such as an employee's right to see his own personnel file or a government's right to specific information. While these issues are real, I do not see the need for a separate information officer or group to oversee this process.

The MIS director has the responsibility to view information as a resource and incorporate the necessary measures within his operation. Setting up a separate entity in an already complex MIS world is, to my way of thinking, counterproductive. IRM is too fundamental a concept and too integral to the operation of MIs to be embodied in an outside agency. The concept of looking at a business as a system has been covered earlier.

Raw material and piece parts are fabricate and assembled into whatever products the company produces. The product process utilizes the necessary resources owned by the company. During the planning phase for any new product, an assessment is made of the resources' availability, cost, and adequacy. More often than not, a similar assessment of the information resource is lacking-and situations where products were seriously delayed as a consequence. The point is that information is a resource of the company and MIS has become part of the business rather than just supporting it. Information must be considered in planning any major company changes. The concept of IRM broadens the conventional definition of MIS. In reality only a small fraction of the informations used throughout a corporation is under the control of MIS, as MIS has traditionally been understood. Information more broadly conceived includes the letters and memos typed by secretaries, the coping process, the mailroom, telephone service, manuals and catalogs, files and records, and so on. Many firms are using this broader definition to reorganize functions within the company. The thinking is that management of information should not be confined to that portion that is currently in electronic form.

The full benefit of integration is not realized unless all information is managed as an entity. Significant efficiencies can be achieved by optimizing the total flow of information. A simple example should illustrate the point. An executive writes a report, which is typed, edited, corrected, copied, and sent to twenty people within the company. Each recipient has a different time frame in which the information is valid, so each reads and/or files the report for later reference according to his or her need. If the report were produced initially in electronic media, it could be accessed by each executive on a need-to-know basis. When called for, the report could be delivered electronically over a communication line either as hard copy or as a video display.

Teleconcferencing, too, can be used to augment the communication process. The point is that by integrating and coordinating all the information and its communication, we can make it both more effective and more efficient. Mobile Oil Corporation is experimenting with this type of organization and presented a model at a conference sponsored by Business Week in early 1981.

A typical MIS organization performs the duties in the boxes entitled System Support Services, Planning controls and Technology, and Processing Services. Though some MIS groups have a few of the information responsibilities listed under Communications and Distribution Services, Reprographics Services, and Records Services, usually these are separate entities managed by other organizations. However, there is much to commend in a plan that phases these functions under the MIS director. The concept of IRM broadens the scope of MIS and causes a healthy rethinking of what constitutes information and how it should be controlled.

This integration has come to be called the convergence of technologies. James McKenney and Warrant McFarlan, writing in Harvard Business Review, termed it the information archipelago, the three islands that comprise it being data processing, communication, and office automation. These started as individual islands or entities within a company, often controlled and managed under separate departments.

The authors state their case for providing bridges or links to connect these islands because they must play an integrated role within the operation of a business. Whether they fall under the same direct management is less important than whether plans, controls, and general management of the functions are integrated by cross-function standards, policy, and strategy.

John Rockart, director of MIT's Center for Information System Research, has written extensively about a concept he calls critical success factors. By analyzing a variety of companies and executives, he has found that a relatively few elements determine whether a particular company or executive will be successful. CSF's are those key areas where high performance is necessary to achieve personnal and company goals. Further research analyzed CSF's for the MIS director. Dr. Rockart interviewed directors who, by company and industry standards, were considered highly successful.

The objective was to bring out those elements or characteristics that appeared to produce success. Synthesis of the data indicates what the nine successful MIS directors thought was important to them. The following is my interpretation and summary of Dr. Rockart's study. In general, the successful MIs director is a business manager, a leader who is aware and concerned with the business, is politically astute in dealing with top management and user management, and recognizes the concepts of information resource management. He is more marketing oriented than production oriented and begins to promote MIs services through newsletters, annual reports, and the like, taking in general a more outward or proactive approach.

Customer service

— Perception by users in the key

— Mechanisms installed to influence perception (user performance index, independent audit, user sing-off, complaint box).

— Spends increasing amount of time with users.

— Possible charge-out system based on customer-understood and oriented method (charge per transaction or report).

User relations/communications

— Knows customer, their CSF's corporate political leaning, etc.

— User/top management involvement in setting application priorities.

— Viewed as a leader.

— Develops clear, concise user interfaces and respective responsibilities.

People resource

— Ensures maximum utilization of this high-quality component.

— Attention of career development and training.

— Emphasizes management/business focus.

— Interchanges people with line departments.

— Controls turnover.

Repositioning of MIS

— Reports to president or very high in organization.

— Views himself a manager versus a technician.

— Sees a constantly evolving structure; more responsibility to users.

— Focuses on effectiveness versus efficiency.

Activities within a business conform to a triangle with the layers of operational control, management control, and strategic planning. Using this focus to describe the MIS function, the operational control activities cover the gathering of input, he processing of data through the computer shop, and the production of output in the form of reports or terminal display screens. This level of activity is quite similar to a factory operation. Operators key in data, load and unload tapes and disks, and monitor the activity much like production foremen.

In carrying out these functions, the MIS operation, like the business it supports, utilizes the resources of money, people, facilities, material, and information. It is enlightening to realize that MIS is a user as well as a provider of its own services. It is also enlightening to realize that the "shoemaker's children" syndrome holds true" MIS does not often produce information to optimally manage itself. Management control activities include such things as scheduling computer operations, monitoring hardware utilization, reviewing performance and costs, and managing application development projects.

Strategic planning involves the development of an MIS mission or direction statement as well as a long-range plan to project future hardware, software, application, and people resource requirements. Thus it is true the MIS is literally a business within a business, operation as a microcosm of the company it supports. This perspective establishes the importance of the MIS director as a business manager using information to control his or her own operation as well as providing information to support the business in general.

The top MIS executive is commonly given the title of Vice-President. While some MIS executives report directly to the President, most still report to either an Executive Vice-President, a Financial Vice President, or an Administrative Vice-President. A word about the reporting relationship within the MIS department: With the advent of distributed processing, much of the computer hardware is located at user sites. Though the hardware is outside he physical confines of the computer center, it usually prudent to maintain direct control of the people operating the equipment. Users dot not seek this responsibility, as they neither possess the skills not see benefit in controlling the function. It is a different story in the application development group.

Users are very much interested in the applications being developed for their operational area, and matrix type organizations are cropping up. Application developers are assigned by particular business function and become specialists in a particular area. I think this is important in order to establish user involvement and satisfaction rather than to use an expert of a particular function as a requirement for effective system development. The skills of competent systems analyst are transferable between functional areas. If the user is responsible for establishing the specs of the system, then the system analyst's job is to translate then into the most efficient system he or she can design, given time and resource restraints.

The application developers can either report directly to the operating departments with a dotted-line relationship to the MIs function, or other way around. This depends on the local environment, but it is becoming more common to have the solid-line relationship with the operating department. We have placed corporate planning, steering committees, and corporate auditing, since these are the critical outside departments for the MIS executive. The importance of proper integration of MIS plans with corporate here to mention the role of MIS planning, steering committees, and the corporate plans will be emphasized throughout the book. It is appropriate here to mention the role of MIS planning, steering committees, and the corporate MIS audit function.

MIS planning

Planning a job or a project before launching it is logical and practical. While individuals and companies realize the worth of planning specific tasks and projects, the application of planning to a major and complex function of a business is not as readily seen. Projects usually have a one-or two-year time horizon, while planning for a major department or function such as MIS requires a longer time horizon, usually in the three-to five-year range. Examples of effective, comprehensive five-year MIS plans are no as prevalent as they should be. Planning has gone through a stage evolution consistent with the stages-theory concept of information system growth within most companies. It is not just an MIS issue but a corporate one as well.

Managers have always been leery of planning. Planning is hard work, not much fun, ill defined, not immediately rewarding, and can detract from time devoted to the day operations of the business. Also the classic profile of the type A executive indicates a natural block to the planning function. Type A executives are action-oriented, aggressive leaders with short attention spans who are impatient with activities that don't promise concrete and immediate payoffs.

Planning does no fit the natural mind set of the type A manager. As result, during the late fifties and early sixties, there was a negative corporate environment for planning. Since any MIS planning methodology must match and fit the company culture, it was obviously no a good time to do much serious thinking about developing and MIS long-range plan. The late sixties and most of the seventies might be characterized as a complacency era, with corporate leaders exhibiting a laissez-faire attitude toward planning. Executives realized planning was necessary, but they really didn't require much of their personal attention, so hey conjectured.

During this period, managers gave lop service to planning, perfunctorily nodding whenever the subject came up. A sharp dichotomy between planning and doing was drawn, with planners assigned full time to the task but assigned in an ivory-tower environment where they would work separately and not interfere with the nonplanners. Massive documents were produced and put on the shelf, where they gathered dust, except when withdrawn to display to visiting consultants, auditors, college professors, or planners from other companies. These thick tomes were impressive but did not really direct the strategies and actions of the company. They gave management a warm feeling and assuaged a planning guilt complex, but did little more.

The eighties initiated a firm belief in a new concept-action planning, planning that is jointly conducted by executives and planners, that addresses the key business directions of the company and is followed and modified as market changes dictate. The plan is the basis for action, not a book that's put on the shelf for review by he inelligentsia.

What prompted this new and serious look at planning is a bit obscure. It may have been the inflationary economy and its impact on future growth, it may have been the political changes in regulation, taxes, and budgetary direction, it may have been the emergence of foreign, competition and particularly the Japanese model of doing business based on a long-term planning foundation, or it could have been just an awakening by executives to the importance of liking our further and the realization that they had to be involved in the process. Whatever the cause or causes, it has become evident that a manager's job and the success of his enterprises depend on a dual responsibility: to perform to meet the current year's goals and to plan to meet future year's goals. This establishes a healthier and more receptive corporate environment for MIS planning. In the early stages of MIS, applications were initiated and implemented as separate entities without much attention to integration.

The aim was to get a specific application up and running to satisfy a particular user's need. The first emergence of planning was project planning, for it was found hat many of the earlier applications did not really satisfy user needs, once the implementation was completed. Users would say, "That isn't what I told you" or "Your should have done what I meant, not what I said." Projects typically were behind schedule and took more resources than were contemplated-and by an order of magnitude or worse. It soon became clear that identifying the projects milestones, gaining user sign-off on specification, and scheduling management reviews throughout the cycle produces better products.

The proliferation of applications during what has been called the contagion stage resulted in heavy demands for computer time. This initiated the second kind of more art than science. MIS managers had to find a way to project future compute hardware requirements in an era of growing application backlogs. Capacity planning permits the modeling of the current workload in order to project future volume levels and the need and time frame for added capacity. With the increase in computer resources, management became alarmed over the sharply rising cost of data processing services. This led to a third type of planning, resource or budgetary planning. MIS managers began developing annual operational plans, which necessitated looking ahead at least a year to project what hardware, software, people, and facilities were required to run the operation and handle the growing portfolio of computer applications. This ushered in the third or control stage of MIS development. At the advent of stage 4, an assessment of management needs showed a requirement for integrated data files in order to provide meaningful management information to tun the business.

This established the need for another type of planning-long-range planning-to formulate the direction and strategy of the MIS function to support the business in the next three-to five-year period. In considering an MIS long-range plan, we need to keep several precepts in mind.

Planning is a verb, not a noun- Planning is not a once-a-year function that produces a report and gets management blessing. Rather it is a continuous process that takes place throughout the year. The report is reviewed and updated continually; it is a living document. Most planners and executives would agree that the effectiveness of planning is in the process rather than in a particular document that becomes the final output.

— *The MIS plan must be consistent with the corporate business plan*-The MIS plan must dovetail with the corporate plan. Since the MIS plan supports the future business, the future business direction of the company must be known before any meaningful MIS plan can be developed. This usually means that the planning cycle of the MIS plan is in sequence with the corporate planning cycle. A set of corporate strategic guidelines will kick off the planning cycle for the year. The MIS cycle should commence at that point and coincide with the key management review points of the corporate schedule.

— *Management involvement and commitment are essential*— Involvement and commitment go hand-in-hand, in that commitment without involvement is usually lip service, rather than arising from understanding and participation in the review process. In order to achieve this participation, an information steering committee is usually required. Since each manager is involve din his or her own department plan, conservative and sensitive use of managers' time is important. Meetings should be well structured and focused on broad strategic issues rather than short-term tactical ones. The makeup and operation of the management review board or steering committee is extremely important. The plan's content obviously is crucial, but is perception by management can be equally as crucial.

— Planning is everybody's job-Though a specific individual or department is responsible for developing the MIS plan, they are the catalysts or agents, chartered to select a planning methodology and to ensure that the planning process takes place according to that methodology and is consistent with corporate guidelines. They can contribute to the plan's content but are not responsible for it. The key department managers and the MIS executive bear the responsibility for providing the strategic directional content. Planning is not a function to be delegated.

Organizational behaviorists point out that it is difficult for a manager to successfully implement a plan that was dictated from the top without his or her involvement or commitment. Grass-roots planning, where the people responsible for implementing the plan are also involved in the planning process, has proven more workable than ivory-tower planning. It takes several cycles to institutionalize a planning process. We noted earlier that planning is no an easy task and runs against the grain of the action-oriented, hard-driving manager.

Therefore, no matter how should the methodology chosen or how efficient the techniques for developing the plan, it will take more than one iteration to establish the process firmly within a company. Planners instituting the process should not be discouraged the first time around. Often the first year's plan is not completely understood by either the MIS people implementing it or the MIS users supported by it. An assessment should be made at the completion of the first planning cycle in order to improve the process during the next cycle.

Modifications may include items such as an off-site half-day workshop to review the final version, a different composition of the steering committee, or a change in the scheduling of various milestones. Remember that planning is a verb; it is a continuous process. The contents of an MIS long-range plan into fifteen categories. The contents answer six basic questions:

1. Where are we?
2. Where do we want to go?
3. How do we get there?
4. When will it be done?
5. Who will do it?
6. How much will it cost?

While the contents will vary between different companies, MIS groups, and stages of development, presents a good starting point. Some sections will be emphasized one year and deemphasized in another. For example, at a particular development stage, the establishment of MIS management control techniques may be of principal significance, while being downplayed in subsequent years. This is true also for other areas such as polices or transition strategies. Often planners feel that if a plan doesn't change dramatically each year, it is no a good one or they are not doing their job.

This is not the case, because if a good solid vision of the future is established and if meaningful, well -founded strategies are put in place, they may hold with but minor fine tuning for several years to come. An extremely useful technique is to develop a difference document which summarizes the key changes of this year's plan from that of the preceding year. Management is particularly interested in this focus.

The fifteen sections of the plan include the following:

1. Corporate guidelines
   (a) Strategic-markets/products
   (b) Volume indicators
   (c) Functional/organizational changes
2. Environment
   (a) Industry trends
   (b) Technology scan
   (c) Government regulations
   (d) Work-force composition
   (e) Customer/supplier relational changes
3. Current operations
   (a) Budget/organization

- (b) Strength/weaknesses
- (c) Strategy/projects
- (d) Opportunities/potentials

4. Mission/direction statement
   - (a) Purpose or reason for MIS
   - (b) Main business of MIS
   - (c) Objectives of MIS
   - (d) Scope of users
5. Objectives/goals
   - (a) Targets and time frame
   - (b) Results expected
   - (c) Qualitative and quantitative goals
6. Assumptions/risks
   - (a) Internal and external constraints
   - (b) Assumptions and potential consequences
   - (c) Major risks
7. Strategies
   - (a) Major strategies o reach objectives
   - (b) Timing of strategies
8. Policies
   - (a) Major current polices (internal and external to MIS)
   - (b) Projected policy changes required and time frame
9. Programs/projects
   - (a) Current program/projects in process
   - (b) New ones required

10. Management control tools
    (a) New procedures/methods needed
    (b) Timing and approach to develop new control techniques
11. Transition plans
    (a) Old environment
    (b) New environment
    (c) Plan to go from old to new
    (d) Necessary user and operational conditioning
12. Priorities and schedules
    (a) Ranking ad prioritization of programs and projects
    (b) Timing and schedule of programs/projects
13. Organization and delegation
    (a) Organization to manage MIS
    (b) Delegation of authority and responsibility
14. Resource projections
    (a) Equipment projections
    (b) Software projections
    (c) Facilities projections
    (d) Personnel requirements (hiring, maintaining, training, developing)
15. Operating budget
    (a) Incremental budget by new program/project or zero based
    (b) New budget projected for each of planned years

The MIS steering committee has become quite significant in many companies and, if properly utilized and administered, can be an effective tool in developing good user relations. The steering committee, is comprised of group of key users of information services whose duty is to act as a review or overseeing body of MIS plans and development. A steering committee helps formalize the concept of user involvement hat is so necessary for successful systems. It provides a higher-level control that can break log jams or give direction when for one reason or another the MIS activity bogs down.

A properly comprised steering group can present a broader business perspective to situation and can help keep system objectives in balance. Another important function is to sing off on the specifications of a new major application area. Often the specs or requirements of a new application either are not stated at the outset or are not clear to the eventual users, so that they are major surprises once the application is in operation. Output and response time of the system should be reviewed at the outset and referred to throughout the production process to ensure the project will meet its objects. Things inevitably change during the course of a development cycle.

The steering committee can assess the impact of these events and assist in making the most beneficial trade-off decisions.Deployment ad organization of steering committees vary within a company. Sometimes there is only one general information advisory group, while in other situations a hierarchy of steering committees exists. The figure illustrates a hierarchical arrangement of an overall MIS steering group and three decision-level groups focusing on the key operating areas of the company-marketing, manufacturing, and engineering. The top group so responsible for approving the business plan for the entire management information system. The group is headed by a prominent member of top management who must e able to devote a good amount of time to the program; in this case it is the executive vice-president.

The heads or key decision makers of the departments to be affected by MIS are also members of the steering group. The director of MIS and the manager of systems and programming represent the MIS department. This group meets periodically to update the MIS business plan as well as to review the status of the three advisory groups working under it. An advisory group so formed for each of the major application subsystem areas-in this case marketing, manufacturing, and engineering.

The group is chaired by a top executive of the department concerned and includes key people within the department as well as the key MIS personnel involved in system development. Note that in each group there is a system analyst representing the department affected. His or her inclusion is extremely important; it ensures that the department's interests and objectives are represented in the detailed implementation steps as well as in the over all planning. The key system designers within the MIS department, called the marketing, manufacturing, and engineering project leaders, are also members of the group. They are the MIS personnel responsible, together with the department's system analyst, for the full-time direction of the particular application area. Note, also, that there is cross-representation on each of the committees.

The directors of manufacturing, marketing, and engineering are on the steering group, and they also head one of the advisory groups. The director of MIS and the manager of systems and programming also sit on advisory groups. Thus there are continuity and tie-in. It may well be that a less formal structure will suit a particular situation. Whatever the scope, it is important to follow certain procedures.

First, because members of the steering groups all have full-time jobs, every effort must be made to make the meetings crisp, well organized, focused, and pertinent. The purpose of the steering committee is not to cover details or do the work of the MIS department, but to review direction, progress toward objectives, and fit of systems to the company culture. The subject matter should emphasize questions of "what," not "how".

The group should include respected people from the various organizations and not just those who happen to be available. This is probably the most important success factor of steering committees: the people selected should be able to speak for their division or organization. While the expanding scope of MIS makes cross-functional steering groups essential the following pitfalls should be avoided if the committee approach is to be effective.

— Group is too large and diverse (six to eight is optimum).
— Meeting deteriorate into vague, wandering discussion.
— Subject matter becomes too detailed and specific rather than focusing on broad direction, strategy, and priority.
— The necessary staff work is not accomplished before meetings.
— Frequency and length of meetings are greater than management can tolerate.
— Substitutes and substitutes for substitutes begin to show up at meetings.

— Low-level chairmanship or MIS domination of the meeting occurs.

Companies have been expanding the role of their corporate audit function to include MIS auditing. Previously, the MIS audit function concentrated on financial auditing, checking those areas that were involved with cash intake and cash disbursements such as purchasing, order processing, and payroll. However, the role in many instances has expanded to include the overall workings of the MIS function.

The role of working around the computer-that is, inspecting what goes in and what goes out-is changing to include what goes on inside the computer and inside the MIS department. One company lists the following functions under its corporate audit department.

— Review data center procedures and standards

— Check for operational compliance

— Security audits

— Recovery and back-up

— Performance measurements

— Postimplementation audits

— System effectiveness reviews

— Review internal controls

— Ensure auditability of new systems

— Quality assurance

— Review documentation

— Evaluation and verification

The philosophy of some organizations is not to give the responsibility for these functions to a separate audit group, but to include them in the charter of the

MIS department. This is similar to combining the quality control department with the production department. Each approach has its obvious pros and cons . However, if the company adopts he separate audit function, it behooves the MIS director to work with this department, to degree on a set of goals and guidelines, and to perform and be measured against this agreed-to set. All levels of management need information on which to base decisions, to plan, to organise, and to control.

People gather information directly by observing and experiencing events but as organisations become larger and more complex it becomes impossible for management, particularly in the middle and higher levels, to observe or experience all operations. In some forms of decentralised organisation management virtually never see the actual events and have to rely almost entirely on information provided through formal and informal channels.

Although much valuable information is passed via discussions, meetings and casual conversation, such methods generally do not give a complete picture nor do they provide information in the correct form for the intended use.

Informal to formal: As organisation grow there is a shift from informal to more formal methods of disseminating information. The more formal information systems (via reports, operating statements, special analyses, variance returns, balance sheets etc.) have the advantages of comprehensiveness, consistency and reasonable accuracy but may suffer from the disadvantages of not meeting the exact requirements of the problem in hand, a lack of flexibility, time lag from event or operation to report, and cost. In spite of these possible disadvantages the development of Management Information Systems (M.I.S) is vitally necessary in most organisations other than the very smallest.

MIS definition. It is an information system using formalised procedures to provide managers at all levels in all functions with appropriate information from all relevant sources (both internal and external to the firm) to enable them to make timely and effective decisions for planning, directing and controlling the activities for which they are responsible. It will be noted from this definition that the emphasis is on the uses to which the information is processed. This emphasis is correct for it is the end use of the information which is important and not the intermediate processing stage. Influences on M.I.S. Numerous factors influence the overall structure of M.I.S., the more important ones being;

a. The primary function of the organisation. Is it a manufacturing company, a wholesaler, a public authority etc.?

b. The structure and levels of the organisation. Is the organisation composed of numerous sections and levels? What degree of autonomy have the section/departments?

c. The degree of centralisation or decentralisation. Is the organisation tightly controlled at the centre? What decisions/actions are the sections allowed to take?

d. Interaction with environment. To what extent is external information of importance? In what does the organisation need to communicate with its environment to customers, suppliers, trade unions, government departments etc.?

e. What decisions need to be taken. What is the extent of programmed and non-programmed decision making? What levels take the decisions?

What is the urgency surrounding the decision making process?

f. The scale of operation. How many employees? How many branches/departments/sections? What is the volume of orders, invoices, bills, enquiries, transactions etc.?

g. The management style? Is it an authoritarian or participative style? Are procedures and operations routine and closely prescribed? Is management by exception practised?

Value of M.I.S. It must be realised that an M.I.S. has no intrinsic value of its own. It cannot be emphasised too strongly that the value of an M.I.S. can only come from the users of the system, and not from the producers of the information. The users, i.e. management at all levels and functions, can only cause value to be attributed to the M.I.S as a result of actions following decisions taken using the information provided. The values which may be imputed to any M.I.S can only come from actions which,

a. Increase profits

b. Reduce costs

c. Utilise resources more effectively or in some way increase the present or future efficiency of the organisation.

Cost/Benefit evaluation: It will be apparent that the correct cost/benefit evaluation of any M.I.S. involves a comparison of the costs of producing the information against the benefits to be obtained from the improved actions resulting from the information. Care should therefore be exercised whenever phrases are heard such as 'management will receive more information', or 'information will be received earlier'. The important point is, will the increased volume of information or the more timely information enable better decisions to be made? If not, the only thing we can say, with certainty, is that producing the information will incur extra costs. Often heavy capital and running costs are incurred to produce information faster or to provide easier access (e.g by the provision of terminal and V.D.U.'s) whereas an analysis of the improvement possible in the actions resulting from the decisions based on the information may show that such enhancements are not cost effective even though technologically advanced.

M.I.S. and the management structure. A brad division of the information supplied by a M.I.S. is into planning and control information. This division is of importance not only because of the intrinsic nature of these two types of information but also because of their destination within the management structure. The following diagram illustrates the broad relationship between the proportion of planning and control information received and the manager's place in the hierarchy.

Characteristics of planning and control information. There are numerous differences between these major information classifications and these are summarised in the following table which shows the information characteristics under four headings, coverage, time scale, amount of detail, and orientation.

Output from M.I.S. Information reaches managers from an M.I.S by way of a wide variety of analyses, statistics, statements etc. which can generally be referred to as reports. These reports may be classified into three broad categories:

a. Reports providing passive background information. These are produced at fairly lengthy intervals in many cases long after the transactions involved took place, e.g asset records, depreciation summaries, annual production statistics, balance sheets etc.

b. Reports which provide control information to influence and guide current and short term, tactical and operating decisions e.g cost variance reports, credit control information, working capital statements, current sales trends, overtime and downtime statistics, machine loading statements etc.

c. Reports which provide statistical data for forecasting, corporate planning and longer term strategic planning e.g. Investment appraisals, budget models, market research reports and analyses, selective economic trends and data, interfirm comparisons etc.

To be effective the reports produced by an M.I.S. should take account of numerous factors the main ones of which are described below.

Destination of report: Who is to be the recipient of a report? At what level of the organisation is he? In general reports produced for top management will be broader in scope and may cover many functional areas whereas reports produced for a manager at the operational level are more restricted in scope and will be limited to a specifically defined area of responsibility.

Uses of report: What will the report be used for? What decisions will be taken based on the report? The answers to such questions will be easier at the operational and tactical levels where activities and decisions are more structured and defined but may be more difficult to answer for top level management.

Urgency of report. The major factor influencing the urgency of a report is the effect on operations which would be caused by non arrival or delayed arrival of a particular report. For example, a fall in the stock of spar parts below the normal minimum level would be important but not necessarily vitally urgent.

On the other hand a fall in stock level below the normal minimum level for apart used on a car assembly line could have immediate and costly consequences so that the systems should be designed to produce the reports on stock levels mentioned above with substantially different degrees of urgency. The urgency requirements can also have a substantial effect on the way the information is produced and transmitted.

Telephones, telex, visual displays, terminals may all have a place in the speedy transmission of urgent information rather than standard printed to typed reports.

Detail: Detail should not be confused with accuracy. According means that a reports should present a picture which will not mislead decision makers. The correct amount of detail is the minimum necessary for the task in hand. Superfluous detail (even though accurate) may cloud the issue and will add to processing, storage and reading costs. Express quantitative information in rounded figures where appropriate, where possible omit details of calculations and only show answers, and do not fall into the trap of providing masses of detailed information merely because it is easily produced as a by-product of a computer run.

The amount of detail normally varies with the level of management that uses the information. The higher the level the less detail would normally be provided, conversely at the operating level considerable detail would be necessary albeit to do with a closely circumscribed area of responsibility. Averaging, summarising, presenting information in graphical form, are all ways in which detail can be reduced often with an increase in comprehension.

Frequency: Much routine information is produced automatically once per hour, per shift, per day, per week, per month or per year and is often vital for the manger concerned. However, too often reports are produced at set intervals without regard to their real need. Typical of the questions which should be asked are; over what period is a deviation from standard (e.g. labour cost variance) likely to be apparent?, how many observations will be necessary before trends can be identified?, If something catastrophic occurs does somebody in the system have enough information to appreciate the real significance of the situation and bypass the normal reporting procedures? What would be the effects on efficiency if reports were produced more/less frequently or not at all?

Management by exception

Definition: Management by exception cab be said to exist (a) when a subordinate is given a prescribed and defined role to perform with the necessary authority to satisfactorily perform the role (b) where the role definition includes a clear statement of what constitutes normal performance and (c) where matters which are not proceeding to plan are reported upon so that the superior may take corrective action.

Management by exception example: The classic accounting example is that of budgetary control whereby a subordinate, after consultation, is given a budget showing what constitutes normal planned performance and significant variances reported to his superior.

Advantages: Management by exception is more than a method of reporting-it is a style of management. ,It has the advantage that subordinates are given clearly defined objectives and the authority to carry them out. They can see what they are required to do and feel that they are trusted to carry out a meaningful task. Their superiors have the advantage that they need not concern themselves with the majority of items which, hopefully, are proceeding according to plan whereas the items which may require attention are brought to their notice through the reporting system. Wherever possible M.I.S. should be built round management by exception principles. Management by exception is a closely controlled form of delegation and it is clear that the types of decisions that are suitable for delegation within management by exception systems are 'programmed' decisions which were defined.

M.I.S. Examples

The following examples illustrate systems in widely varying parts of a typical manufacturing organisation. The examples are by no means exhaustive and many different types of M.I.S. exist in manufacturing and other types of organisation.

Personal

a. *Scope.* M.I.S. in this area provide information to help Personal and other Management in the selection, recruitment and training of personnel, wages and salaries, administration, and promotion and grading. In addition, information must be provided for the development and operation of policies on Welfare, Health and Safety, Conditions of Employment, and Industrial Relations.

b. Typical Reports Produced.

Wages and Salary analyses
Labour Turnover Statistics
Accident and Absentee reports
Training Returns
Job Descriptions
Joint Consultation reports and minutes
Pension analyses and projections.
Job Evaluation reports
Manpower planning reports and projections etc.

c. Typical Inputs Handled.

i. Internal

Times cards and production data
Application forms
Interview summaries
Staff review data
Factory review data
Factory level trade union data
Training summaries etc.

ii. External

College/University reports
National Trade Union Agreements and proposals
Government legislation (Factories Acts, Labour Law etc.)
Wage and salary comparative data
Relevant economic statistics, e.g. employment trends

iii. Major relationships. Personnel must, of necessity, have close relationship with all functional areas to provide them with services and data on all aspects of staffing but it also has specific operational links with a number of functions including

Accounting (e.g. for Wages and Salary payment)

Production (e.g for absentee and attendance data)

Boundaries: The boundaries of a Personnel system vary considerably from one organisation to another. For example, does the Personnel Department actually engage an employee or does it provide the service necessary to produce a short list of suitable candidates for the appropriate functional manager to make the final decision? Does the personnel department arrange for the putting up and payment of wages or is this considered to be part of the Accounting Function? Does Production Management carry out negotiations with Trades Unions or is this a function of the Personnel Department? These and numberous other boundaries have to be resolved in designing any system.

Information

Effective managers were thought of as having an intrinsic quality for leadership. This philosophy could be expressed as: Managers are born, not made. As businesses and demands for managers grew, management was studied and specific attributes of effective managers were identified. Management skills were subject to being learned through training.

Modern theories describe management as a profession. A professional cultivates and brings an extensive and current body of knowledge to the performance of his or her work. Professional accounts, for example, regularly review information about new tax laws and market analyses to maintain their professional knowledge.

The basis of professional knowledge is information. Information is produced by processing data. This transition, from data to information to knowledge, is the framework for effective business planning. That is, data are processed and presented to planners as information. The information is evaluated by managers to support decision making. Evaluations are conducted according to the existing knowledge base of managers. In turn, decision-making activities are accumulated as experience and integrated into knowledge.

The key word in this discussion is information. Information is the basis of planning, management, and knowledge. The importance of information has grown to such an extent that modern, computer-oriented societies are described as information societies. Consider this quote from a statement by John Diebold:

> Information, which in essence is the analysis and synthesis of data, will unquestionably be one of the most vital corporate resources in the 1980s. It will be structured into models for planning and decision making. It will be in corporated into measurements of performance and profitability. It will be integrated into product design and marketing methods. In other words, information will be recognized and treated as an asset.

This quotation illustrates an important change in the nature of CIS. An asset is something that has value to an organization. A bank could not exist without financial assets. Accordingly, the reliance upon and support of information resources has grown to such an extent that many businesses have ceased to exist when data and information files have been lost due to some catastrophe.

The CIS professional and other professionals in computer-oriented businesses, then, must adjust and incorporate this concept as part of their knowledge base. In fact, these adjustments in perceptions have initiated a new term for the CIS function: information resource management.

The adjustment of CIS professionals to this new view of information is evidenced by the use of the term *information resource management* to describe the function responsible for information processing. IRM professionals are responsible not only for processing data and distributing information, but also for the efficient and effective management of information resources. This new role incorporates knowledge in the areas of business theories and administration, telecommunication, and others. Of course, this knowledge is distilled from information, of which there are numerous sources. Information sources are covered in the sections that follow.

Information gathering

Planners and systems analysts are faced with a constant and ever expanding need for information about business in general and about computing disciplines specifically. Some of the sources available to planners and analysts for gathering information with which to maintain current professional knowledge include:

- Professional press
- Conferences
- Seminars
- Associations
- Peer contact
- User groups
- Research publications

— Analysis groups
— Bibliographic services
— Sales representatives
— Advertising
— Consultants
— Electronic bulletin boards.
— Professional press

Consider that in 1650 there were only two scientific journals in publication. By 1850, the number had grown to roughly 1,000. In 1985, there were more than 100,000 publications for professional audiences and thousands more that emphasized technical subjects-and in both areas the numbers were growing weekly. Of course, the magnitude of this proliferation should arouse a degree of suspicion about the quality and accuracy of content. Judgment should be applied by individual professionals to evaluate the degree of care that goes into the screening and validation of content for published articles.

There are three basic categories of publication-journals published by the professional associations primarily for their membership, publications circulated free to qualified individuals, and trade publications.

Professional associations: Most professional associations publish journals with articles of interest to members. Examples include Computer published by the IIEE Computer Society, Communications of the ACM published by the Association for Computer Machinery Data Management published by the Data Processing Management Association, and The Journal of Computer/Information Systems published by Thy Society of Data Educators. As a point of interest, Computer and Communications of the ACM articles are very technical and often are targeted at computer scientists. Data Management is slanted toward business concerns and emphasizes management and administration. A significant feature of many scientific journals is that articles are contributed by appropriate, recognize experts.

Free publications: Many publications are distributed at no charge to qualified organizations or individuals. Requirements for receiving such publications may include the job classification of manager or purchasing authority for computing equipment and supplies. Qualifications generally are reviewed annually.

The best known publication in this category is Datamation. This magazine is published twice each month by *Technical Publishing*, a part of the Dun and Bradstreet Corporation. Other publication examples include T*he Office and Hardcopy.*

Article in these magazines generally address current topics and may be written by external contributors or staff writers. In most of these publications there is a section that contains a series of short comments on current events and outlooks for the future. A valuable source of information in these magazines is advertisements. A brief scan of advertisements usually provides a general overview of trends in hardware and software. IRM professionals also may use advertisements to locate vendors and/or specification for products.

The trade press: Many publications specialize in computing and information system topics. Popular examples include *Computer world*, *BYTE*, and *PC World. Computer world* is a weekly newspaper covering the computing industry. In each issue, a specific topic is given extensive coverage. Often, an interview with an expert in the featured area is included. *BYTE* and *PC World* appeal to users of microcomputers.

Trade shows and conferences are another source of current information for IRM professionals. Many trade shows and conferences are sponsored by one or more professional associations. Topics of these conferences vary in content and in degree of technical depth. That is, some shows are generic, or overview presentations. Other are vertical conferences that focus on specific technical topics of individual industries or disciplines. Depending on the size of the association, regional, national, and/or international conferences may be held.

Common features of conferences and shows include exhibits of computing hardware, software, and/or support items; technical presentations; workshops; and tutorials. In fact, many professional organizations hold smaller, regional or special-interest conferences. For example, DPMA conferences concentrate on business applications of computer technology. ACM conferences explore the technical aspects of computing and are targeted at computer scientist and systems programmers. The IEEE-CS emphasizes scientific concepts and directs technical sessions and materials toward engineers and computer scientists.

The TCA specializes in voice and data communications. Interface Group is a private organization that present technical conferences, such as COMDEX, that attract builders and marketers of computing equipment. The American Federation of Information Processing Societies is an umbrella organization of eleven associations for computer professionals. AFIPS conferences hardware, software, and applications sessions for the attendees. AFIPS sponsors the National Computers Conference and the National Computer-Telecommunications. Seminars are similar to conferences, but differ in that seminars tend to feature specific topics. Because seminars generally focus upon a single topic, IRM professionals can obtain concentrated instruction in specific subject areas. Most professional associations, such as ACM, DPMA, and IIEE-CS, sponsor technical seminars open both to members and the general public. For example, the DPMA sponsors regular one-day seminars designed to increase the attendees' personal capabilities, such as listening skills.

Several private organizations also sponsor seminars. Examples include. The Interface Group, The Wang Institute, and The American Management Association. Seminars and conferences motivate *technology transfer*. That is, these gatherings are opportunities for IRM professionals to seek answers to pressing questions, to hold individual finding up to the scrutiny of other professionals, and to reap the benefits of this synergy. In other words, the development of knowledge is enhanced by the give and take of information at seminars and conferences.

IRM professionals, by definition, should strive to maintain currency in their knowledge and experiences. Through this chapter, professional associations and the services they provide have been discussed. Active participation in one or more of these associations can provide significant benefits to IRM professionals. Meetings are held regularly and provide opportunities to maintain regular contact with professional peers. Newsletters that detail important events and/or conferences and seminars usually are sent to members.

Meetings may be the most valuable function of professional associations. In effect, meetings are a forum for explanations and discussions of common problems. In addition, IRM professionals can accumulate a list of professional contacts who can be reached by telephone for exchange of ideas and information. Meetings also communicate the interest of members to association leaders. Subjects that are of interest to members may be slated for a conference or seminar at a later date. Notice the references to peer contact. Peer contact cannot be stressed enough as a source of information for IRM professionals. Input from peers is universal and may come from sources as diverse as fellow workers, friends, neighbors, fellow association members, and religious or fraternal organizations.

Peers provide input based upon their own experiences or knowledge of the experience of others. The benefits of this input are twofold. That is, information can be gathered about possible solutions to current problems and about the difficulties that can result when other problems are solved. The computing industry has spawned many *user groups.* User groups generally are organized according to common interests of people who have installed particular equipment.

The advent of the microcomputer has spawned a great number of user groups. Members of user groups meet periodically to share ideas and information on how to use the equipment more effectively. These groups also may be a source of software for particular equipment. Occasionally, user groups from a network; members are given access to electronic bulletin boards or mailboxes to exchange information. Large groups of this often are sponsored by manufacturers. Examples include SHARE and GUIDE for users of large IBM computers and DECUS for users of Digital Equipment products.

In addition to the sources discussed in other parts of this chapter, many professional research organizations now specialize in publishing reviews and summaries of hardware, peripherals, software, and services. Some of the reports are extensive and detailed and may involve considerable effort to maintain. Updates may be sent regularly to subscribers for accumulation in a blinder or file. Other reports of this type may contain only a list of the main attributes of a device or software package. Specifications such as speed, capacity, and price are included in research reports.

Most reports of this type are indexed to facilitate the location of specific pieces of information. Examples of prominent research organizations include Auerbach Reports, Computerworld Quarterlies, Data Sources, and Datapro. Analysis groups are private research organizations that focus on areas of interest rather than specific products. Leading organizations of this type include the Yankee Group, International Data Corporation, and The Gartner Group. Analysis groups research topics, such as computing or communications, and distribute results to clients through publications, seminars, executive briefings, or telephone query services.

Telephone query services provide IRM professionals with immediate access to comprehensive information about a variety of topics. Another source of information for IRM professionals is bibliographic retrieval services. These organizations differ from analysis groups in that in bibliographic services provide professionals with possible locations of data. Professionals then use these references to gather needed data. Some organizations that offers bibliographic services include Lockheed, Systems Development Corporation, Source, and the Computing Reviews of the ACM.

Vendor representatives also are a valuable source of information. Naturally, vendor representatives are biased toward the products they represent and IRM professionals should evaluate information from salespeople in this light. But sales representatives usually are knowledgeable about their products, under development by their organizations, the competitive market in general, and future trends. Further, vendor representatives are backed by resources that include research and development capabilities and support capabilities that include seminars and training sessions.

Each computer user represents a segment of the market for sales organizations. Therefore, the feedback provided by customers can effect the shape and capabilities of future products. Planners should review promotional advertising regularly. There is no shortage of source materials for this task. Recall the previous discussion of technical publications, and publications of professional organizations. Many of these publications rely on advertising revenues and dedicate large portions of space to advertising.

A careful review of advertising also can indicate trends and developments in hardware, software, and other areas of interest to IRM professionals. In addition, advertisements and announcements of seminars and conferences are a good indication of future developments in any area. This is because seminars and conferences often emphasize subjects on the leading edge of technical evolution. Consultants often are hired by IRM organizations for their expertise.

However, IRM professionals need to study their requirements and the capabilities of consultants to make sure they are appropriate. The use of consultants provides many advantages, including their experience on other systems, cost savings from not having to retain a permanent employee, and the short-term nature of the agreement. Disadvantages arise when IRM functions rely too heavily on consultants. In this situation, IRM functions are vulnerable when the work is finished or if the relationship is terminated. Historically, systems designed and built with the assistance of consultants have presented maintenance difficulties. Electronic bulletin boards are introduced in the section on user groups. Electronic bulletin boards are public or private forums in which participants are linked through telecommunications.

Information evaluation

Evaluations of system benefits are included in the feasibility analysis phase of new system development. It is also necessary to evaluate the efficiency and effectiveness of existing applications and hardware. Proposed additions are evaluated by comparison to alternative, competing hardware and software. Quality is defined as excellence or fitness. It is not absolute concept; it is defined within a context. An application has quality relative to its primary and secondary users, operations personnel, control personnel, maintenance personnel, and so forth. Perfect quality is very costly and virtually impossible. Quality should be within acceptable limits as defined by the organizations. The quality limits reflect the consequences of lack of quality and the cost of achieving it. For example, lack of quality in the development process may result in applications that are not used or that have a very seeks to make sure the application is perfect will never be completed.

The basic organizational mechanisms for control and quality assurance in information systems follow the patterns established for other activities such as production. There are management duties relative to quality and control, and there are also special functions within the information systems organization. The users of information systems resources also have responsibility for quality assurance. The role of top management in information system quality control is to establish the overall organization structure, select the information system executive, approve the information system plan and budget, and evaluate performance. Some examples of top management duties are:

— Establish domain of responsibility and authority of information systems function

— Select information systems executive

— Approve the information systems charter, the information system long-range plan, and the yearly budget

— Approve major hardware and software systems

— Approve major applications

— Review results against plan and evaluate information system performance

— Review and approve information system procedures for quality assurance and control

The top management responsibilities listed above may be exercised by individual top management personnel, or a committee structure may be used to do much of the work prior to final decision making by top management, In the committee approach, an information system steering committee composed of top management of the organizational functions performs evaluations and makes recommendations for action.

The information systems executive has the responsibility for organizing and supervising the various control and quality assurance activities in information systems. Examples of duties are.

— Establish and supervise quality assurance procedures for applications developed in-house or obtained as packages.

— Establish and supervise various information system control functions.

— Establish and monitor procedures to measure and report evidence of quality: error, downtime, reruns, application repair maintenance, etc.

There are certain control and quality assurance functions that need to be performed in information system operations. In large installations, performance of these functions may require a special staff; in small installation, they may be part-time duties for an individual performing other activities. The major functions are;

1. *Librarian:* This function maintains custody of programs, files, and documentation. These resource are issued based on an authorized of uses or special authorization. The custodial activities include record keeping.
2. *Processing control:* This includes logging in and checking input, checking progress of jobs, reconciling control information for applications, checking output and distributing it to authorized recipients, maintaining error logs, and following up on error correction.
3. *Access control:* This function is responsible for control of physical access to the installation and control of access through terminals. Duties include follow up on violations of systems access rules.
4. *Database administration:* This include control over access to and use of the database, enforcement of data integrity rules, and establishment and enforcement of standards.
5. *Back and recovery:* This functions is reasonable for preparing backup copies of programs, files and database, etc.

6. *Application development quality assurance*: This function includes review of controls planned for an application and review of adequacy of testing during development.

Users have quality assurance duties as participants in application and database development and maintenance. There are also special control and quality assurance considerations when users develop their own systems, to be discussed later in the chapter. Users quality assurance duties require knowledge of context of data, user participation in both input and output, and the organizational control principles of separation of functions.

Knowledge of context means that users are able to identify individual data because it does not fit or is not reasonable. This ability represents situation-dependent data validation because the validation criteria may not be formulated until the user is faced with the specific invalid instance. For example, the user may recognize a personnel record showing that a person was born in 1961 and graduated from a university in 1975 as probably being in error. A validation test for this relationship could have been designed, but it is likely to have been overlooked. The user should be responsible for reporting such probable invalid data; procedures should exist to facilitate reporting to such instances and provide feedback that they have been corrected.

When a user prepares input for a batch system and also receive the output, this is one bases for quality control duties. For instance, the user may develop a control total of input data provided to data processing and check control totals on output against the input control total. The user may check output with other data such as checking the total on listing of accounts receivable with the accounting ledger total for accounts receivable.

The organizational control principle of separating functions that a person should not be responsible for incompatible functions in terms of ability to make errors or commit fraud. The same person should not have custody of assets and do all accounting for the assets. The initiation of transactions should be separated from the data processing of the transactions to produce financial records. The separation of functions increases the probability than an error by one person will be detected by another. Also, separation of function reduces the likelihood of fraud because it would require collusion. In the case of information processing, the division of functions is manifest in:

— Requirements that a transaction in error be returned to the initiation area rather than being corrected by data processing.

— Policy that data processing may not initiate transactions or master file changes.

— User controls and user control duties in applications

A large proportion of the procedures related to an information system application related to quality assurance. These include handling of exceptions, detection of errors, error correction, and various exception error, and control reports. In a typical application, from 25 to 50 percent of activities and program code are for quality assurance. The same factors apply to database. Quality assurance is therefore a significant issue in application design, operation, and maintenance.

There are three conditions that underlie quality control in application: organizational commitment to quality, information processing discipline with respect to operations, and redundancy to achieve error control in the application design. Specific quality assurance procedures rely upon these three conditions. The organizational commitment to quality in the results of information processing is not merely a statement of support; quality assurance requires extra effort and extra expense both in development and in operation. However, there are significant differences in quality requirements among applications.

There are different quality requirements by different organizations and different functions within the same organization. This means the commitment to quality may differ among organizations and applications, but the commitment should be appropriate to the conditions. Information processing discipline is an element in overall organizational discipline.

The term "discipline" is used in the sense of diligently following established procedures. It implies an acceptance of the need for careful attention to quality. Information processing discipline is institutionalized in the use of forms, screen design and procedures for input, output, and error handling. It is transmitted to new employees by training, supervision, and example. For example, and older employee tells about the time she stayed until midnight locating an error caused by a sloppy transaction document.

This transmits a message about the seriousness of errors and the diligence expected of employees in locating and fixing them. As a new employee gains experience, acceptance of data processing quality assurance procedures is strengthened. The success of many quality assurance procedures depends on the existence of such information processing discipline in the organization. Redundancy was explained in connection with information concepts. Redundancy in information processing consists of an extra element, process, or procedure that would not be required if there were complete assurance that the data and procedures were without error. Some examples of redundancy in computer data processing are;

— Parity bid to detect errors in electronic circuitry or data communication lines

— Longitudinal parity bit on magnetic tape blocks to detect and correct errors

— Check digit added to identification codes

— Control totals on batches of data

— Run - to -run control totals

— Echo of input at VDT entry

— Verification of input data by rekeying and comparing

Redundant data or redundant processing procedures provide the basis for very effective quality assurance procedures. However, there are three costs associated with the redundant elements; the cost of obtaining the redundant data or doing the redundant processing, the cost of error detection and error correction for the redundant elements, and the cost of the assurance procedures themselves. For examples, a control total comparison used to detect loss or nonprocessing of data in a batch of data items requires the control total to be computed, the control total to be recomputed if there is a difference between the control total and the processing total, and either manual or programmed comparison of the two totals. The development cycle is designed to support quality assurance in terms of developing a system that meets requirements. Some quality assurance processes are:

— Information requirements determination processes to ensure complete and correct requirements.

— Sign-offs at each phase of development to assure adequate review and agreement on the system to that point.

— Program development procedures for quality control. These include structured design, structured programming, independent review of program logic, and program testing.

— Conventional installation testing.

Development quality assurance procedures can be operated in a cooperative mode, an adversary mode, or a combination. In the cooperative mode, quality assurance is considered a responsibility of the entire development group. Finding errors is viewed as an aid to assist members of the group to achieve a better result. An examples of the cooperative approach is a structured walkthrough for programmers.

A member of the project team "walks through" program logic and procedures with the rest of the group the objective is to improve the program, not to evaluate the programmer or analyst. In the adversary mode, a separate quality assurance or testing function is established. The persons doing the quality assurance and testing receive organizational rewards for finding weaknesses and errors and identifying the source of the errors.

The staff of the quality assurance function monitors application development projects and evaluates them in terms of processes being applied to achieve quality and in terms of the quality of the result. The separate function provides an independent evaluation of both project management relative to quality assurance and the application that is produced. The quality management relative to quality assurance and the application that is produced. The review consists of an independent evaluation of project risk and project plans in the light of the risk.

Project reviews are conducted on a periodic basis during the development to assess progress. Special reviews may be made to deal with problems that arise.

The advantages of the separate quality assurance function are independence of the function, demonstration of organizational time and resource commitment, and specialization in quality assurance. The disadvantages are primarily that quality assurance is then divorced from application development and resistance to separate quality assurance personnel may reduce their effectiveness.

Applications designed with high regard for quality assurance in operation tend to have low error rates. Some examples of features that aid in assuring quality and low error rates are the following;

— Design of input documents and screens to elicit input in natural sequence with labels, boxes, and menus that clearly identify what is to be input.

— Expanded echo of input data to provide data provide opportunity for visual verification.

— Presentation of sufficient information on output for recipient to verify processing. "70 dozen widgets at $0.72 per dozen = $50.40."

— Control totals on output to allow checking against other control totals.

— Audit trail references to allow tracing of end result back to constituent parts or tracing a part up to the result.

The cost of data increases with the quality requirements. A tendency to request higher quality of data than is required can be costly. Accounting data on cash, customer billing, etc., needs to be very exact;

data on sales by product by area can be less exact and yet be completely satisfactory. Additional accuracy and completeness are achieved at the cost of redundant data and controls at a variety of points in the processing cycle.

According to system theory, a system will run down and become disorganized unless matter and energy are applied to overcome the natural tendency to entropy. For information system applications, the negative entropy is application maintenance; this refers to either repairs of errors or enhancements. If repairs are not made, users lose confidence in the system and fail to use it or to provide inputs. If enhancements are not made, users may switch to alternative source of information.

The process of maintenance follows a cycle of identification, analysis, performing changes, and testing. The identification to errors and proposed enhancements in crucial to the maintenance of system quality. Procedures need to be established for feedback from users on need for changes and from maintenance personnel to users. If the applications is "owned" by one function, this function can assign responsibility for working with maintenance personnel. If there are many users, there may need to be a suer group responsible for resolving conflicts.

The principle of entropy also applies to stored data. The maintenance of data quality requires continuous inputs or resources. In assessing the establishment of databases, an important factor to be considered is the probability that the integrity of the data can be maintained. The assessment should also consider the risk from a degradation of data quality. The ability of an organization to maintain data quality depends on both organizational factors and data factors.

1 *Length of error-effect cycle:* If errors have an immediate effect, organizational resources will be applied more readily than if the effect of error is longer term. Errors in the billing file are therefore more likely to receive attention than error in the employee information file.

2. Regularity *of measurements*: Data collection that is scheduled that is scheduled at frequent, regular intervals is more likely to be regularized through institutional procedures. Occasional, ad hoc data collection is likely to be forgotten or done poorly. A regular, weekly report of competitor intelligence from sales as part of expense reports is more likely to have high integrity than an occasional intelligence report.

3. *User-provider link:* It is more difficult to maintain high quality when the function providing the data has no organizational link with its users. If the data is received from an external source, the organization cannot impose its own quality control stands.

4. *Provider data discipline:* The extent of data discipline in a function is a result of the background, training, and culture of the function. For example, the accounting function tends to have greater data discipline then marketing.

5. *Ease of verification*: Some data items can be easily checked by comparison with other stored data or by comparison with physical evidence. The credits to accounts receivable are easily verified by the debits to cash.

Given these factors affecting data quality and the difficulty of maintaining data quality over time, organizational procedures can be applied to increase the probability of maintaining suitable quality. There can be regular comparison with physical evidence, such as inventory counts.

The objects of data collection may be requested to review their records for correctness and completeness. Records may be reviewed on a cycle basis by persons who can recognize errors. For example, the purchasing department may review two percent of the vendor files each week. Training and supervision may be utilized to instill and appropriate level of data discipline.

User-developed applications are an approach to overcoming problems of backlog of new applications, system that do not meet user needs, and implementation failure. Users are provided with application development tools and given training and assistance; they take over the responsibility for requirements determination, development, implementation, and maintenance. There are unique quality assurance problems associated with user-developed systems, primarily because of the elimination of the analyst role in the design of controls for the application.

Development tools can be used which automatically include control procedures or prompt users to include them. Some also provide appropriate documentation as a by-product of user development. The policy approach is to establish policy for adequacy of testing and documentation. For example, a policy may establish different testing and documentation guidelines depending on the importance of the problem, the duration of the system, and the task interdependencies involved. Four levels of testing might be:

— No testing or non-developer review

— Minimal testing and peer review

— Medium testing and external review

— High level of testing and formal external review

The quality assurance procedures summarized above reflect a balance between letting users have complete responsibility for developing their own systems without organizational controls and having a formal quality assurance process that must be applied to all user-developed systems. The same level of formal process for all cases would stifle creativity and experimentation, but the lack of any organizational controls subjects the organization to an unacceptable level of risk.

The last phase of the system development life cycle is a post audit. This is review by a task group. The audit group reviews the objectives and cost-benefit representations made on behalf of the project and compares them with actual performance and actual costs. If also review the operational characteristics of the system to determine if they are satisfactory. Documentation is reviewed for backup and maintainability considerations. Control and security provisions are examined.

The results of the post audit are intended to assist in improved cost justification and management of future projects, improvement in the application under review, or cancellation of the application of it is no longer justified. Applications may be evaluated in terms of measures of system value. They may also be compared with the reports of technical, operational, and economic feasibility by which they originally justified.

One of the most severe problems with the post audit evaluation is the difficulty of determining system value. The ideal measure, as of any investment of organizational resources, is a determination of the impact of the system on organizational effectiveness. Since few changes can be isolated so that their effects on overall organizational functioning can be measured, substitute indicators must be used. The most logical place to look for such measures of system value is the immediate environment where the system is being used. Methods can be determined for measuring the *effectiveness* of the user as a result of having received the output or service from the system. Some methods of indirectly measuring system value are:

Significant task relevance	Results of system use are directly observable. For instance, an office support system results in improved turnaround of documents. For a decision support system, task relevance is improved decision quality which is often difficult to observe but sometimes possible to approximate through users' subjective estimates.
Willing to pay	Users may be asked to specify how much they are willing to pay for a specific report or system capability.
System usage	System logs may permit measures of system use, or users may be asked to estimate their user of the system. This is only appropriate for systems whose usage is voluntary.
User information satisfaction	Users are asked to rate their satisfaction with such aspects of the system as response time, turnaround time, vendor support, accuracy, timeliness, format of outputs, and confidence in the system.

Measures developed according to any of the above methods are probably most effective if given both before and after a new system or system enhancement is introduced. This provides a comparative indicator of improvements.

System value assessments should not be made shortly after a system is implemented; an excess of program errors, difficulties in learning and adjusting to new procedures, and general resistance to change may bias significantly both user satisfaction and system usage. With many voluntary-usage systems. Initial use may be very high and will gradually taper off to a steady level once the novelty of the system has worn off. Another caution is that some applications cause subtle changes in the structure and behaviour of organizations in ways that were not anticipated, and these changes may be difficult to uncover through the simple measures described above. An information system faculty member who did significant amounts of writing plus some administrative duties acquired tow microcomputers. One was provided to his secretary. The other one was placed in his study at home where he did much of his writing.

Communication was established for transfer between the two machines. After a year and a half of experience, some roles and duties had changed.

— The faculty member now composes at the keyboard where previously all keying was done by the secretary.

— Faculty member frequently keys in all text and data for document and secretary puts in final form, including page breaks, checking for misspelled or mistyped words using software, and printing on letter-quality printer. Previously, he read for errors and format.

- — Faculty members sometimes dictates to secretary who keys text. To do further work, he either takes diskette or receives text over communications line. He makes corrections directly at his microcomputer and sends corrected text back to secretary. Previously, he always marked changes in pen which secretary keyed.
- — Secretary writes programs, using microcomputer application development system to do complex reports.
- — Secretary builds files on the microcomputer for administrative lists, mailing, etc.
- — Secretary has learned to send files to a large computer for special printing and to prepare graphical output. Previously, faculty member was responsible for all computer technology.

The question asked during a technical evaluation are similar to those used to determine whether the application was technically feasible. When applications are installed, subsequent evaluation may disclose that they operate ineffectively because the technical capabilities of the hardware or software cannot support them properly. An online realtime operation may be very slow because the computer involved has insufficient capacity to handle the workload. A communications network may adequately handle the workload but the more costly than had been anticipated. Another common problem is that transaction volumes were underestimated, so that secondary storage for online processing has inadequate capacity.

Operational considerations relate to whether the input data is properly provided and the output is usable and used appropriately. Evaluation of application should examine how well they operate with special reference to input, error rates, timeliness off output, and utilization. Some research on utilization of output suggests the need for periodic evaluation of applications. In a study by Gee, 64 line managers at the middle management level of manufacturing companies were interviewed and asked to evaluate control information items they received as being used substantially or as being irrelevant or background information. Of 579 items, 46 percent were considered to be irrelevant or useful only for background. In a further investigation, 49 middle managers were asked to classify items of control information as vital important, or background.

There is a tendency not to terminate a report once it is started. Even though it may not be used, there often is a feeling that it might have utility in the future. Various methods can be used to identify unused reports:

— Termination of the report to see if anyone asks for it when it does not arrive

— Periodic review of all reports by a task force

— Transfer pricing for reports to provide incentives for managers to eliminate those that are unnecessary.

The original proposal for an application included an economic evaluation. In the post audit economic evaluation, the actual costs are compared with actual benefits. The costs can be estimated with reasonable accuracy at post audit, but many benefits may still be difficult to measure. After making these estimates, an economic evaluation may be computed. For example, a revised return on investment may be calculated.

The economic evaluation may be useful beyond the specific application examined. For management purposes, the evaluation may aid future decision making to identify the costs of applications for which an economic return was not expected or could not be estimated. For example, the reasons for the application may have been:

— Mandated by law or changes in external systems
— Required in order to meet competition
— To establish or maintain a competitive advantage or innovation
— Improvements in organizational performance that are expected are difficult to measure.

If economic evaluation shows that the return-on-investment objective will not be achieved or other benefits. In other words, the costs of development already incurred are no longer relevant; they are sunk costs and cannot be altered by the decision. Frequently, therefore, an application that has less benefit than anticipated may still have sufficient future benefit to pay for operating costs and future maintenance costs.

The purpose of evaluation of existing hardware and software is to determine if all resources are needed, if some resources should be replaced with improved hardware or software, if a rearrangement of resources will improve effectiveness, or if additional resources will increase the effectiveness of the system. Some examples of actions resulting from performance evaluation of the existing hardware-software system are:

— Addition of a new data channel or dropping a data channel not being used
— Replacement of a low-speed data channel with a high-speed channel
— Addition to main memory capacity

— Change in disk storage units

— Change in disk organization

— Change in database management software

— Change in communication network

— Replacement of order entry application package

The methods and tools for evaluation of the hardware-software system are hardware and software monitors, system logs and observations, and simulation.

Hardware monitors are sensing devices attached to selected signal lines in the computer hard ware to measure the presence or absence of electrical impulses. For example, a sensor might be attached to measure the time that the CPU is in wait state. Another sensor might measure channel activity. The monitoring device does not affect the operation of the computer hardware. It requires no primary storage and the CPU cycle times. The data from the sensor probes is routed to counters.

Periodically the data in the counters, together with the time determined by an internal clock, is written onto magnetic tape or other output medium in computer-readable format. It is periodically summarized by use of a computer program and reported in an analytical format. Monitors can collect data on both CPU and peripheral device activity such as disk storage. The major shortcoming of hardware monitors is that they cannot identify the program which is being measured unless monitors is that they cannot identify the program which is being measured unless the location of the program in memory is known.

Most computers of reasonable size use relocatable programs and have more than one program in memory at a time; this reduces the effectiveness of hardware monitors for measuring specific program efficiency. The operating system normally resides in a fixed partition in memory, so its activity can be measured. *Software monitors* are computer programs. They reside in main memory and require execution time; they interrupt the program being executed to record data about the execution. They therefore slow down the execution of the programs they are monitoring. One approach to reduce the amount of interruption is to sample the activities being executed rather than to measure them continuously. Software monitors can identify particular programmes or program modules within the operating system environment. Peripheral device activity is not measured directly but can be estimated from the CPU commands.

Hardware and software monitors can be used to detect idle resources, bottlenecks, and load imbalance. Inefficient use of resource owing to excessive wait time can be measured. This wait time may be caused by insufficient channel capacity, excessive seek time by disk storage devices, inefficient overlapping input-output and processing, etc. The monitors assist in identifying the causes of inefficiency. Some remedies to be applied following performance monitoring and analysis of the results include;

- Changes in equipment
- Recording of program segments
- Redesign of disk storage files
- Restructuring of access to disk storage records

The results from "tuning" of hardware-software systems have been significant. A 25 percent reduction in execution time for the few jobs which normally take most of the processing capability is not unusual.

The system log may provide data useful for evaluation. This is especially true of small installation which maintain simple logs of jobs, job times, etc. An analysis of the system log may indicate problems with reruns, variations in job running times or excessive machine failure. The log may also be used to develop a distribution of jobs by time required. Such a list generally reveals the impact of, for example, few large jobs or a stream of small jobs.

Observation of computer operations is useful in detecting inefficient scheduling of resource use and inefficient applications. Some of inefficient scheduling or poor operating procedures are:

— Processing delays for operator to locate files, mount tapes or disks, load forms, or perform similar functions

— Excessive requirements for operator response at console

— Delays caused by lack of training in proper restart procedures when processing is interrupted

Simulation is used primarily to chose a new system can also be used to study the effects of proposed changes or addition to existing installations. In this approach, the analysts defines mathematical models of representative computer runs and descriptions of the existing or proposed computer configuration and operating system. These are input to a software package which produce a series of reports representing how the workload will be processed. Simulation is useful, once a problem has been identified, in analyzing various alternative solutions. Its drawbacks are that it is expensive to set up and run. A frequent decision in information systems is the acquisition of new or replacement hardware or software. These are often major purchases with significant organizational implications.

The process of evaluation for a new or major replacement hardware software system will vary depending on the level or experience by the organization using computers, the urgency of replacement, and other factors. A general approach consists of steps such as: requirements study, preparation of specifications, obtaining vendor proposals and evaluation of proposals. The basis for this approach is that the organization should undertake sufficient analysis to specify its requirements and request proposals from vendors based on the specific requirements.

The vendor proposals are systematically evaluated relative to the requirements, and a decision is made. This approach is in contrast to a common method of asking a single vendor to propose hardware and software without any organizational study and specification. If the hardware or software acquisition is major, a high-level study group or committee should be formed. Some smaller acquisitions may benefit from an advisory group of users.

The high-level study group will be described as the model for both groups. A high level committee should usually consist of middle-management personnel who represent the principal functions of the business, plus an executive from the systems function. The study group should be provide with technical staff support. For an organization that already has a computer installation and is studying the value of a new or expanded system, this support can come from the data processing systems staff. For an organization without prior experience, the use of outside consultant for support is frequently advisable. The purpose of the requirements study is to investigate the present hardware or software system, evaluated the need for a new or replacement system outline the characteristics of a tentative system, evaluative the cost and effectiveness of the tentative system, and evaluate the impact of the tentative system on the organization.

From the information obtained in the requirements study, the group formulates the characteristics of one or more tentative hardware and software systems, then makes rough estimates of cost and ability of each alternative to meet performance objectives. From these tentative systems, one of which should usually be a modified version of the system in use, a tentative system having the specified characteristics is selected as the preferred solution and is then analyzed further in terms of personnel impact, cost-benefit, and suitability to the firm's needs. The system solution is by necessity very general, since it is not tied to a particular hardware or software vendor.

The cost-benefit study summarizes the benefits to be expected from the system, the expected cost, and expected savings, if any. A reasonable life estimate for medium-to large-scale equipment is five years; for microcomputers, the life before obsolescence is considered about three years. The results of the hardware-software requirements study together with the recommendations of the study group are summarized and presented for top-management approval. If the project is approved, the next step is to prepare a manual of specifications for use in procurement. The manual of specifications defines specifically what is to be accomplished by the proposed hardware-software system. It is a fairly detailed document based on data collected in the requirements study.

The document serves both as a summary of the proposed system for internal purposes and as a statement for use in inviting proposals from vendors of hardware and software. Evaluation may be simple if only one vendor can satisfy the specifications, but in general several vendors will respond with proposal worthy of consideration.

Since there are a number of considerations, both quantitative and subjective, one evaluation method is to rank each supplier by a point system. For each criterion for evaluation, a number of points is assigned as a potential total, and then each vendor is rated by being award part or all of the potential points.

— Operating system evaluation

— Very high level language evaluation

— Procedural language evaluation

— Database management system evaluation

— Software package availability evaluation

— Other software evaluation

The major questions that need to be addressed are whether the proposed hardware or software will perform the job in the time allowed, its relative cost, and its flexibility to expand as more applications are needed. Most computer systems can provide for growth by the addition of equipment options. for example, a stripped-down minimum-memory computer may have its power increased by addition of faster input-output, more storage, or special software packages. A compatible "family" of computers allows the organization to move from one computer in the family to a larger size without reprogramming.

The evaluation should include not only the existing software but also the probability of promised software being available on schedule. In evaluations of hardware and software it is usually desirable to run test programs. The vendor will usually provide time for testing.

When equipment is being evaluated, the alternative of a mixed system should be considered. Several firms offer "plug compatible" peripherals which have higher performance at a lower cost than the computer vendor's units. The main disadvantage of these independent peripherals is in the added management problems of dealing with more than one vendor and coping with responsibility for equipment-caused failures. For a new computer system or major software package, the study group should conduct an independent analysis of system performance.

The real criterion for measuring system performance is throughput; if actual jobs cannot be run and timed, then substitute measures must be used. There are several substitute comparison methods, but the most common is standard benchmark analysis in which standard problems of a type normally performed are code and time to perform the standard task is estimated or measured by running it.

Organizations use auditors as independent evaluators. There are basically two types of auditors: independent auditors and internal auditors. Auditors who specialize in auditing activities related to information systems are generally termed EDP auditors. The roles of independent and internal auditors are different, although they perform many activities that are similar. Auditors can have a significant effect on quality and control of computer processing.

A major role of independent auditors is to attest to the fairness of financial statements. This professional judgment is based on evidence obtained and evaluated by the auditor during an examination.

If computer are used in activities that effect the financial statements, independent auditors must include a study of internal control in EDP systems as part of the overall study and evaluation of internal control. This process includes the following procedures:

1. Preliminary phase of the review in which an initial assessment is made of the role of computer data processing in the preparation of financial records. A preliminary evaluation is made of the existence of general controls over data processing and controls in applications relevant to the audit. The assessment from the preliminary phase is the basis for planning the completion of the review. the result may be to tentatively rely on the internal control in data processing and proceed to complete the review or not to rely and to collect alternative evidence.

2. Complete the review of internal control in computer data processing by more detailed study of controls. By interviews, checklists, study of documentation, and observation, the auditor determines the set of controls the company says are operating. If these controls provide a reasonable basis for internal control, the auditor proceeds to test whether the controls are functioning.

3. Compliance tests of the controls. Controls may be established but not operating or operating improperly, incorrectly, or irregularly. The purpose of the compliance tests is to obtain evidence on how well the controls are operating. The tests include examination of evidence of compliance such as signatures when they are required, control total comparisons, library control records, etc.

4. Evaluation of the reliance that can be placed on internal EDP control and decision on the substantive tests that need to be performed to provide evidence other than internal control.

Substantive tests by the independent auditor can be performed by manual procedures; they can also make use of both independent, auditor-supplied software and company software. For example, an auditor may make use of a generalized audit software system to test files by counting records, summing dollar amounts, selecting records for followup, analyzing characteristics of data in the file, etc. An auditor may also make use of system software to select records, print files, etc., and database management software to retrieve data from databases. The procedures followed by an independent auditor will generally provide sufficient evidence for making a judgment about the financial statements of the organization; it is not sufficient to detect all instance of fraud or other misconduct. Presumably, major frauds that have a significant effect on the financial statements will be discovered, but relatively minor ones will not. If fraud is suspected, a special fraud audit may be conducted. Independent auditors can also be engaged to perform management advisory services with respect to data processing. Examples are evaluation of information services, evaluation of security procedures, and performance evaluation.

Internal auditors are employees of the company. The usually have a reporting relationship within the company that provides independence from those they are auditing. Internal auditors perform control assignments, do more detailed auditing than that performed by external auditors, and do evaluations.

Index